JOURNEY TO MINDFULNESS

Mid-1990s. In the forest at Bhavana Society, West Virginia.

Journey to Mindfulness

THE AUTOBIOGRAPHY OF
Bhante G.

EXPANDED ANNIVERSARY EDITION

by
Bhante Henepola Gunaratana
with
Jeanne Malmgren

Wisdom Publications
199 Elm Street
Somerville MA 02144 USA
www.wisdompubs.org

Library of Congress Cataloging-in-Publication Data
Names: Gunaratana, Henepola, 1927– author. | Malmgren, Jeanne.
Title: Journey to mindfulness: the autobiography of Bhante G. / by Bhante Henepola
    Gunaratana with Jeanne Malmgren.
Description: Expanded anniversary edition. |
    Somerville, MA: Wisdom Publications, 2017. |
Identifiers: LCCN 2017020697 (print) | LCCN 2017021344 (ebook) | ISBN 9781614294580
    (ebook) | ISBN 1614294585 (ebook) | ISBN 9781614294429 (paperback)
Subjects: LCSH: Gunaratana, Henepola, 1927– | Buddhist monks—Sri Lanka—
    Biography. | Spiritual life—Buddhism. | Spiritual biography—United States. |
    BISAC: BIOGRAPHY & AUTOBIOGRAPHY / Religious. | RELIGION / Buddhism /
    Theravada. | BIOGRAPHY & AUTOBIOGRAPHY / Personal Memoirs.
Classification: LCC BQ960.U767 (ebook) | LCC BQ960.U767 A3 2017 (print) | DDC
    294.3/91092 [B] —dc23
LC record available at https://lccn.loc.gov/2017020697

ISBN 978-1-61429-442-9   ebook ISBN 978-1-61429-458-0

21   20   19   18   17
5   4   3   2   1

Cover designed by Jim Zaccaria.
Interior designed by Gopa&Ted2. Set in Minion 11/15.
Photo by ᑊᖇᖇᖇᖇ; courtesy of Bhavana Society.

♻ This book was produced with environmental mindfulness.
For more information, please visit wisdompubs.org/wisdom-environment.

Printed in the United States of America.

Please visit fscus.org.

Contents

Preface

WRITING AN AUTOBIOGRAPHY might seem like an inappropriate exercise for a *bhikkhu*, a Buddhist monk, since we bhikkhus strive to eradicate the ego, not glorify it. Through meditation and mindfulness we want to let go of attachments and practice selflessness. Why then would I write a whole book about *me?*

The idea, oddly enough, came from my meditation retreats.

Whenever I teach a retreat, I invite attendees to write questions on slips of paper and put them in a box. Each evening, after my formal Dhamma talk, a lecture about the essence of the Buddha's teachings, I pull a few of the slips out of the box, one by one, and answer whatever question is there.

Usually people want to know about meditation: how to keep up the momentum they've built at the retreat; what to do when they are so agitated they can't sit still; how to practice if they don't have a good teacher nearby. Sometimes, though, someone asks a question about my life:

"How long have you been a monk?"

"What was it like, growing up in Sri Lanka?"

"How do you maintain monastic discipline in this world full of temptations?"

When I answer those kinds of questions, I tend to ramble. I tell stories about my life and people seem to enjoy them. The meditation hall, usually a silent place, fills with laughter. Often the students say, "Bhante, you should write your autobiography!"

I've read a few life stories of spiritual men and women, and in them, it always seems like miraculous, wondrous things happen to the main character. Sometimes, the main character may even be the one performing miracles.

Reading these amazing stories, one might conclude that spiritual people are somehow very different from regular people. As for me, I can claim no miracles. I have been a simple person all my life. Early on I learned that if I worked hard, I would usually get good results—nothing supernatural about that. In many ways my life is probably much like yours.

And so I was hesitant to write the book my students were suggesting. I worried that it would appear to be an exercise in ego. I was afraid people might think I had grown vain and self-absorbed in my old age.

"Not necessarily," a friend told me. "You might be able to do some teaching by telling your own story." I thought about that. I thought about my life and realized that, yes, this might indeed be an opportunity to show how the Buddha's teachings can be an extraordinary guide, leading a simple person like myself to a life of great happiness, great fulfillment.

As a monk, I have dedicated my life to protecting and maintaining the Buddha's teachings. I have found that because of that, the Dhamma has protected and maintained me as well. That's what I have learned in my seventy-five years. And that's the essence of what I want to share with you in all these rambling stories about my life.

For example, I can say sincerely that whenever I was arrogant in my life, I suffered a great deal. As a young man in monks' college, I spied on other students, I gossiped, I was always looking for others' faults. And because of that, I was miserable.

In fact, I'd say that has always been my greatest weakness: finding fault in others. Rising above that defilement even a little bit took many long years, through much trial and error, and even now I occasionally struggle with it. But more or less, I'm happy to say, I can now pretty much accept people as they are. And my life (not to mention theirs!) is so much smoother as a result.

By relying on the Buddha's teachings, I have learned slowly to withdraw from conflict rather than charging into it or, worse still, going looking for it. That, too, has made life immeasurably more peaceful.

With the help of the Buddha's teachings and the practice of mindfulness, the greatest change I have made in myself, I think, is that I can easily forgive people now, no matter what they do, and believe me, this skill didn't come easily! I had to work long and hard at it. But my own anger, contentiousness, and judgmentalness were fertile ground for practice. Just because a person becomes a monk, by no means is he immediately free from all defilements of character or empty of worldly concerns. As you will see over and over in this book, even in the supposedly noble world of spiritual work, I encountered—in myself and in others—petty jealousies, backstabbing, indifference, and cruelty.

When I reminisce now, I can see that all those things that seemed so awful at the time have ultimately led to positive outcomes. All the people and situations that I thought were painful were also teachers pushing me in the direction I was supposed to go, pointing out what I needed to learn to become happy.

In retrospect, I am grateful for the mysterious chain of causes and effects that unfolded in my life, even though many of them felt awful and unlucky at the time. If my father had not been such a strict disciplinarian, I might not have left home to become a monk. If my teachers hadn't punished me so severely, I wouldn't have gone off to missionary school. If I hadn't lost my memory and needed a "cure," I might never have taken an interest in meditation. If I hadn't fallen sick working with the Untouchables of India, I wouldn't have left to go to Malaysia. If my visa had been extended in Malaysia, I probably would never have ventured to America. And if things hadn't fallen apart so bitterly at the Washington Buddhist Vihara, I might not have started Bhavana Society. But this has been my life, and I am grateful for all of it.

Even so, it pained me to write about some of these things, to dredge up the memories of old hurts and conflicts. Several times I nearly lost my nerve and withdrew from the plans for this book. In my periods of doubt, I kept remembering the words of Mark Twain: "Only dead men tell the truth."

I thought about the sometimes ugly truths of my life, and I worried. If I wrote about them honestly, I would be displaying my weaknesses, my shortcomings. But hiding the truth—well, that didn't feel right either. And furthermore, it seemed so un-monk-like to write about unpleasant conversations and situations that happened decades ago, to reveal people who were unkind to me, especially when many of them aren't around anymore to defend themselves.

Adding to my worries was the fact that my native culture does not prize open discussion of conflict. When my Sinhalese nephews read an early draft of this manuscript, they were aghast. "You can't talk about people this way," they said. "Why do you want to rehash these old problems? It can only cause trouble."

People in Sri Lanka don't want to hear about a monk's mistakes or character flaws. They prefer to think of him as an exalted holy man to whom they can bow down in reverence. In the spiritual economy of Asian Buddhist monastics and laypeople, honoring a venerable bhikkhu by giving him gifts or supporting him brings spiritual merit. To find out that he is anything less than worthy would disturb a layperson's sense of order.

But in Western culture, the truth is highly prized. So I couldn't tell my life story and leave out the bad parts; that would be a "sanitized" version and would perhaps be perceived as dishonest. And if I portrayed myself as never having struggled with difficulties and shortcomings, my story certainly wouldn't help anyone see the value of the Dhamma in dealing with life's slings and arrows.

The first of the Buddha's noble truths is that life contains suffering. We cannot avoid suffering. Our only option is to work at overcoming the defilements within ourselves that cause suffering: greed, anger, and delusion. Overcoming these defilements is a lifelong task, as I hope the story of my simple life, my own journey to mindfulness, will show.

But I also hope my story will illustrate that, no matter how strong they may be, the sources of suffering can be overcome in your life, too!

had married and left home before I was even born. Two girls were born after me, but one died as an infant. My birth was attended by a midwife, who received a measure of rice and a coconut for her trouble. I came into this world at home in a dimly lit hut with no windows. While my mother was in labor, she alternately squatted and lay on a mat made of palm fronds spread over the floor. As was the custom, the midwife tied a rope to the roof beam; it hung down over my mother's mat so that she could pull on it as a distraction when the pain became unbearable. She delivered all eight of her children that way.

Two weeks after my birth, when it looked likely I was hearty enough to survive, my father went to visit the chief of a nearby village. All births and deaths had to be officially registered with a local chief, but Henepola was too small to have its own chief, so my father walked a half mile to the nearest village, Dehideniya. There, he told the chief the name he had given his third son: Ekanayaka Mudiyanselage Ukkubanda.

Ukku means small and *banda* means treasure. It's a fond name adults use to refer tenderly to a baby. Often the name, even though it's used for an infant, would remain into adulthood.

As I got older, though, my parents decided to call me Kudabanda, which means something like "small boy." That made sense, I suppose, because I was the last boy in the family. But I never asked them why they called me that instead of my legal name.

My father built our house himself. It was maybe thirty by forty feet. The roof was made of straw, dried fronds from coconut trees, and scraps of tin. The walls were made of mud, reinforced with strips of bamboo. Along the front and back of the house were open verandas, with walls that were made of mud on the lower half and a wooden lattice on the upper half.

Compared to many huts in the village, ours was spacious. It had two rooms. One was a small, dark kitchen; the other was a storage room for my father's papers, books, and tools. The furniture was sparse, and all of it handmade, consisting of a couple of small, crude benches and a chair woven of beech strips. I remember my father sitting upright in that chair after meals, smoking a cigar or chewing betel nut while he told us stories or gave us lectures. My mother sat on a bench, never in Father's chair. We children sat on the floor.

The floor was made of mud, like the walls, but every so often my mother and sisters smeared fresh cow dung over it, using their bare hands. Manure was considered a germicide, its odor the smell of freshness. We walked on that floor every day, barefoot.

There were only two beds, each a crude wooden platform topped by a cloth sack stuffed with dried coconut husks. Those "mattresses" were only a little softer than a pile of rocks. My oldest brother, Tikiribanda, slept in one bed, which was on the veranda at the front of our hut. My other brother and I slept near him, on the bare floor. The other bed, on the back veranda, was my father's. Never once did I see my mother lying in that bed with him; she slept with my sisters on the floor. I never saw my parents kiss or hug or even have a private conversation.

Our parents did, however, share a deep devotion to Buddhism. Every morning we children woke up to the singsong chant of them reading Pali suttas. These daily recitations served as our lullaby at night, too. Before we even learned the alphabet, we could recite Pali devotional stanzas from memory, and we knew what the words *kamma* and *rebirth* meant.

Day after day my parents went about their routines without grumbling. Every morning my father went off to work in the rice paddy, or on our small rubber estate. My mother stayed home and took care of the house and us children. When my father came home, she would have a meal ready for him.

Both of my parents knew how to read and write in Sinhalese, which was a rarity in our village and in most of rural Ceylon. Because my father was literate, and was known as a man of dignity and strict moral principles, he was the most highly respected man in Henepola. The other villagers often came to him to settle their disputes. With his own family, though, my father could be a terror. Sometimes he would suddenly start fighting with my mother. I never understood why. And he showed his temper in a violent way. Punishment for us children was swift and painful, and sometimes he even beat my mother. When that happened, all of us hid. We were afraid that if we made a sound, his rage would turn on us.

My mother had no formal education, but she was very intelligent. She taught herself how to read and write, and she knew a lot about herbal medicine. Her intuition was powerful.

I was very close to my oldest sister, Dingiriamma. When I was almost two, she gave birth to her second child, a girl who died a couple of weeks later. Although I had already started to eat solid food, I still loved to drink milk, but our family had no cow and my mother's milk flow had long since stopped. So, for almost a year after her baby died, Dingiriamma took me to her breast and fed me as if I were her own child. She and her husband lived in a village called Gunadaha, three miles away, and a couple of times a week, she would walk to our house and nurse me. To this day, I still consider her my second mother. We were perhaps closer to each other than to all of the other five siblings.

My mother and sisters had the job of gathering firewood for cooking fuel. In an area forested mostly with palm trees and cocoa plants, wood was scarce. Often, they had to rip dead branches off rubber trees.

Since we had no electricity, we relied on the dim light of coconut oil lamps. Sometimes, when we didn't have enough oil for the lamps, my mother made a torch out of nuts from the kekune tree. She would remove the hard shell from ten or fifteen nuts, and then impale them on a stick. The natural oil in the nuts would burn for hours.

Although our village didn't have running water, our family was lucky because about two hundred yards from the house, we had a private well. This well was fed by a spring that ran year-round, and although it was only about five feet deep, it was a generous six feet by four feet wide. We used the water for bathing, drinking, and washing clothes.

My mother and sisters hauled the spring water to the house in large earthen pots, which had round bellies and small mouths. I remember how water stayed so cool in those pots.

For bathing, we used primitive buckets made of fibrous sheaths shed by areca palm trees. Those sheaths were sometimes five feet long and three feet wide. We could fold one into a bucket shape and carry two or three gallons of water in it.

No matter how clean we kept our bodies, our clothes, and our mattresses, we all suffered the agony of bed bugs. I vividly remember scratching the swollen, red places on my body where bed bugs had bitten me. Although the itching was terrible, I never thought to wish for anything else; it was just a part of life. We had mosquitoes and flies, too, but those you could combat by burning coconut husks. Bed bugs, on the other hand, were nearly impossible to get rid of. They were barely visible, and hid in the coconut husk mattresses. Even though we often washed those mattresses and dried them in the sun, the bed bugs always came back. Some people would move their mattresses away from the wall or place little tin cans of oil under each leg of their bed, but the bed bugs were determined. If they couldn't climb up the legs of the bed, they crawled up the wall and dropped down from the ceiling like tiny kamikaze pilots.

Leeches were another problem. Whenever my brother and I went exploring, we'd come home with leeches clinging to our legs or burrowed between our toes. We would pull them off, but often their minute teeth stayed imbedded in our skin. A couple of days later, there would be open wounds where the leeches had bitten us. Sometimes blueflies laid their eggs there. Those eggs would hatch into maggots, which of course made the wounds worse.

Maybe because I was malnourished, my body didn't have enough strength to fight the bacteria in those wounds. They would heal slowly, and badly. I still have scars on my legs.

My father had inherited several acres of land: a one-acre rubber estate, a half-acre tea plantation, a one-acre rice field, and the cleared acre on which he built our house. In addition to farming rice, tea, and rubber, my father also enjoyed gardening. In the clearing around our house, he planted bougainvillea and hibiscus. Next to the house, he planted a mixed hedge of jasmine and roses, which he neatly trimmed with a large knife. He also grew numerous cash crops: sweet potatoes, tapioca, beans, eggplant, okra, bitter gourds, cabbage, and coffee. However, even with that much food growing nearby, there was still never enough to feed us all.

In addition to our property, we had two water buffalo, which my father used to pull a plow across the rice paddy. Luckily, we did not have to feed the buffalo produce from our fields and gardens; they ate grass or the thorny, discarded shells of jackfruit.

My father traded his crops for dried fish, spices, sugar, salt, kerosene oil, and other supplies we couldn't grow or make ourselves. To do his trading, he walked three miles to a town called Galagedara, where there were some shops run by Muslims and Hindu Tamils. Often he couldn't find what he wanted; everything seemed to be in short supply.

To help support his seven hungry children, my father also did carpentry work for our neighbors. Unfortunately, people could rarely afford to pay him. Maybe it was the constant financial worries that made him so cross. He was a severe disciplinarian. He kept a stick hidden on the roof of the house and used it quickly and forcefully to punish us for any slight wrongdoing. His shout was so frightening that we would tremble when we heard it. My brother Rambanda and I knew that sound, and the stick, well. We were quite mischievous.

One of our earliest pranks was throwing stones at cows and birds. One day we saw a dog with puppies. My brother picked up a handful of stones and told me to climb a nearby tree. His plan was to harass the dog while we were safely ensconced in the tree. I told Rambanda the tree was too high to climb, that I was too small.

"Please don't," I begged. "She'll bite me."

But he was intent. He swung himself up into the tree, then started pelting the dog with stones. I ran as fast as I could, but the dog was faster. I fell down and she bit me.

When my brother and I got home, we had to explain why I was bleeding. My father beat both of us for being cruel to the dog.

Rambanda and I always seemed to be hungry. Edible fruits or nuts we found while playing were great treats. If they were growing on someone's property, we'd ask the property owner's permission. If they said no, we took the fruits anyway. One day my brother and I were on our way to our family's rubber estate. Halfway there, we passed a small field belonging to a poorer family. There were about fifty corn plants growing in that field. One plant near the road had a ripe ear of corn hanging on it. My brother looked around and saw no one, so he picked the ear and broke it in half. One piece for him, one for me: delicious!

On our way home, we passed the cornfield again. This time, for some reason, we decided to be honest. My brother went to the owner's house and asked her for an ear of corn. The woman said there was one just next to the road, and we were welcome to it. She came out into the field to show us where it was, but when we reached the corn stalks by the road, the woman saw that the ear she intended to give us was gone. Then she noticed a small footprint in the mud. She asked my brother to place his foot in the footprint. He did, and it was a perfect fit.

We were obviously guilty, but the woman didn't appear angry. She said, "You boys go home. I'll bring you some more corn."

We started off happily toward home.

When we reached our house, however, the woman was already there. She had told our father the whole story and he was waiting for us, stick in hand, angrier than I had ever seen him.

This was a doubly bad deed. Not only had we broken the Buddhist precept against stealing, but we also had stolen from a lower-caste family who had very little.

Father thrashed us until our backs began to bleed. My mother tried to stop him, but he kept beating us. Even the woman, the victim of our crime, begged him to stop. Everyone was crying, but our father would listen to no one. He beat us until he was too tired to beat us anymore.

This, of course, would be labeled child abuse today. But seventy years ago in Ceylon, it was standard practice for parents to punish children by thrashing them. As a devout Buddhist, my father was determined to teach us the difference between right and wrong, and his methods were simply those of his generation and culture. Truly, I can't fault him for that.

As a child, I wore a long shirt of rough cotton. It was blue and red plaid, and came down to my knees. That was the uniform for young boys and girls. When I was eleven, I began to wear two pieces of clothing: a regular shirt and a skirtlike sarong. Throughout my childhood, I never wore shoes or even sandals; they were too expensive. We children had to be careful with our clothes because we only got new outfits at New Year's, which Ceylonese celebrated in mid-April.

My siblings and I also had no toys. We played with sticks, dry palm fronds, coconut shells, and frayed pieces of discarded rope. Our playground was the sand in front of our house, the rice fields, or the threshing grounds where farmers separated rice from its stalks. I also loved to climb trees and explore the forest.

One time I was out exploring and discovered an old woodshed in the forest. I found some rope and slung it over one of the beams in the shed, to make a swing. It was great fun for about thirty seconds. As soon as I started swinging, the beam cracked, broke in two, and fell on top of my head. Everything felt numb for a moment, then warm liquid began to pour down my forehead and over my face. I stumbled outside and found an areca palm sheath on the ground. I pressed it to my head, thinking I somehow had to collect all that blood. My mother, who seemed to have a sixth sense for knowing when I was in trouble, quickly found me. She took me home, tenderly washed the wound on my head, and applied one of her herbal ointments.

In the evenings, my brothers, sisters, and I would play hide-and-seek until dinnertime, which was usually around 9 P.M. As soon as dinner was over, we fell asleep, on the bare floor, without a pillow or blanket. There was no such thing as brushing our teeth or taking a bath before we went to bed. To lull us to sleep Mother told beautiful stories, some of them folktales and some Jataka tales, which are stories of the Buddha's previous lives.

As a child, one of my favorite Jataka stories was about Sasa, the generous rabbit who offered to jump into a fire and sacrifice himself so a hungry old man could have something to eat. I think I liked that story because I used to gaze at the full moon and would see in its craters and valleys what looked like a rabbit. I dreamed of being generous enough to reach the moon, where I could sit beside that rabbit and look down on the earth. My parents always told me the Buddha was soft and gentle like moonlight, shining his brilliance on everyone without discrimination. So when I thought of the moon, I thought of the rabbit in the moon, of Sasa the generous rabbit, and of the Buddha—all three were interwoven in my mind.

It's ironic that I liked the story of a self-sacrificing rabbit, because I myself was actually very greedy, especially about food. I was always on guard over my food, lest someone grab my meal away from me. If someone even looked at my plate, I would get angry and throw it on the ground. That was completely foolish, of course, because food was too precious to waste. But I had a flash temper, perhaps like my father, and I didn't control it any better than he did.

Sometimes my brothers and sisters stared at my food just to set me off. Once, when that happened, I flew into such a rage I threw my plate of food out the door. Father gave me a beating, then made me go and pick up the plate, and of course I didn't get any more food that meal.

One day, my third sister, who was four years older than I, took a wooden stick and drew a pumpkin in the sand. I took another stick and scratched it out. She was so upset that she hit me with a broom. I grabbed a wooden bench and chased her into the house, then I threw the bench at her. It hit her big toe and ripped the nail completely off. There was a lot of blood and immediately she started wailing. When my mother heard her, she rushed in to help and I ran outside.

That was the first time I remember doing something mean to one of my siblings. I was seven or eight years old. Luckily, my father was not home when it happened, and neither my mother nor my sister told him exactly what happened. I guess they feared my father's wrath as much as I did. They simply let him believe my sister's bandaged toe was the result of an accident.

When I was growing up, there were no cars or even bicycles in our village; walking was the only mode of transportation. To get to a main road, we either had to walk two miles down a steep hill in one direction or three miles along a flat road in the other direction. When people were seriously ill and unable to walk, they were tied into a chair or onto a board and carried three miles to the nearest hospital, in Galagedara.

In 1933, when I was five, a malaria epidemic swept Ceylon. My whole family was sick, off and on, for three years. The British government distributed quinine, as well as free rice and other food staples, because no one was strong enough to work. However, there was a catch: We had to walk three miles each week to get our allotment. We took turns making the trip; whoever was least sick would go. I remember walking those three miles with a terrible fever, just to get the food and medicine.

I recall two other medical emergencies.

When I was about eight or nine I abruptly lost my night vision, probably because of malnutrition. After dark, it was as if I were blind. I couldn't see anything at all, even with the light from a kerosene lamp.

My brothers and sisters teased me about it, saying I was pretending, but my mother was very concerned. She consulted the village medicine man, who gave her a bitter-tasting potion for me. It was made from an herb, but he wouldn't tell her its name. Many people believed herbal medicines had mystical powers, and their components were often kept secret.

My mother was supposed to grind the herb into a paste and feed it to me every day until my eyesight improved. The paste tasted wretched, and to make matters worse, I was supposed to take this foul concoction early in the morning, when my stomach was empty.

To get me to take that medicine, my mother used the power of love. Before anyone else in the house was awake, she would take me onto her lap. She would hug me, kiss me, and tell me stories in a low whisper. After a few minutes, I was so relaxed and happy that I would have done anything she asked.

That was the moment she would put the medicine in my mouth and tell me to swallow it quickly. She always mixed the bitter paste with sugar, though it still tasted awful. But after several months of that daily ritual, I completely recovered my eyesight.

Now, many years later, I understand the power of *metta,* or loving-friendliness. In a way, it helps us swallow the bitterness of life. It smooths over the rough moments, the disappointments, the hurt. The Buddha used the power of metta to "conquer" many of his enemies. He even instructed monks living in the forest to use metta when confronted by poisonous snakes. And the Metta Sutta is one of the most beautiful of his discourses.

It is a very short sutta, but one that Buddhist monks usually chant at every formal gathering. It describes a way of thinking and acting that can bring peace to the practitioner and to those around him or her.

The Buddha told his disciples that the practice of metta is a meritorious deed. Therefore, while cultivating thoughts of loving-friendliness, we are happy, feeling the kind of deep happiness that comes from performing a meritorious deed. It's a sense of peace.

What's more, the calming effect of metta is immediate. We feel it that very moment. When we speak or act with loving-friendliness, we feel happy. When we work or do physical labor with thoughts of metta filling our minds, we feel happy.

Whenever I teach people how to formally practice loving-friendliness, I give them the following phrases to repeat:

May you be well, happy, and peaceful.
May no harm come to you.
May no difficulties come to you.
May no problems come to you.
May you always meet with success.

May you also have patience, courage, understanding,
and determination to meet and overcome inevitable
difficulties, problems, and failures in life.

The first person to whom we direct thoughts of metta is ourself:
"May I be well, happy, and peaceful. May no harm come to me. May
no difficulties come to me…"

Why start with yourself? some people ask. Isn't that terribly selfish?
To love yourself before anyone else?

Not necessarily. It is easiest to summon up metta for ourselves
because, among all beings on earth, we love ourselves best. (Well, most
of us do!) So we can quickly generate those warm feelings of loving-
friendliness for ourselves. We can saturate ourselves in it, fill our bodies and minds with it.

Then, as the goodwill spreads through our being, it naturally spills
out. We have surplus to share. And we do, with the next most logical
group of people: those near and dear to us. Spouses, life partners, children, parents, brothers, sisters, other relatives, close friends, perhaps
a spiritual mentor. We picture them in our mind's eye and we repeat
the phrases, with those cherished ones as the recipients of our metta.

The next group is the largest. It includes all those beings we encounter every day, but aren't as close to. The passing acquaintances—
sometimes complete strangers—who move in and out of our lives.
Classmates, coworkers, neighbors, the checkout clerk at the grocery
store, the person sitting in the car next to you at a stoplight, a friendly
dog with a wagging tail, someone who whizzes by you on a bike trail.
We extend loving-friendliness to all these beings, human and nonhu-
man, and wish them well.

The last group is probably—hopefully!—a small one. It consists of
your adversaries, those difficult people who pop up in your life to provide what we might politely call "challenges." This is where metta practice becomes sticky for many people.

Wish your enemies well? Hope for their success, when they're
going after the same promotion you want? Send them peaceful

thoughts when they've just insulted your child or cut in front of you in traffic?

Yes, said the Buddha. And here's why: If we wish that person well, and hope that he has success, maybe he will develop spiritually. That's the kind of success we're wishing for him—spiritual success. And if he evolves spiritually, he probably won't be our adversary anymore. There won't be any need for that. He'll be more peaceful; his noble qualities will emerge. We'll all be able to coexist more harmoniously.

But the practice of loving-friendliness shouldn't be confined to formal repetition of the phrases. We should cultivate metta in our thoughts, words, and deeds, the Buddha said. Every step, every action, every reflection should be one of metta. Whatever a person repeats again and again will become his or her own mental state. If you practice metta constantly, you yourself will be full of metta. It will become your nature. And you'll realize that others have this soft, gentle nature buried within them, too.

My mother understood and lived the words of the Buddha. She made sure all her children heard stories of the Buddha's life and learned about his compassion and wisdom. She herself was a walking example of metta, always treating anyone she met with gentleness and soft words. In many ways, I considered her almost a holy person.

About a year after my mysterious bout of night blindness, my mother had an accident that changed her life.

One day she climbed a cocoa tree to pick some cocoa fruit, something she did often. She would cut open the fruit, take out the fleshy seeds (each about the size of a walnut), and dry them in the sun. Father would take them to market and sell them for about five cents a pound. Dried cocoa seeds were a great delicacy because they could be pounded into cocoa powder.

That day, my mother's routine turned to tragedy. When she was high in the tree, a branch gave way under her and she fell. I heard her cry out, and when I ran over, I found her lying on her back on the ground, unconscious. Two of my sisters came, as well, and when they saw her, they started crying.

Apparently the neighbors heard my sisters crying and they tried their best to help. When Mother woke up, one of the neighbors offered her a folk tonic: a drink of brandy with an egg yolk stirred into it. She refused to drink it. All her life she had followed the Buddhist precepts, which include a dictum against alcohol. She didn't want to break the precept, even if the brandy would dull her pain.

Someone ran to alert my father, who was working in the rice paddy. My father, in turn, ran to fetch the village medicine man.

Several people helped carry my mother to our house; her back was hurting so much she couldn't walk. The medicine man sent people in several directions to collect the leaves and roots of particular herbs. When they returned, he ground the herbs into a paste and rubbed it on my mother's back. He left us with a supply of the paste, and told us to reapply it twice a day.

Every Ceylonese village had both a Buddhist monk and a medicine man, and the two worked cooperatively. Before preparing any of his herbal medicines, the medicine man would chant Buddhist stanzas in front of his home altar. He didn't charge anything for his services, but people routinely gave him gifts of vegetables, coconuts, spices, tea, or betel nut. It was believed that if the medicine man was a good Buddhist, his potions would have more power. Therefore, his healing power depended on his purity as a Buddhist.

Even after the British set up a system of local government with a chief in charge of each village, the medicine man and head monk still had the greatest authority. The chief always consulted with the head monk and the medicine man before making decisions about how to punish a criminal or settle a dispute.

Several days after her fall, my mother was no better. She couldn't move her legs or stand up; all she could do was moan in pain. She barely ate or drank anything except for a little rice soup and some orange juice. It was obvious she needed more medical care, but my parents didn't trust hospitals.

My mother said she wanted to go to her parents' house, about thirty miles from our village. That was a long journey, but the medicine man in her parents' village was supposed to be powerful, and my mother said she would be more comfortable in her childhood home. So Father and a few other men eased her onto a board and carried her to the nearest town. There, my father hired a car and took her to her parents' house.

During their trip, we children were left alone. My second oldest sister was eighteen by then, so she did the cooking and looked after us younger ones.

After a few days, my father returned without my mother. She had remained at her parents' house to recuperate. But she never recovered entirely. When she finally came home several months later, she was hunchbacked and on crutches. Her right leg wouldn't bend at all, and she couldn't even walk the short distance to the temple.

At age seven, I started school. The nearest one was in Medagama, about a half mile from our house, and was run by Catholic missionary nuns. I loved it, mainly because of the delicious lunches we were served each day. Before eating, we had to say Catholic prayers, our heads bowed over the little food trays placed on our desks. I closed my eyes and mumbled the words, but my mind was on the tantalizing aromas wafting up to my nose.

I attended the Catholic school for about a year before the Buddhist temple in Dehideniya opened a primary school. All the children of Henepola, perhaps thirty or forty of us, switched schools. The first year at the Buddhist school was pretty cramped. The temple's preaching hall, an open-air structure, served as the only classroom, and it was always noisy because there were so many of us in one room.

A year later, the government granted a small plot of land next to the temple for a separate school building. The villagers worked together to build a simple rectangular, one-room building, which was about one hundred feet by thirty feet. It had five-foot-high walls with only bare openings instead of windows or doors, and the roof was made of coconut palm fronds. This new building had long tables and hard wooden benches. During our first year in the new school building, we used slates and slender stone slabs for writing our lessons. By the second year, however, the government provided pencils and paper exercise books, a real luxury!

Every morning when the teacher walked in, we stood next to our benches and bowed, hands folded in front of our chests.

"Good morning, sir," we chorused, as he greeted us with a similar bow.

Then it was inspection time. The teacher walked along the rows of students and looked at our teeth and fingernails to make sure they were clean. Everything had to be neat, including our clothes. If something wasn't, we got a thrashing with his long cane. In fact, if we did anything wrong at all, our backsides met that cane. And sometimes the teacher used his knuckles to rap our skulls. It didn't occur to anyone that this was cruel, or anything other than usual.

Before lessons began, in Pali we all recited the three refuges—refuge in the Buddha, Dhamma, and Sangha—and the five precepts of Buddhism. Even the youngest children knew these recitations by heart, because everyone had heard their parents chanting them at home every single day of their lives. The school curriculum included Sinhalese grammar, history, science, arithmetic, and of course, Buddhism.

Every day, on the way to and from school, I walked past a small, swift-flowing creek. Neither my brother nor I could swim, and my mother was petrified that we would drown in that creek. Every day she would stand in the doorway of our house and wait for us to come home from school. She knew what a magnet the creek was for adventurous kids, how my brother and I longed to throw down our schoolbooks, tear off our sarongs, and jump in the cool water. And some days, we did just that! My mother, ever vigilant, would scream at the top of her lungs as soon as we set foot in the water, and we would reluctantly climb out.

Once, though, we got away with it. We jumped in the water and Mother didn't see us. Almost immediately, I was trapped in a small whirlpool where the stream flowed under a stand of bamboo. I flailed my arms and tried to stay afloat, but the eddy was pulling me down with a terrifying force. Somehow my brother managed to grab hold of me and pull me out. He saved my life.

That would not be my last experience of near-drowning. To this day, even though I have traveled all over the world and crossed oceans countless times, I am still uncomfortable around large bodies of water.

One day, when I was perhaps nine years old, I was coming home from school with several other boys during a heavy rainstorm. We had to cross a rice field, which had narrow dividers between the rows of rice plants, with irrigation ditches bisecting the dividers. We came to one particular ditch swollen by the monsoon rains. It was like a small river, with a swift current. All the other boys jumped over the ditch, but I hesitated, holding my schoolbooks against my chest.

Finally, as I was working up my courage to jump, I slipped on the edge of the bank and fell into the water. My books and slate were immediately carried away by the current as I struggled to keep my head above water. The harder I tried to swim, the faster I seemed to sink. My brother, Rambanda, jumped into the water and pulled me out. I was scared and wet, but all right.

We never told our parents about it. We knew what would happen if we did.

The Buddhist temple, which was about a quarter-mile from our house, was the center of our village. Only one monk and his assistant, a layman, lived there.

The compound included a preaching hall, a shrine room, a little mud hut that served as a kitchen, and an outhouse. In a corner of the courtyard stood a Bodhi tree, to remind us of the tree that Shakyamuni Buddha sat under when he attained enlightenment. A brick wall surrounded the tree, to keep children from climbing its sacred limbs.

The temple was maintained by a board of directors and a willing force of volunteer labor. People from the village cheerfully helped with construction, cleaning, cooking, and organizing celebrations. Buddhists believe that such good works earn merit in this life and the next. Most people went to the temple nearly every day, even if only for a short visit.

The daily rhythms of the temple also regulated our daily lives. Every day at 6 A.M., either the monk or his assistant would ring a large, gong-like bell in the temple courtyard. That was the signal for morning devotions. It meant the monk had completed his hour-long meditation and now was going to the shrine room to chant devotional prayers. Everyone in the village could hear that bell. When it rang, we knew it was time for our individual rituals, too. We would put fresh flowers on our home altars, light incense, and settle down to chant.

The temple bell would ring again at 11 A.M., when the monk was beginning to eat his main meal of the day. That bell was our only way of marking time, as no one had clocks or wristwatches.

Every evening, Rambanda and I went to the temple. We loved it there. The monk let us play on the temple grounds and often gave us candy or leftover food.

We were not supposed to eat temple food, because it had been offered by villagers for the monk's consumption. Our parents had told us that eating temple food would cause bad kamma for us, that we'd be dragged into hell by that kamma. But the monk was so friendly, and our hunger so strong, that we forgot about hell. We eagerly ate whatever he gave us: boiled rice, spicy fish, cooked lentils, rice-flour sweets, maybe a ripe mango.

My father built the temple's preaching hall, a thirty-by-thirty-foot building with a cement floor, brick walls, and a tile roof. Inside was a square platform about six inches high, with four tall wooden pillars at its corners. The only thing on the platform was a chair, surrounded by a wooden lattice and covered with a cloth canopy that was draped over the pillars.

On full-moon and new-moon days, laypeople spent the whole day and night at the temple. Monks from neighboring villages would also come to our temple and take turns sitting on that throne and delivering sermons.

First thing in the morning, a monk would recite one of the Buddha's discourses in Pali. Because Pali is similar to Sinhalese, most of the laypeople could understand what he was saying. The morning recital was short, usually only an hour, because the monks also had to perform a devotional service before their lunch, which was at 11 A.M.

In the afternoon, another monk would explain the meaning of the Pali discourse that had been delivered that morning. Then the temple visitors were free for several hours to meditate, ask the monks questions, or read Dhamma books.

In the evening, a solemn ceremony unfolded. After all the laypeople assembled in the preaching hall, a learned monk was carried in by two men folding their arms together to make a seat. There weren't many of these highly respected monks. Some of them could recite the entire Pali canon by memory and knew all the commentaries as well. They were skilled in picking apart a discourse and explaining every point, in marathon sermons that lasted as long as ten hours. They were usually renowned for their storytelling abilities and their sweet chanting voices.

The monk's procession was accompanied by drum-beating, conch-blowing, flute-playing, and loud calls of *"Sadhu! Sadhu! Sadhu!"* which means, "Excellent! Excellent! Excellent!"

The monk was gently lowered into his chair on the platform, then wrapped in a white cloth up to his neck. A curtain was drawn in front of him, leaving only his face showing. Other men came forward with tea for the monk, or a tray full of sugarcane candy and a chewing mixture of betel nuts, areca nuts, lime paste, and tobacco. A spittoon was placed before him.

First the monk took refuge in the Buddha, Dhamma, and Sangha, the Triple Gem of Buddhism. His voice was beautifully nasal, his chant hypnotically singsong as it floated out from behind the curtain:

Namo tassa Bhagavato Arahato Sammasambuddhasa.
Namo tassa Bhagavato Arahato Sammasambuddhasa.
Namo tassa Bhagavato Arahato Sammasambuddhasa.
(Homage to the Blessed One, the Worthy One, the Fully
   Enlightened One.)

Buddham saranam gacchami.
(I go to the Buddha for refuge.)
Dhammam saranam gacchami.
(I go to the Dhamma for refuge.)
Sangham saranam gacchami.
(I go to the Sangha for refuge.)

Dutiyam pi Buddham saranam gacchami.
Dutiyam pi Dhammam saranam gacchami.
Dutiyam pi Sangham saranam gacchami.
(A second time I go to…)

Tatiyam pi Buddham saranam gacchami.
Tatiyam pi Dhammam saranam gacchami.
Tatiyam pi Sangham saranam gacchami.
(A third time I go to…)

Then the monk would administer the five precepts to the villagers,
a traditional beginning for any Buddhist gathering. He chanted the
phrases in Pali, and the laypeople repeated after him.

After those preliminaries, the sermon would begin around 8 P.M.
Sometimes it lasted all night. Children fell asleep on the floor beside
their parents. The adults, however, were supposed to stay awake. To
help them, an old man with a long white beard sat in front of the
platform. Every time the monk paused to take a breath, the old man
said very loudly, "YES, Venerable Sir!"

Sometimes I would wake up in the middle of the night and find the whole room asleep, save for the monk and that old man. It amazed me that anyone managed to stay awake.

Around 5 A.M., the drum-beaters began thumping a beat, and people would begin to stir. By then the monk had moved into the last part of his sermon, explaining how Maitreya, the future Buddha, will appear when the teachings of Gotama, our present Buddha, are no longer in practice.

At 6 A.M., the monk would open the curtain and stretch out his legs, which had been folded in the same position all night. Several men would approach him, carrying a pan of warm coconut oil. For fifteen minutes, they'd massage his feet and legs with the oil. Then the monk would descend from the platform and retire to his room to wash before breakfast.

Watching all this as a young boy, I was deeply impressed. The laypeople's pious attitude and respect for the monk was inspiring. I told my parents that I wanted to become a monk: I wanted to deliver sermons and be carried to my chair by reverent people.

Not only that, but I would teach Dhamma in English, I boasted. My oldest brother had taught me the English alphabet, as well as a few English words. Nobody else in our village knew any English at all, even though it was the "official" language of Ceylon under British rule. We villagers were allowed to use Sinhalese, but English was clearly the language of the elite—those with government jobs, those in high society, those wealthy enough to travel. So I thought if I could learn English, I would be the ultimate educated monk.

My parents listened to my childish dreams, and they laughed.

CHAPTER TWO

The Homeless Life

As I GREW OLDER, my interest in becoming a monk intensified. Before I became a bhikkhu, I loved pretending I was a bhikkhu. I would wrap a piece of white cloth around myself, the way monks wrap their robes around them, and sit down under a tree in the forest. I imagined that the other trees around me were people, and I preached to the crowd of silent listeners, reciting a few Pali stanzas I'd heard at the temple. I would also sit and pretend to be deep in "meditations," though I had no idea what meditation was.

Even then, I believed it was somehow my kamma to become a monk. This is not to say that it was my "fate" to be a monk, for Buddhism has no such notions. Rather, because of all the accumulated causes and conditions in my past, however long that may have been, I now wanted to be a Buddhist monk. Perhaps I had been a monk in a previous life—not a totally successful one, because I obviously hadn't achieved enlightenment in that life, but not a complete failure, either, because I had the good fortune to have been reborn as a human being, with another chance to better myself spiritually. But even putting such notions aside, the impulse to ordain and that deep longing to wear the saffron robe flowered in me very early.

By the time I was eleven years old, I had lost interest in the boyhood mischief and pranks Rambanda and I used to enjoy, but I'd also lost interest in school. I wanted only to enter the two-and-a-half-millennium-old order of Buddhist monks in the ancient Asian tradition. Stories of young boys in the time of the Buddha who had had similar aspirations to become monks captivated me. One such story was about a boy called Culapanthaka.

Culapanthaka was born at the side of a road as his mother traveled to her parents' home. In ancient India, it was the custom for a pregnant woman to return to her ancestral home to deliver a baby, and often the rigors of the trip induced labor. Prince Siddhattha Gotama (called in Sanskrit Siddhartha Gautama), who would later become the Buddha, was born in a grove of trees near a roadway because his mother, Queen Mahamaya, was on her way to her parents' house.

Culapanthaka's mother had two sons, both of them born in this fashion, by the side of a road. The first, she named Mahapanthaka— "big traveler." The second one's name, Culapanthaka, meant "little traveler." Because she was extremely poor, she left the boys in the care of her parents in Rajagaha.

Mahapanthaka often accompanied his grandfather to hear the Buddha preach, and that inspired him eventually to become a monk. Young Culapanthaka followed in his brother's footsteps several years later.

Mahapanthaka wanted to teach his brother Dhamma, but found him to be a poor student. Culapanthaka could not memorize one simple stanza even in several months' time. Mahapanthaka was very disappointed and thought it was wrong for his brother to continue as a monk if he could not learn Dhamma.

"You should take off your monk's robe and go home," he told his younger brother.

Culapanthaka was devastated. He loved the monk's life and loved being a disciple of the Buddha. He didn't know what to do, but he knew he didn't want to leave the robe.

Not long after, Jivaka Komarabhacca, who sometimes served as the Buddha's physician, requested that Mahapanthaka invite the Buddha and all the monks in the monastery to have a noontime meal at his house. Mahapanthaka accepted the invitation on the monks' behalf, adding, "By tomorrow, however, Culapanthaka will no longer be at the monastery. I have asked him to disrobe. But I will come with the Buddha and the rest of the monks."

Overhearing his brother's decisive tone, Culapanthaka grieved bitterly, and with tears in his eyes, he packed his few belongings and left the monastery. But as he was walking out, the Buddha met him and asked him why he seemed so sad. He told the Buddha what had happened.

"Come, come," said the Buddha. "You don't have to leave the robe and the monk's life just because you couldn't memorize one stanza. Here, I'll teach you something that you can learn easily."

The Buddha gave him a piece of white cloth and said, "Take this cloth and sit in the sun. Put the cloth in the palm of your left hand, and rub it with your right palm, saying over and over, 'Cleaning, cleaning, cleaning.'"

Culapanthaka did exactly what the Buddha asked him to. He sat in the sun, rubbing his right hand in circles over the cloth, repeating the unusual mantra the Buddha had given him as an exercise in mindfulness.

After a while he looked down. The white piece of cloth had turned dark, stained by the oils in his hand. Even though he had been chanting a mantra about cleaning, he had made the cloth dirty!

All of a sudden, Culapanthaka realized that everything is impermanent. All that he loved, all that he encountered, all that he resisted, everything without exception was as impermanent as that clean white cloth. At that moment, clearly realizing the impermanence of all things, Culapanthaka became enlightened. He went to the monastery, sat under a tree and, using the mysterious psychic powers of a fully awakened one, created hundreds of monks exactly like himself.

Meanwhile, the other monks of the monastery had gone with the Buddha to Jivaka's house. The Buddha did not see Culapanthaka and thus declined to eat when the lunch was served.

"What is the matter, Venerable Sir?" asked a nervous Jivaka. "Is something amiss?"

"Are you sure that all the monks in the monastery have come here?" asked the Buddha.

"Yes, Venerable Sir, I am sure they've all come. Venerable Mahapanthaka confirmed that."

"Nevertheless," the Buddha said calmly, "send somebody to the monastery and see if any monk was left behind."

Jivaka sent a man to the monastery. The man returned very quickly, pale as a ghost.

"Venerable Sir, the entire monastery is full of monks!" he said. "Some were meditating, some sewing their robes, some cleaning the compound, some fetching water, some walking, some reciting whole discourses on the Dhamma."

Then the Buddha asked the man to go back to the monastery and ask for Culapanthaka. He did. And when he did, all the monks— hundreds of them—said, in one voice, "I am Culapanthaka."

The man was dumbfounded. He went back to Jivaka's house and reported what he had witnessed. Then the Buddha asked him to go back and catch one of the monks by his robe. "If you do that," the Buddha said, "the other monks will disappear."

That was what the man did. And he brought the one named Culapanthaka back for lunch. When they finished eating, the Buddha asked Culapanthaka to deliver a sermon. His brother, Mahapanthaka, and the rest of the monks were shocked. Why would the Buddha honor such an inferior person, a no-good monk who couldn't even memorize so much as a stanza of the teachings?

But Culapanthaka delivered a wonderful Dhamma sermon, taken directly from his own realization of impermanence. Everyone was astounded by the depth of his intellect.

According to the story, in one of his previous lives he had been a very smart monk, but had laughed at a dull colleague who was trying with difficulty to learn a certain passage by heart. So in Culapanthaka's next life, his kamma came to fruition: On the one hand he could not learn one stanza in four months, and on the other hand he was able to attain enlightenment and supernatural powers. Both were the results of his own previous kamma, good and bad. A dual-purpose story: both inspiration and warning!

Like Culapanthaka, I was steadfast in pursuit of my goal. I pestered my parents about becoming a bhikkhu long enough that they gradually began to take my request more seriously, as something more than a passing whim. I was still too young to ordain fully, but I could live in a temple and train as a novice. Many young boys did that, and many of those became monks when they were old enough.

It was considered very auspicious for a family if one of its sons entered the order. When a boy ordained, all his relatives received the benefit of spiritual merit. Even if a young man had already married when he decided to become a monk, it was no shame for him to leave his wife. She, too, would acquire merit by her husband's ordination.

So, with some reluctance, my father finally agreed to let me try temple life. My mother cried because she hated to see me leave home, but she saw in my determination that it was inevitable—my birth horoscope had even predicted it! And my mother was certainly not the only mother in Ceylon to give her youngest son to the religious life; because Buddhism was so pervasive in our culture, this happened all the time.

My father consulted the village astrologer to determine a lucky day for me to leave home. In those days, astrology dictated the main events of our lives. People consulted the stars for deciding when to plant a crop, when to marry, when to cremate the dead, when to cut a child's hair for the first time, when to start an important job, even when to dig the foundation for a building.

Although astrological principles may seem contrary to the Buddha's teaching of the kammic law of cause and effect, belief in astrology coexisted nonetheless alongside Buddhist practices, and no one thought this was a problem in the least.

On the chosen day, my mother cooked some milk rice for me. That was a wonderful treat, made only for very special occasions. When a child reads his alphabet for the first time, his mother makes milk rice.

When a child goes to school for the first time, his mother makes milk rice. To celebrate a birthday or the new year, people make milk rice. The first harvest of rice every year is used to make milk rice that is offered to the monks.

And, of course, it was milk rice that the village girl Sujata offered to an emaciated Siddhattha Gotama, after he decided to give up asceticism. He accepted the refreshment. It revived him to the point that he was able to meditate strongly beneath the Bodhi tree and attain enlightenment and then teach about the Middle Way.

While I was eating the milk rice my mother had prepared for my home-leaving day, I saw that tears were beginning to roll down her cheeks and my sisters'. Rambanda also was trying to keep from crying.

As the time to leave approached, my father appeared, dressed in his best white sarong and shirt. He told me it was time to get going. I put on a white sarong and shirt, too.

By then my brother was crying openly, and suddenly it became very hard to leave. Mixed feelings swirled into a knot in my throat. I was happy at last to be going to a temple, but I felt very sad to leave my family. With this departure I was symbolically renouncing home life to take up what is called "the homeless life," the life of a Buddhist monk.

The family gathered in front of the house to see me off. I knelt before my mother and touched my forehead to the sand at her feet.

She stroked my head with both of her hands.

"May the Triple Gem protect you," she murmured, her voice thick and choked. "May all the gods protect you. May you live long in good health. May no harm come to you."

And then she started sobbing.

I stood up and she kissed my forehead and gave me a strong hug.

My father and I walked many hours along dusty roads to reach the temple that would be my new home. We had no appointment, and my father had not told the temple I was coming. The stars said it was an auspicious day for my home-leaving, and that was that.

Late in the day we reached the town of Kosinna, in Rambukkana district. The temple was on a coconut estate at the end of a dirt path.

The compound included a preaching hall, monks' quarters, and a separate shrine room. In the open center of the compound were several chairs and lots of flowering plants, as well as beds of betel shrubs, which yield the betel leaves that the monks chewed for their mild narcotic effects.

My father presented me to the resident monk, who was a small man about sixty years old. I would later find out that this man had been married before he ordained, and had lived in a house at the edge of the coconut estate, and that he had a grown son.

My father stayed with me at the temple for about two hours; then he left. I was very tired and wanted only to sleep. Already, my home and my childhood seemed distant.

The next morning, the head monk gave me a book of basic Pali, the language the Buddha spoke and the one used in Theravada Buddhist chanting. He told me I would need to memorize everything in the book to prepare for my ordination, and he outlined what would be expected of me.

I and the three other boys living at the temple were required to walk around the estate collecting fallen coconuts and stacking them in various places. We also had to sweep, collect firewood for cooking, haul water, wash dishes, and do laundry. Basically we were unpaid laborers—slaves, of a sort.

Our religious duties included picking flowers to be placed on the altar in the shrine room and attending devotional services every morning and evening.

The other boys cooked our meals every day. My job was to go to the head monk's former home and fetch special food prepared for him by his former wife. Only he was allowed to eat those dishes.

The three other boys who lived at the temple were all older and bigger than I was. These "temple boys" were not novice monks, as I would eventually be, but they had the opportunity to have a religious education by living at the temple and working in exchange for their room and board. One of them was in charge of the betel shrubs. The other managed the kitchen. The third took care of the many dogs roaming the compound. Generally, they did jobs that a monk was not allowed to do because of his vows, such as cooking or shopping.

This was to be my new life.

But I lived in that temple for only about three months.

One day I was in the kitchen washing a pot. Two of the other boys stood nearby having a heated argument. One boy threw a rock at the other and it hit me on the wrist. My hand swelled immediately and was very painful.

I wrote my father a letter and told him what had happened. Several days later, he arrived to take me home. "I don't want my boy at any temple where there are violent people," he said. He felt it was reasonable that a father might hit his son, but did not think this kind of behavior had any place in a temple. I went back home with my father.

My mother and sisters were overjoyed to see me again, and it was wonderful to be back with Rambanda. We all seemed to take up right where we had left off.

I spent most of my time running back and forth between my parents' house and the house where my oldest sister lived with her husband and daughter. They told me they would love to have a boy in their house, so why didn't I come live with them?

It was tempting. I loved them both very much, and my niece was like a sister to me. And my situation, at that point, seemed very uncertain. I was almost twelve and hadn't been in school for four months.

But the desire to be a monk still burned in my heart. I missed being in the robes. So I asked my father to find another temple that would take me.

Several months later, in January 1939, my brother-in-law told my father he had heard of another temple, this one in the village of Malandeniya, looking for a boy to ordain. It was called Sri Vijayarama, which means "prosperous and victorious." My father and brother-in-law thought that Malandeniya was about six miles from our house, but they weren't sure because none of us had ever been there.

My second home-leaving was much like the first: my mother's rice milk; a clean white sarong; tears and feelings of both excitement and sadness on my part. I felt happy anticipation of my future as a monk. At the same time, reflecting on my experience at the previous temple, I was filled with anxiety over going to live in another strange place with strange people.

This time, both my father and brother-in-law would accompany me on the trip. As we left, my mother told my brother-in-law, "Please take care of my boy. Since you live close to that temple, bring me reports about my boy."

Then we set off on foot, as my mother stood by the house. I kept turning around to look at her, and each time, she was still standing there, farther and farther away, until I could no longer see her—and it was longer still before the tears dried on my cheeks.

There was no road to follow from our village to Malandeniya. We walked along a footpath that crossed rice paddies, small creeks, and rubber tree plantations. Every once in a while, we passed through other small villages. Each time we asked directions to Malandeniya, someone would send us a little farther along the way.

Finally we approached a temple compound that was surrounded by barbed wire. We later learned that this was to prevent the neighbors' cattle from coming in and eating the small coconut trees on the grounds. At the gate, strips of bamboo covered the wire so that it didn't rip people's sarongs as they stepped through.

When we walked in, we were greeted first by a pack of barking dogs, then by a few boys, and eventually by the head monk, a man of medium height, with sharp eyes and a very long nose. He smiled, showing teeth stained dark by betel nuts.

My father, my brother-in-law, and I immediately knelt in the dirt and bowed three times. The monk motioned us inside the temple and pointed to mats on the floor where we could sit.

The monk's name was Venerable Kiribatkumbure Sonuttara Mahathera. The title Mahathera, "great elder," signified that he had been a bhikkhu for at least thirty-eight years. He was then almost sixty years old and seemed very friendly; he smiled often.

My father introduced me to him and told him that I would like to live at the temple and ordain. The monk looked me up and down, then nodded.

It was that simple. I had been accepted.

My father and brother-in-law stayed about an hour, chatting with the monk, and then left. The moment they disappeared from sight, I felt a great wave of loneliness wash over me. I longed to run after them and tell them I had changed my mind, that I wanted to go home.

I started to cry, and I couldn't stop for hours.

Venerable Sonuttara consoled me, saying that at the monastery I would have a very good home and I would learn Dhamma from very good teachers. Then he gave me a worn mat and a dirty pillow to spread on the concrete floor for my bed.

The shrine room contained a wooden platform raised on pillars four feet high. Its centerpiece was a very old, very ugly Buddha statue made of clay. That Buddha, I remember, had terrible, mean-looking eyes. It was nothing like the serene statues seen in most Buddhist temples. Evidently whoever sculpted it had not been schooled in the special qualities of the Buddha that are supposed to be depicted in statues of him.

On one side of the scowling Buddha was a picture of blue-skinned Vishnu, one of the chief Hindu deities. On the other side was a portrait of Huniyam Devata, a god revered even today by some Sinhalese for his viciousness. Some people say prayers in front of this deity to invoke its power against their enemies. Vishnu and Huniyam were strange choices for the altar of a Buddhist temple, and the cumulative effect of these three statues was unsettling indeed.

In a separate building, about twenty feet from the shrine room, were three rooms, all of them dirty and dingy: the head monk's sleeping quarters, a guest room for visiting monks, and a storeroom. The kitchen was reached by way of an open-air corridor. There was a small area for eating, also very dirty, and a wood cookstove with three stones on top, where pots could be placed over the fire.

Behind the kitchen was an outhouse exclusively for the use of the head monk. We boys were told to relieve ourselves in an open area at the back of the temple compound. And whenever we did so, the neighbors' pigs would come and clean up after us.

Just as in the first temple, I had many duties assigned to me. I was to split firewood for cooking, bring water from the well, sweep the grounds, pick flowers for the altar, cook, wash dishes, and feed the dozen dogs and cats that roamed the temple compound.

Between chores I was supposed to be memorizing Sanskrit stanzas from books called Sataka, which literally means "one hundred" but generally refers to "one hundred verses composed in praise of the Buddha." When we memorized all of one book, we moved on to another. One of the Sataka books explains the hundred and eight names of the Buddha, another presents the nine admirable qualities of the Buddha, and so on.

The purpose of forcing young boys to memorize those stanzas was threefold: to teach us correct Sanskrit pronunciation; to introduce us to the qualities of the Buddha; and most importantly, I think, to arouse faith and devotion in our young minds.

Each evening, as we recited our day's memorizations, Venerable Sonuttara would turn the kerosene lamp very low so that I couldn't cheat by reading my texts. If I made mistakes or hadn't memorized enough verses, he would get angry and slap me. His slaps were more like "teaching aids," not quite the same as the violence that made me want to leave the first temple.

Usually, though, I did well at the recitations. I seemed to be a quick learner, and my teacher was pleased. Within three months, he announced that I had progressed well and was ready for novice ordination.

Venerable Sonuttara consulted an almanac to choose an auspicious day and time for the ceremony. Then he sent word to my parents and invited twenty monks from other temples in the district. The oldest monk in the district, Venerable Alagoda Sumanatissa Nayaka Mahathera, would act as preceptor and administer my vows. The day before the ceremony, the temple was a flurry of activity as guests arrived and villagers from Malandeniya prepared food for the visiting monks.

Many of my relatives came for the big day, including my father, brother-in-law, and Rambanda, my dear brother. My mother could not travel that far because of her back injury. She was heartbroken she couldn't be there, my father told me, and I was very sad, too.

At ten o'clock in the morning, everyone gathered on a ten-by-forty-foot porch of the monks' residence. Normally an ordination ceremony would have been held in the shrine room, but because so many guests were there, my teacher decided the ceremony should be in the bigger space.

I wore a clean white shirt and sarong. My father walked with me toward the assembled monks, who were sitting on the floor next to a makeshift altar, facing the crowd.

I knelt before the senior monk, Venerable Sumanatissa, and bowed three times. He told me to seek permission from my father to enter the homeless life of a mendicant. So I knelt in front of my father and repeated the ritual of three bows, each time touching my forehead to the floor at his feet to express respect. I remember my father's solemn face looking down at me.

When I returned to the monks, Venerable Sumanatissa cut a few strands of my hair with a pair of scissors and told me to repeat after him: "Hair on the head, hair on the body, nails, teeth, skin." The parts of the body were to be my first subject of meditation. It is a traditional assignment given to all novices, reflecting the Buddha's First Foundation of Mindfulness, the physical form.

In one of his key discourses, the Mahasatipatthana Sutta, the Discourse on the Four Foundations of Mindfulness, the Buddha laid out four subjects toward which we should direct attention: our body, our feelings and emotions, our consciousness itself, and the mental objects of consciousness.

If we really look at those four things with total, undivided, and clear attention, we begin to see that they're all in flux all the time. They move and flow, changing from one moment to the next, leaving no possibility to cling to any one moment's experience. Contemplating those four constantly fluctuating objects, we see the impermanence of everything manifest in our own being.

Moreover, we see that there's no difference between ourselves and others. We are, each and every one of us, a conglomeration of body, feelings, consciousness, and mental objects. Understanding this, we become more magnanimous with others. Jealousy and separateness fade, and are replaced by growing compassion and loving-friendliness.

But not for a twelve-year-old boy in the midst of his novice ordination—all of that, of course, is still a distant goal on the day a novice monk receives his first subject of meditation. The older bhikkhus might equally well instruct a novice to work with any of the other four foundations of mindfulness, but they always choose the body because it is very easy, even for the beginner, to perceive. The body is, so to speak, right there, in all its lust-producing, pain-creating, pride-swelling physicality. And as I knelt before my preceptor, I had only the dimmest idea of what I would later learn about that first foundation of mindfulness.

The senior monk dropped the locks of my hair into my open palm. That was a signal for a junior monk to come forward and lead me out to have the rest of my head shaved.

The head-shaving ritual, symbolic of a monk's giving up material and worldly attachments, is always done in private, away from the audience of laypeople. Once my head was bare, I was sent to take a bath in the temple well, behind the kitchen. Then I dressed in white clothes again.

When I reentered the hall, I was carrying a folded bundle on top of my head—my monk's robes. I knelt before my preceptor. Chanting in Pali, I asked the Venerable to receive the set of robes I had, and to ordain me as a novice monk so that I would be able to end all suffering and attain nibbana (nirvana, in Pali).

Again, three bows.

Then Venerable Sumanatissa administered the three refuges and the ten precepts that were to become the moral basis of my new life, chanting them in Pali with me repeating after him.

> I go to the Buddha for refuge.
> I go to the Dhamma for refuge.
> I go to the Sangha for refuge.
> *(The three refuges were chanted three times each.)*
> I undertake the precept to abstain from killing.
> I undertake the precept to abstain from stealing.
> I undertake the precept to abstain from sexual activities.
> I undertake the precept to abstain from lying.
> I undertake the precept to abstain from taking intoxicating
>   drinks and drugs, which cause infatuation and heedlessness.
> I undertake the precept to abstain from eating after noon.
> I undertake the precept to abstain from dancing, singing, playing
>   musical instruments, and visiting theatrical shows.
> I undertake the precept to abstain from wearing garlands,
>   perfumes, unguents, cosmetics, and beautifying the body.
> I undertake the precept to abstain from using luxurious chairs
>   and beds.
> I undertake the precept to abstain from accepting gold and silver.

After reciting these things, I made the formal request of my preceptor that he share the merits I had earned by this act of ordaining: "Venerable Sir, please rejoice in all the merits I have acquired and allow me to rejoice in all the merits that you have acquired."

Then I made three more bows to him and bowed to all the other monks as well.

Finally, Venerable Sumanatissa announced my new name: Gunaratana, "Jewel of Virtue."

Now I was a novice.

I was given a little cushion and told to sit among the other monks, though not too close! I sat, and a small parade of laypeople came forward, each one bowing and laying a small present before me. There were towels, bars of soap, an umbrella—practical items useful to me in my new, simplified life.

The day concluded with a sumptuous meal. I ate with the other monks, sitting on the floor. The food offered at temples by laypeople is expressly for the monastics, and so I had never before been allowed to legitimately partake of it. It was delicious.

That day was truly a high point in my life. Everything was perfect, except for one thing: My beloved mother was not there. I missed her very much.

Two weeks later, I went to see her. She was overjoyed to see her youngest son, now with a shaved head, wearing the burnt-orange robes of an ordained bhikkhu.

She spread a clean towel at my feet and, sinking painfully to her knees, prostrated before me. Three times her forehead touched the towel.

It was a reversal of the day I left home, when I had bowed to her. Now she was paying her respects to me. It was a powerful and moving moment for both of us.

"My dear little monk," said my mother, tears in her eyes, "you should never disrobe. The monk's life is the best for you. It is the life of freedom. Never think of disrobing."

From that day onward, whenever I visited home, Mother repeated this ritual and this request of me, always saying, "Never disrobe, my son."

After my ordination, life at the temple changed, yet it didn't. There were still religious texts to memorize, chores to perform, punishments to endure. Meals were certainly different, though. Now, according to the precepts, I could not eat solid food after midday. Basically, we had one large meal a day. It was collected by going on alms round in the village. As the resident novice, that was my job.

Every day, after my morning chores, I left the temple at about 9:30 A.M. A large metal bowl, about the size of a soup tureen, hung from a wide cloth band around my neck, its mouth covered by a cotton cloth.

My duty was to collect food to feed both the head monk and myself from each of the sixty or so houses in the village. Villagers stood in front of their huts, pots of rice or dahl or vegetables or sweet cakes in hand. As I walked slowly by, maintaining silence and avoiding eye contact, they would place a spoonful of their offering in my bowl.

The alms round is still practiced today in villages all over Asia. It's a beautiful sight—long lines of monks walking silently, barefoot, and stopping in front of laypeople's homes. The devout villagers bow as they place food in the alms bowls. Not a word is exchanged.

This practice is an ancient tradition bringing to life the interdependent relationship of monastics and laypeople. The bhikkhus, who are not allowed by their vows to cook food, receive sustenance from the laypeople. The laypeople, by offering food to the bhikkhus, receive spiritual merit and support the continuation of the Buddha's way.

But for me, alms round was always stressful. I had to visit all sixty homes and return to the temple precisely at 11 A.M. If I was just five minutes late, my teacher would refuse to eat. Monastic rules specified that our meal must be completed before noon, and my teacher didn't want to eat hurriedly. So I rushed through the village, not daring to miss even one house, because that would deprive its occupants of the merit of offering alms food, and then they would complain to my teacher and I'd receive a reprimand.

There were many dogs in that village, and they were hungry. When they saw a small boy carrying a bowl of steaming, fragrant food, they became aggressive. I tried to fend them off with the umbrella I carried to protect me against the blazing sun. But I was never very successful.

Sometimes I tried to run away from the dogs, but with a heavy bowl hanging around my neck, that wasn't easy. Invariably I would fall, spilling food in the dust. The dogs would rush me, snarling and snapping. Many times I returned to the temple with bleeding legs and a half-empty alms bowl.

Some of the villagers seemed to feel sorry for me. Whenever a particular dog had bitten me, they would come to the temple a few days later and announce that that dog had "died." This outcome was not at all something I would have wished for, but it was nonetheless what happened.

Every day after lunch, I helped the two temple boys clean the kitchen, then I left for a two-mile walk to a temple in the next village, where the head monk would drill me in Pali lessons. I was able to memorize the verses easily, so this monk liked me very much. Then, after my lessons, I would rush back to my temple for evening chores and devotions, a ritual of reciting the qualities of the Buddha, Dhamma, and Sangha.

After that service, we had tea and I studied some more. We were usually in bed by 9:30 P.M. The wake-up gong sounded at four o'clock the next morning.

Like my father, Venerable Sonuttara had a temper. He used abusive language to insult me and the temple boys. If we broke any rules or strayed from the daily schedule in the slightest, he didn't hesitate to hit us with whatever he could lay his hands on: rocks, sticks, bricks, a broom, even a knife.

So I tried hard to follow the rules. As soon as I got up at 4:00 every morning, I would begin to cook breakfast and heat water. By 5:00, my teacher expected the water, so he could wash his face. Then I had to pick fresh flowers and arrange them on the altar for morning devotions at 5:30.

Breakfast was to be ready precisely at 6:00. Venerable Sonuttara wanted the dogs' plates placed next to where he sat, so he could feed them with his own hands. We could not eat until he finished, then we had to gulp our food in order to get to our next chores quickly. After I was ordained a novice, I was allowed to eat near my teacher, but he sat on a chair and put his plate on a table. I was nearby, sitting on the floor, with my plate on a low bench in front of me.

When I returned from alms round at 11:00, we went through a similar ritual of serving lunch and gobbling our own meals.

At 1 P.M. our teacher expected his tea on a special table. Then I went to the other temple for my Pali lessons, returning no later than three in the afternoon.

By 5:30, the flowers and garden were to be watered and then I had time for a quick bath before evening devotional chanting at 6:00. At 6:30, I was expected to serve the Venerable his tea. At 7:00 I recited my memorized verses for him. Afterward, I prepared his betel chewing mixture, to be served at 7:30. Then there was final cleanup and bed.

On full-moon and new-moon days, we enjoyed a break from the routine. Instead of manual laborers, we were hosts to the villagers who would come to spend that special day at the temple. Most of them were elderly and could not read or write. In most temples, monks would read Jataka tales to the laypeople and explain their significance.

The whole collection of Jataka tales is 550 stories, each one illustrating how the Buddha in a previous rebirth manifested a certain noble quality: generosity, say, or moral integrity, renunciation, wisdom, effort, patience, truthfulness, determination, loving-friendliness, and equanimity. Sometimes in the Jataka tales, the Buddha is some kind of animal; always he is a bodhisattva, or one who is in the preparatory phases of becoming a Buddha.

Because I had a fourth-grade education, I was something of a hero to the uneducated villagers who came to our temple. They loved to listen to me recite the tales in my girlish, prepubescent voice.

One day I remember telling a story from the human life of the Buddha. I said that after leaving his father's palace and cutting off his hair, Prince Siddhattha became an ascetic. He wrapped a length of yellow cloth around himself and collected food in an alms bowl.

One of the villagers listening, an old man who reminded me of my grandfather, said, "Little monk, I think you are wrong. I think the yellow robe and alms bowl were not introduced to the world until Siddhattha became the Buddha and began his order of monks."

I answered him: "Sir, the Sanskrit word for bowl is *patra,* which literally means any kind of container open at the top. Certainly such items were in use prior to the Buddha's coming. They were commonly used by mendicants. And the Sanskrit word for yellow cloth is *kashaya vastra,* which refers to any piece of yellow cloth. Why couldn't Siddhattha wrap himself in a length of yellow cloth?"

As I recall, my answer pleased the old man very much.

But not everything that took place at the temple was so lofty. One day the temple boys, who were older than I was, invited me to smoke tobacco with them. I did, and thus an addiction was born. We could not afford to buy cigarettes, so we stole tobacco from the head monk's room, where he kept a supply of it to mix with betel and areca nuts, for chewing.

We'd wrap the tobacco in scraps of newspaper and smoke secretly. Every once in a while our teacher would discover us smoking and beat us for it. But that didn't deter us; we just became more and more careful about not getting caught.

One day after returning from alms round, I lit a small roll of tobacco in the kitchen and began to smoke it. My teacher appeared, carrying a bucket, on his way to bathe in the well.

He stopped and looked directly at me: I was caught red-handed.

"I'm not going to beat you this time," he said. "But what should I do to you if I catch you doing this again? You tell me."

I swallowed hard. My teacher's anger was intimidating. I knew there was only one answer to that question.

"If you see me smoking again, you should beat me as much as you wish," I said.

But I didn't stop smoking; I was thoroughly addicted. A couple of weeks later I was caught in the act again. Venerable Sonuttara beat me with his bare hands.

After that, he locked up his tobacco so we couldn't get at it. Again, we were undeterred and simply became more resourceful: We sold coconuts, towels, handkerchiefs, and rice, whatever we had on hand—usually gifts from laypeople—to buy our tobacco.

As I got nearer to my teenage years I felt stirrings of independence. I was no longer so afraid of Venerable Sonuttara's unpredictable rage. His extreme punishments seemed unfair and cruel and I began to resent him.

I also began to feel that my education was lacking. I was thirteen years old and I had only completed the fourth grade—an accomplishment in those days, but still not enough for me. Neither my teacher nor the monk in the neighboring temple who taught me Pali had any formal education. I wanted to learn more, a desire that would stay with me for my entire life.

The temple began to feel like a prison. This was not the luminous religious life I had dreamed of.

One day, after lunch, Venerable Sonuttara went to take a nap. One of the other boys decided he wanted an orange from the tree outside our teacher's room. He started throwing rocks into the tree to knock down an orange.

The noise woke our teacher. He came out of his room, furious, and demanded to know who had been making such a racket. One of the other boys said it was me, that I was throwing rocks.

And now suddenly I was furious, too. I asked the boy, in very unpleasant language, why he was lying to our teacher. Venerable Sonuttara turned on me. He said I was disrespectful. He said he didn't care who had been throwing rocks and that because I was being disrespectful, I was the one to be punished.

He seized a broomstick and hit me over and over until I fell to the floor. I could hardly breathe.

That was the last straw for me.

Later in the afternoon, I gathered my books as usual. It was time to go to Kebilitigoda temple for my Pali lessons. I started out the door just as my teacher and the other boys headed toward the back of the compound to dig a new latrine. I watched them go, then I quietly went back inside and threw down my books.

I went into the room where the temple boys kept their clothes and grabbed a white shirt and a sarong. Without a pang of regret, I took off my robes and put on the shirt and sarong.

Exhilaration rising inside me, I slipped out the front door of the temple, through the barbed-wire gate, and onto the hard-packed road.

I was no longer a novice monk. I was free.

CHAPTER THREE

Escape

WHEN I DISROBED and left the temple, there was no question in my mind where I was headed: home.

First, though, I stopped at my sister's house. My brother-in-law seemed only mildly surprised to see me. He had heard of my struggles and, smiling, he said, "It's good that you left that place. Stay here awhile, and I'll find you another temple." But I was afraid that if I stayed there, Venerable Sonuttara would come looking for me. So I ran home to my parents' house.

My mother was shocked to see me. She asked why I had left the temple, so I told her what had happened. She didn't say much, just started to cry.

In the evening my father came home from working in the rice paddy. I told him about the abuse I had endured at the temple. I could see from the expression on his face that he didn't believe me, but he stayed calm. My brother and sisters all seemed glad to see me, but no one had much to say. They simply accepted my being there.

We all seemed to know it couldn't last, though. It was taboo for a monk to disrobe. It brought bad luck, even disgrace, to the whole family.

The next afternoon my teacher arrived at the house. My parents, out of respect for the monk, didn't ask him to explain why I had run away from him. They pretended not to know anything about what had happened.

After a few minutes of casual conversation, Venerable Sonuttara asked me to return to the temple with him. I looked at my parents, silently pleading for their help, hoping they would rise to my defense and say they wanted me to stay with them.

For a minute or two, no one said anything. There was complete silence. My parents seemed unable to look at me. Then my teacher repeated his request.

My father nodded his head and said quietly, "Yes, you must go with him."

My heart sank. I knew that if I stayed, my father would simply force me to return to the temple the next day, or the day after that. And I didn't want to bring disgrace on my family.

So I left with Venerable Sonuttara. As soon as we got back to the temple, he ordained me again, in a ceremony much less elaborate than the first one. For the second time in my life, I put on orange robes. I could only hope it would go better this time.

My teacher, as a member of the monks' council, a governing body of our sect, had to spend the month between the full moon of June and the full moon of July in Kandy. During that month, the council held higher ordination ceremonies for novice monks, sometimes conferring full monkhood on as many as thirty young men a day. During my teacher's absence I was to serve as head of the temple, even though I was barely thirteen years old and still a novice.

One day, while my teacher was gone and I was in charge, a man came to the temple asking for oranges. We had two orange trees on the premises, so whenever villagers needed oranges they came to us. He gave me a little less than one rupee, the equivalent of about twenty-five cents.

One of the temple boys had gone to Kandy with Venerable Sonuttara, so only the other boy, named Hinnimahattaya, was there with me. Normally we shared everything, like partners. So as soon as the villager left with his sack of oranges, Hinnimahattaya asked me for his share of the proceeds.

"He only gave me twenty-five cents," I told Hinnimahattaya, "and out of that we have to buy sugar, tea, and some kerosene for the lamps for tonight."

Hinnimahattaya got very upset and let loose a string of filthy words. I beat him up.

Another time, we had run out of matches to light the kerosene lamps. I asked Hinnimahattaya to run to a neighbor's house and bring back a burning stick. That was very common in those days, to "borrow" fire from your neighbor.

But Hinnimahattaya refused to go. So I threatened him: If he wouldn't go get the burning stick, I wouldn't give him half of my next cigarette. (Normally we shared cigarettes; I would smoke one half, then give him the other half.) But Hinnimahattaya was unpersuaded. He was willing to give up his half of a smoke in return for not running the errand.

So I went myself, and when I came back with the burning stick, I used it to light a cigarette. Eagerly Hinnimahattaya watched me. As soon as half of the cigarette was gone, he asked me for the second half.

"Forget it," I said. "A deal is a deal. I ran the errand, and so you don't get the cigarette."

Hinnimahattaya started to curse me. Enraged, I pushed him up against the wall, held him there, and used the cigarette to burn both corners of his mouth.

It also happened that, during the Venerable's trip to Kandy, several teenage boys from the village came to the temple and stayed with us. We played lots of games. Of course, as a novice monk I wasn't supposed to be entertaining myself with games, but who cares when the teacher is not around?

One of our favorite games was called *panca ganahava*, which means "play with five." It involved tossing small seashells onto the floor and earning points based on whether the shells landed right-side up or not.

One day our next-door neighbor came over and said that he wanted to teach us a card game. He showed us a game and got us interested.

He made sure we won several games in a row, then he said, "If you have money, you can bet on this game. Today is your lucky day. You seem to be winning."

I told him I only had one rupee. He said, "That's good. Let's play for money."

I bet my one rupee and immediately won two more! I was hooked. He encouraged me to play again. Of course, that time I lost. The neighbor pocketed the three rupees and left, smiling.

That was the end of my short gambling career and one lesson I learned in just a single try.

On the afternoon my teacher returned from Kandy, the very first thing he did was examine the bowl we used for offering food to the Buddha statue in the shrine room. Our instructions had been to empty it each day before noon.

That day, the Venerable found it still full at one o'clock. I was in the kitchen at the time, preparing tea for him. He called me and I came out of the kitchen and started down the steps into the main building.

Suddenly I saw an object flying toward me—the alms bowl from the shrine room! My teacher was so upset that he had thrown the bowl at me before even asking why it was still full. The bowl hit me square in the forehead, hard, and I fell to the ground, bleeding.

I still have a scar on my forehead, to this day.

Our teacher also noticed the burn marks around Hinnimahattaya's mouth.

"How did this happen?" the Venerable asked me.

I had warned Hinnimahattaya not to tell our teacher about the incident with the cigarette. If he did, we would both be in trouble for smoking. Fortunately, Hinnimahattaya said nothing.

I told Venerable Sonuttara that the temple boy had cursed me, so I burned his mouth as punishment. Curiously, he seemed to accept that story and said nothing more about it.

That was one of the rare times when I got away with something, though. My teacher's temper was uncontrollable and the beatings continued, often for the slightest infraction of the rules. He was the dictator, and we had to accept his every command without question or discussion.

Yet for all that, Venerable Sonuttara did have a kind streak. He had a real soft spot for animals; that's why he fed all the stray dogs and cats in the area. And if sick people came to the temple seeking help, he gave them free herbal medicines. Occasionally one of the temple boys would run away, taking something of value with him, such as a brass oil lamp or even one of the Buddha statues.

"Let him go," my teacher would say. "He is poor. He can sell those things and get a little money. We can replace whatever he stole."

In reflecting now upon my teacher's behavior, I think that Venerable Sonuttara really did want to see me become a good monk and not be led astray by my natural adolescent urges for independence. And he "encouraged" good behavior by using the normal form of punishment in those days: physical beatings.

Of course, I couldn't see it that way until later, when I was an adult. At the time I lived in his temple as a novice, I was miserable. I chafed continually under his dominance.

At one point, I began to talk to one of the temple boys about leaving. He was very unhappy, too. Both of us were saving up money and hoarding candles, and we planned to run away some night. One day we agreed to escape that night. We both worked harder than usual that day, in order to please our teacher so that he wouldn't suspect anything.

That night, after everyone in the temple went to bed, I removed my robes and put on a sarong and shirt. My accomplice and I sneaked out the back door.

First we had to go through a cemetery, which unnerved both of us. Then we found ourselves on a wooden bridge over a small creek. We had heard the local stories that this was a place where wicked demons and goblins grabbed people. The legend also said that the first sign of their appearance would be a big black dog.

Normally, if people had to pass over that bridge they would go in a large group, everyone talking loudly and carrying bright torches to scare away the demons. But because we were running away, we had to be quiet and we couldn't even light the candles we had brought with us, for fear someone would see us.

We crossed the bridge at exactly midnight. We were trembling, dry-mouthed. Our hair stood on end. We didn't utter one word to each other, just walked slowly in the pitch dark.

Suddenly, a big black dog appeared in front of us, and my heart began pounding even harder. Then we were both slapped so hard in the face we nearly fell off the bridge and into the water.

It turned out that the big black dog was our temple dog and the slaps came from our teacher, who had heard us sneaking out the back door and followed us to the bridge. On his orders, we followed him back to the temple, where I was immediately ordained a third time, in the middle of the night.

None of the other temple boys ever heard about that incident, nor did the villagers. The next day, back in my bhikkhu's robes, I took the alms bowl and went into the village to collect alms as usual.

When I was fifteen or so, I became interested in a girl from the village who was about my age. Every day she would stand in front of her house as I came by with the alms bowl. She was near my height, with long black hair. She had a round face like mine, with skin lighter than the normal Sinhalese complexion, and a perfect set of teeth that showed whenever she smiled. I thought she was beautiful. One day, as she ladled rice into my bowl, we had a very brief, whispered conversation—very much against the monastic rules.

That evening, when I went to our well to take a bath, I deliberately banged the bucket against the sides of the well to make a noise loud enough for her to hear at her house. That was the signal we had agreed on.

Within moments she ran to the well, carrying a pot as if she needed to fill it with water. I was thrilled to see her coming.

For about ten days, that was our routine. I would bang the bucket in the well; she would grab a pot in her house and, if it was full of water, pour it out so that she had an excuse to come to the well. Even though we were too shy to share our budding feelings for each other, we had long, lovely conversations, and each time, they got longer and longer. I told her that temple life was like a prison. We gossiped about other people in the village. She told me about her life at home.

Eventually my teacher began to wonder why I was taking so long at my bath, and one day he came to check on me and caught us there, talking and laughing.

Of course he was upset. Monks of any age are not supposed to have close contact with females. He ordered the girl not to come to the well when I was there. Back at the temple, he reprimanded me in very strong language and ordered me to take my baths later at night, at a time he thought would be too late for her to come to the well.

Actually, that suited me fine because I knew we would have even more privacy to talk after dark, when no one would see us together. So we continued our clandestine meetings.

Inevitably, my teacher caught us again, and this time his rebuke was even harsher. He told the girl never to come to the well again. He said that he was going to report her behavior to her parents.

She cried and begged him not to tell her parents. She promised not to go to the well anymore, and she didn't. I never saw her again.

When I look back on that incident now, after years of Dhamma study and practice, I see it as evidence that boys perhaps should not be ordained so young, as was customary in my childhood. They should first receive a secular education and be allowed to enjoy games, sports, friends, and parties—all the things that young people crave. Then, when they have grown into adults, they can make a mature decision about whether to be ordained. Joining the Sangha is a serious commitment, and I don't think a very young person is prepared to make an informed choice about it. And it would be a rare boy who was emotionally ready to cope with the rigors and restrictions of monastic life.

The traditional thinking in my country was that boys, with their vigorous young minds, could memorize sacred texts more easily than adults. Their personalities could be shaped and molded early into the peaceful demeanor of a contemplative monk. But now I'm not so sure that's true. I have seen plenty of men who became monks in middle or old age, after being married and having raised children, and they make fine bhikkhus. And I've seen too many monks, on the other hand, who were ordained before puberty, continue to behave like children.

After Venerable Sonuttara cut off my budding romance with the girl at the well, my dissatisfaction with temple life deepened. I was a teenager, with a mind of my own and a desire for a more formal education than this teacher could offer me. I wanted to remain a monk, but not under the yoke of this particular Venerable. I could think of no solution except to run away again, but where to? I knew I could no longer go home. My parents would be heartbroken if I disrobed again. I couldn't bring them into this shameful plan.

About that time, a father and son came to live at the temple. The son's name was Gunawardhena, and he and I became very good friends. He kept telling me that he knew another place that was better than this temple, so we hatched a plan to run away together. This time, I intended to do it right. I would run away so that no one would ever find me.

On the chosen day I had the village barber shave my head as usual. The whole day I was in a fever of anticipation; so was Gunawardhena. At eleven o'clock that night, I went to the outhouse, and when I came back I left the front door slightly open.

At about twelve-thirty, we heard our teacher snoring. We picked up several candles and walked to the kitchen, where I slipped off my robes and, yet again, pulled on a sarong and shirt.

Leaving the temple grounds, we headed in the direction opposite the one I had used in my last getaway. As fast as we could, we ran through rice fields to the main road two miles away. All around us were the sounds of nocturnal birds, frogs and crickets, and dogs barking in the distance.

Once we reached the road we slowed down to a walk. Soon we saw two people holding lanterns coming toward us. It was 1942, during the Second World War, and a dusk-to-dawn curfew had been imposed over all of Ceylon.

Nervously, Gunawardhena spoke to me, using not my ordained name but my lay name. "Ukkubanda, those are policemen. They're going to ask us all kinds of questions. What shall we tell them?"

In a flash I made up an entirely fictitious story: "Tell them my mother died yesterday, and that somebody came to the temple to give us the message. We missed the bus to go to her funeral, so now we're walking along the road, and are hoping to catch another bus in the morning."

The policemen reached us and eyed me suspiciously. I had a handkerchief tied around my shaved head, and another tied around my neck. Because I had no belt, I was wearing another handkerchief around my waist to hold up my sarong. The bundle of candles in my hand, too, was wrapped in a handkerchief.

"Look at this rascal," one of the policemen said. "He has handkerchiefs all over him."

They separated me from Gunawardhena and took us about ten yards apart, then asked each of us the same question: Where were we going in the middle of the night?

Both of us told the same story, so the policemen let us go, not even mentioning the curfew. All they said was to be sure to use a candle as we walked.

Within two hours we arrived at Kurunegala, about eleven miles from the temple. Now we felt safer and were pretty sure Venerable Sonuttara wouldn't follow us this far.

Just as it was starting to get light, we came upon a roadside shelter, one of many typical structures known as pilgrims' rest houses. The hut had low walls, a straw roof, and a dirt floor upon which people rolled out straw mats to lie down on. Most of the time, these primitive, open-air huts were occupied by travelers resting in the shade and beggars cooking whatever food they had scrounged.

Gunawardhena and I were lucky. This particular shelter was unoccupied that morning. Gratefully, we sank to the ground and were asleep almost immediately.

Several hours later, we woke up and washed our faces with cold water from a well. We started walking again, not knowing exactly where we were going. We just walked.

The scenery changed constantly. We passed coconut groves, rubber and tea estates, terraced rice paddies, banana plantations, and small vegetable gardens outside one-room huts. There seemed to be stray dogs everywhere, many of which had completely lost their fur, and more with numerous wounds from bites of other dogs or beatings by humans. Often we saw wild monkeys swinging in the trees or running on the ground. In the distance, every so often, we could hear elephants trumpeting.

There were occasional cars, trucks, buses, motorcycles, and rickshaws, all honking their horns to warn pedestrians and people sitting in the road.

But most of the traffic was human. We passed men, women, and children simply walking or herding cows and chickens. Some rode in primitive wooden carts pulled by oxen.

Along the roadsides were small mud huts that functioned as shops. People sat in front of them, chewing betel nuts and drinking tea and gossiping. Travelers could stop and buy tea, small loaves of bread, areca nuts, dried fish, ropes made of coconut fiber, and occasionally staples such as sugar, salt, rice, lentils, and kerosene.

Most everyone smoked. People would buy one or two cigarettes at a time, or maybe a bidi, the poor man's smoke that only cost about one-fifth of a cent. It was basically just a dry leaf filled with a pinch of tobacco—meager, but serviceable.

Gunawardhena and I had a little money we had stolen from Venerable Sonuttara's room before leaving the temple, so we bought a couple of loaves of bread. On somebody's land next to the road we saw a heap of coconuts. We stole one and broke it open by smashing it against the ground. The flesh of that coconut, and the bread, was our first meal on our journey.

We walked twenty-five miles that day. Late in the evening we arrived at a town called Dambulla. We found another empty pilgrims' rest house, spread some palm fronds on the floor, and lay down. We were exhausted.

The next morning we woke to find ourselves covered with ticks and sand flies. We went to a nearby well, and there, we broke sticks from a bush and started to brush our teeth with their fibrous ends.

A monk approached us, eyeing me carefully. I tried to ignore him.

"Have you been a monk?" he asked, looking at my hairless head.

"No," I lied easily. "I've been sick. I just got out of the hospital yesterday."

"You don't look like you've been sick," he said. "I think you're a monk. Come with me. I'll ordain you again, at my temple."

I considered his offer. I still had a desire to be a monk, deep inside me. I had only disrobed because Venerable Sonuttara had been so cruel. This monk seemed kinder. But of course, I couldn't go without consulting my friend.

I turned to Gunawardhena.

"What do you think?" I asked him. "I really don't want to disrobe. Here is a chance for me to be a monk again."

"Are you crazy?" Gunawardhena said. "Don't you remember what our teacher did to us? All these monks are alike. They have no heart. They only think about their rules and regulations. Don't be a fool, let's go."

The monk sweetened his offer. He said that he knew some British officers at a nearby military airport. He could get Gunawardhena a job there, he promised. We could both live at the temple, and I could be a monk while Gunawardhena worked at the airport.

Gunawardhena would hear none of it, and I didn't want to abandon my friend. So we left the monk and started walking again.

The next day we ran into a man who said that he worked for a civilian contractor. "If you want to work, come with me," the man told us. "We have plenty of jobs available."

We agreed.

Our job turned out to be hard manual labor. We were given two shovels and two bamboo baskets and told to collect sand from a creek bed, then pile it in large heaps for collection.

For several months we worked there, part of a crew of about twenty young men. We worked from 7 A.M. to 7 P.M. Our pay was 1.2 rupees a day, the equivalent of about fifty cents. Out of that salary, the boss deducted about twenty-five cents for our meals. Breakfast was a cup of tea with sugar, and dinner was rice with lentils. We slept in hammocks made by tying a gunny sack between two trees.

The jungle was alive with mosquitoes. They bit us night and day, and sure enough, before long, Gunawardhena came down with malaria. He had a high fever and could not work.

I asked our boss for two days off, so I could take care of my friend. He refused.

"I've worked for you for months, seven days a week, twelve hours a day," I said. "All I want is a couple of days' break."

Again, he refused. Either I had to keep working, or both Gunawardhena and I had to leave the work camp.

"All right," I said. "Give us the rest of our salary."

The boss paid us, and we left.

Thus began our life as beggars. By day we wandered along dusty roads. By night we shared other beggars' meager meals in the roadside huts, telling jokes, singing, and dancing to pass the time.

For several weeks we didn't bathe. Our clothes were filthy and we smelled bad. Every morning the other beggars would leave for "work" and ask us which area we planned to beg in that day.

"We don't know," was always our answer. The truth was, we didn't beg at all. We just ate whatever food other people were willing to share with us. We were lazy beggars.

Gradually Gunawardhena recovered from malaria and regained his strength. But then, one morning I woke up with severe pain in my right leg. I felt feverish. Looking closely at my leg, I found a red blotch on the thigh about four inches above my knee. One of the beggars sharing our shelter peered at the wound and declared it a snakebite. The pain was excruciating, and I could barely lift my leg.

Gunawardhena and I stayed behind when the other beggars left. After about two hours, I struggled to my feet and limped out of the hut.

We had barely walked ten yards when we ran into a man about twenty-five years old. Neither of us had ever seen him before. For some reason I couldn't understand, he and Gunawardhena struck up an instant friendship. They started joking and laughing like old buddies. Probably Gunawardhena was feeling weighed down by me and my lame leg; he was relieved to run into someone who was more fun.

The three of us walked together, with me lagging behind. Within five minutes, Gunawardhena turned to me.

"Ukkubanda, since you can't walk very fast, why don't I go ahead with this man? You take your time and walk as slow as you need. We'll wait for you in Lovamahapaya."

I was immediately struck with fear. Lovamahapaya was a six- or seven-hour walk.

"No, don't leave me alone," I begged. "I can't walk by myself. I need your help. Please stay with me."

Then the incomprehensible happened: Gunawardhena ignored me and simply walked away with his new friend.

I sat down and started crying. My leg was throbbing. I couldn't believe what was happening.

How ungrateful Gunawardhena was. We had planned our adventure together, weeks ahead of time, and I had given up the monkhood to run away with him. When he got sick in the jungle, I had given up the construction job. All these months, we had been traveling friends. We had depended on each other. And now, when I needed him most, he had abandoned me.

I had no companion, no home, no money, no food. I was at rock bottom, and I was utterly alone.

What in the world was I going to do?

CHAPTER FOUR

A Monk Once Again

For an hour after Gunawardhena had abruptly left me by the roadside, I just sat there, alone and confused. What had started out as the great adventure of running away from our temple had turned into a frightening ordeal. I had a leg badly swollen from snakebite, I was hungry, and my traveling companion was gone forever, for all I knew. I had never felt so low in my life.

Eventually, though, something inside me commanded me to get up. "Keep moving," the voice seemed to say.

So I got to my feet and started limping along the deserted road. I walked for several hours until finally I came upon a girl sitting in the shade of a tree. She was selling fruits, nuts, bread, tea, and vegetables.

I sat down on a rough bench.

"Why are you limping?" she asked me.

I explained that a snake had bitten my leg the night before.

The girl asked me more questions: what my name was, where I came from, and why I was traveling alone. I told her my whole story.

She gave me a piece of bread with lentil curry, and a good cup of hot tea. Gratefully, I accepted the meal.

She went inside her tiny hut and came out with a piece of lemon. She rubbed the lemon on the wound in my thigh, then massaged some oil into it. She asked me to stay there until her father came home from work, but I said that I needed to get to Lovamahapaya to meet my friend. I was hoping Gunawardhena might indeed be waiting for me there.

I started down the road again, still limping. Pretty soon I arrived in the town of Anuradhapura. One of the first places I saw was a restaurant called the Siyasiri Hotel (restaurants were called hotels in those days). The manager greeted me, then asked why I was limping. I told him about the snakebite. He asked why I was alone. I told him how I couldn't keep up with my traveling friend, so he had gone on ahead to Lovamahapaya.

"Everybody who passes through here comes to this hotel," the manager said. "Stay here. If they come through this town, when they arrive you'll see them."

I agreed, and sat down to wait. By 11 P.M., my head was nodding. The manager could see I was very tired.

"You should stay overnight," he said. He gave me a straw mat to sleep on.

And that was the last thing I knew until eight o'clock the next morning.

As soon as I woke up, I asked the manager if Gunawardhena had arrived.

"No," he said, shaking his head. "Nobody came looking for you. But you stay here, I can give you a little job."

I didn't know what else to do, or where else to go, so I accepted his offer.

And thus I became a waiter at the Siyasiri Hotel in Anuradhapura. It was a pleasant enough job. Several other young people worked at the restaurant, and we all got along well. I waited on customers, cleaned tables, and washed dishes.

One day, several weeks later, I came down with a malarial fever and felt too sick to work. While resting, I wrote my mother a letter to let her know where I was. I felt guilty, knowing that she probably had heard the news of my running away from the temple, and that she must be worried sick about me.

A few days later, when I was back at work, I went to the nearby well to draw water for the restaurant. Another boy was there, too. I borrowed his bucket and used it to draw some water and pour it in my bucket. As I handed his bucket back to him, the boy dropped it into the well, rope and all. He started to cry, knowing how much trouble he would be in for losing the bucket.

But I had customers in the restaurant waiting for fresh water for their tea. I had to hurry. I told the boy that I would take my bucket of water to the restaurant, then I would come right back and help him fish his bucket out of the well.

But when I walked into the restaurant carrying a full bucket of water, my eldest brother, Tikiribanda, was standing at the entrance. As soon as he caught sight of me, he demanded that I come home with him. Mother was crying nonstop, he said, ever since she had heard the news of my escape from the temple.

My brother was almost as intimidating as my father. I dared not disobey his command.

I forgot all about the poor boy waiting at the well for me to come and help him retrieve his bucket. I forgot about the kind restaurant manager who had given me a chance to start a new life.

"I have opened a small shop," my brother told me. "You can come and help me run it."

Later I found out that the day after Gunawardhena and I left the temple, Venerable Sonuttara had reported our disappearance to the police. My father went to the temple and demanded my teacher find me and return me home. By then, Father realized that Venerable Sonuttara was an angry, cruel man, and that my problems at the temple were not just due to my misbehavior. My father knew that my stories of being abused at the hands of my teacher were not lies, but by then, of course, it was too late. I had left the temple, and that time, I didn't run home.

Meanwhile, police officers were combing the countryside for me.

Then came my letter from Anuradhapura. Mother and Father immediately dispatched my oldest brother to fetch me.

My parents, especially my mother, were overjoyed to see me alive and well, but it was uncomfortable being in their house again. All the neighbors called me "ex-monk," which was a great insult. My father didn't want to have an "unlucky" son around; he asked me to reordain.

To keep away from Father so that we didn't have to talk much, I kept busy at a series of small jobs. One of them was digging flood-control ditches on a rubber estate near our house.

This estate was run by a large company. They paid a meager salary, and the work was backbreaking. I would fill bucket after bucket with soil, and then women carried the buckets to a dumping ground. One time, one of those women saw the deep blisters on my hands from the shovel, and she offered to trade jobs with me. So for a while, she dug the soil and I carried the full buckets.

After that job, I picked tea leaves. That also was monotonous, hard labor. I would have preferred to work at my brother's shop, of course, but he had closed it only a couple of months after opening. People in the village were too poor to support his shop. Most of them couldn't afford to buy even the simplest staples.

I spent much of my free time at my sister's house, the same sister who had nursed me when I was young, the woman I called my second mother. Since her husband had died, there was no adult male in the house. It was only my sister, her infant son, and her one daughter, my niece, who was just five months older than me.

They were very kind to me and I felt more at home with them than with my own parents. So a few weeks after I had returned home, I moved from my parents' house to my sister's house. That was a more peaceful arrangement, but I still wasn't really comfortable with the life of a householder. My original desire to be a monk still burned within me, despite everything that had happened.

I began to think more and more about my teacher and the temple I had left five months before. I felt regret for having run away. My mind had softened toward Venerable Sonuttara, and I remembered his good qualities. I thought that I should at least apologize to him.

One day, when my sister had gone to visit her dead husband's relatives, I decided I would secretly go to see my teacher. It was an overnight visit because of the distance, but I figured I could be back before my sister returned. I knew she wouldn't approve of this visit. She wanted me to live at her house permanently and give up my dreams of being a monk.

As I was preparing to leave, my niece cried and asked me not to go. I told her not to worry and that I'd be back the next day. She continued to cry as I walked off in the direction of the temple.

When Venerable Sonuttara saw me he was relieved. Even though he wasn't always the kindest teacher, he wanted to keep me in monks' robes as much as I wanted to be in them. I apologized for running away, and he asked me if I was ready to ordain again.

"Yes," I answered, certain of my decision. "But I don't want to live in the temple as a novice. I want to go to monks' school."

He agreed immediately.

Two days later, after a simple ceremony, I was wearing the orange robes again. This time, I would never take them off.

Venerable Sonuttara contacted another monk, Venerable Siyambalangamuwe Dhammakkhandha, who ran a small primary school for monks in the Gampaha district. It was about sixty miles from the temple. Because Venerable Siyambalangamuwe and my teacher were friends, he readily accepted my application, and in April 1944, a month after my most recent ordination, I began my formal monastic education. I attended school at Vidyasekhara Pirivena (*vidyasekhara* means "crown of learning," and *pirivena* means "a school for monks"). About twenty young bhikkhus and three teachers lived there. We studied Ceylonese history and important Dhamma texts such as the Anguttara Nikaya (the gradual sayings of the Buddha) and the Majjhima Nikaya (the middle-length discourses). We also were taught a whole host of languages: Sinhalese, Tamil, Hindi, English, Pali, and Sanskrit.

I was very happy at my new school, living among other teenage monks and spending my days studying. But I hadn't been there long before Venerable Siyambalangamuwe came to me with a request. He said there was a temple in the village of Napagoda, and the head monk had disrobed, leaving the temple with no one in charge.

He asked if I would go there and run the temple. I thought this would be a temporary arrangement, that I'd live there for a few weeks and then return to the monks' school, so I agreed.

As it turned out, I lived in that temple for eight months.

There were no Dhamma or Pali studies there, just the usual monastic chores, the weary round of endless labor. One day there was nothing to eat. So I asked the temple boy, a youngster about my own age, to go buy some bread at a shop in the village. He refused. I asked him again. He refused once more. "I'll ask somebody else to buy me some food, then, and I won't share it with you," I told him.

His response was to curse at me. I kicked him several times.

Later that day, another monk who had been living with us for a time returned to the temple. He happened to be the older brother of the temple boy. He asked me what had happened, why the temple boy was no longer there. When he heard my story, he got very upset.

"Well, since you chased off the only boy who was here to help us, it's now your job to climb a coconut tree and get me a coconut."

I refused. "Monks don't climb trees," I pointed out. "It's against our rules. And besides, my teacher didn't send me here to climb trees and pick coconuts."

After seven months of such frustration and petty disputes, my desire to learn made me so restless that I wrote to my teacher. "Please send me back to the monks' school," I begged.

I was jubilant when, soon, I received a postcard from Venerable Siyambalangamuwe that said, "Yes, you can come back to school."

I immediately hired an ox cart to take me to the train station in Veyangoda, four miles away. I couldn't wait to get back to Gampaha and reenroll in school.

When I got to the train station, I saw that the train to Gampaha didn't leave for five hours, so I went to visit a temple nearby.

In that temple there was a young novice, maybe eight or nine years old, who took a liking to me. He invited me to go swimming with him in the river next to the train station and I hesitantly agreed.

Although nearly seventeen years old, I had never learned to swim, but I was too proud to tell that to the young monk. Little did I know that this single prideful act would soon threaten my life.

Pride, in the Buddha's teaching, is one of the last of the five fetters that falls away when a person attains enlightenment. It's one of the twenty-seven mental impurities that the Buddha warned can trip us up. To overcome infatuation with ourselves, he recommended a series of reflections a person should use:

> I am of the nature to decay; I have not gone beyond decay.
> I am of the nature to be diseased; I have not gone beyond disease.
> I am of the nature to die; I have not gone beyond death.
> All that is mine, dear and delightful, will change and vanish.
> I am the owner of my kamma, heir to my kamma, born of my kamma, related to my kamma, I abide by my kamma. Whatever kamma I shall create, whether good or evil, of that I shall be the heir.

At the river, the novice took off his outer robe and jumped into the water. He swam like a fish. I stood on the bank, admiring his easy, elegant strokes. It didn't look so difficult, but the last thing I wanted to do was jump into the muddy, fetid water.

The young boy saw me hesitating on the bank and urged me to join him. Reluctantly I took off my outer robe and tied a knot in the folds of my inner robe so that it wouldn't come off. Then I held my breath, and jumped.

Within seconds I was in trouble.

My feet reached for the bottom, but all I felt was soft mud. There was nothing solid to stand on. I felt like I was sinking, and I started to struggle. Panic rose inside me like an electric current. My arms and legs flailed, and as I gasped for air, I swallowed the foul river water.

The little monk saw what was happening and tried to help. He swam over to me, took hold of my ears, and pulled my head out of the water—ouch! But he wasn't strong enough to pull the rest of my body above the surface. I grabbed at his robe frantically, and in a moment it came loose.

Three times I went under, clutching that robe as if it would save me. Three times I struggled back up, searching for help.

The last time, all I could see was the color red filling my entire field of vision.

I was losing consciousness.

CHAPTER FIVE

Monks' School

WHEN I AWOKE, I was lying on the ground next to the river with a man kneeling over me. I started coughing up river water as a large crowd stood around me and stared. Later I was told that the young monk who had been swimming with me wouldn't get out of the river because I had torn off his robe in my panic to stay afloat. Naked, he had stood in waist-deep water at the edge of the river and screamed for help.

Apparently, a man came out of a tea shop next to the train station and asked what was the matter. The young monk pointed to a spot in the river and said that I had drowned.

"He must be dead by now," the monk had shouted.

The man from the tea shop jumped into the river, fully clothed, and searched underwater until he found me, unconscious, at the bottom. He dragged me up onto the riverbank and started giving me mouth-to-mouth resuscitation as a crowd gathered.

Eventually I sat up, coughing and sputtering. I was a little shaken, but otherwise all right. The young monk fetched his teacher, and together they walked me back to their temple, which was just fifty yards away. They gave me a cup of hot coffee with lots of sugar, and a set of dry robes. It was not long before I started feeling like myself again.

The head monk was very kind. He asked me my name and where I was going. When I told him, he sent an attendant to the train station to buy me a ticket to Gampaha.

After a few hours' rest, I was on my way again. Ironically, when I arrived at the monks' school in Gampaha, the first person I talked to asked me why I sounded like a drowned person.

"I just have a cold," I replied. I was too embarrassed to tell the truth.

But the next day, there was my picture on the front page of Ceylon's leading newspaper, along with a story about the teenage monk who nearly drowned in the river at the Veyangoda train station. My fellow students at the monks' school teased me about that for years.

Although tuition at the monks' school was free, boarders were required to donate about five rupees a month. Unfortunately, I didn't have any money to pay the fee, so I was given an abandoned shed to sleep in. The shed had a dirt floor, partial walls about four feet high, and no door. I scavenged some gunnysacks, bamboo sticks, and ropes with which I fashioned a crude door and window shade. For light, I had one earthen lamp that burned coconut oil. This was my first *kuti,* the one-room hut that some monks live in, and I was delighted to have it.

I did most of my studying in my kuti. Very quickly I became known as the smartest student in the school. I discovered I had a photographic memory, clearly a gift of good kamma. In ten minutes, I could read a long book and retain everything in it. I don't know how this worked; I just know that each page stuck in my mind like a picture.

I was very proud of my gift and asked my friends to challenge me by posing questions from books. I could answer them with the page number, and even the punctuation, of the sentence in question.

Perhaps because of this, the principal of the school liked me and selected me to be his assistant. I was also named treasurer, which meant that I organized and stored all the donations that came into the school—things such as robes, medicine, and toiletries. Then I would dole them out to the student-monks as needed.

Because of my privileges and responsibilities, several of my fellow monks became jealous of me, and it didn't help that I had developed the habit of reporting other students' weaknesses to the principal! In short, I was a rat. I filed report after report, detailing the wrongdoings of other monks. I knew that I should be more concerned with my own behavior than with finding faults in others, but I wanted so much to maintain the approval of the principal.

It's too bad that I didn't take to heart the words of the Buddha, in the Dhammapada:

> Easily seen is the fault of others, but one's own is difficult to see. Like chaff, one winnows another's faults but hides one's own, even as a crafty fowler hides behind sham branches. He who seeks another's faults, who is ever censorious, his cankers grow. He is far from destruction of the cankers.

On full-moon days I gave half-hour Dhamma talks at the school. Usually they were based on books I had read, but one time I decided that this might be boring for my audience. So I decided to "wing it." All I did was memorize a three-page sutta, one of the Buddha's sermons called Visakhuposatha Sutta. Then I repeated it to my audience.

The experimental sermon was a disaster. I was finished reciting within ten minutes, then I simply babbled on for five more minutes—about what, I can't even remember. It was embarrassing, and it taught me a valuable lesson about the value of diligent preparation. From then on, I carefully prepared for each of my Dhamma talks. I would choose a stanza from the Dhammapada and explain it using stories from the commentary. The Dhammapada contains 423 stanzas, most of which teach about ethics and morality. There are also hundreds of stories elsewhere in the Buddhist canon that illustrate the topics mentioned in the Dhammapada. I enjoyed telling those stories, offering listeners a grounding in Buddhist morality.

It wasn't until much later in my career as a monk that I again felt confident enough to give sermons without preparation.

At the monks' school, at age seventeen, I was finally able to give up smoking. It was a habit I had had for several years, but unfortunately, I only exchanged one addiction for another. My new habit was chewing betel nut.

In time I became the comedian of the school. Every night, I would hold court for an hour or so, telling jokes to the other students. I enjoyed making them laugh.

One of my jokes was about a supporter of a temple who became angry that the monks there never shared any of his offerings with the Buddha image. So he wrapped a rope around the neck of the Buddha statue and hung it from one of the rafters. When the monks discovered what he had done and demanded to know why, he called it a suicide. "The Buddha statue said it couldn't continue living in such a place," he told them.

Amazingly, the principal did not object to such irreverent comedy. Usually, after my performance was finished, we went to his room and enjoyed a chew together. He was a wise man when it came to dealing with teenage monks. He was strict, but also very gentle. He knew how to motivate us without forcing us, which might have destroyed our interest in learning. He encouraged us to be disciplined monks. "Laypeople will look up to you," he would say. "They know you have sacrificed sensual pleasure to devote your lives to the practice of Dhamma, so you must earn that respect."

I almost never had any money, but it didn't matter. My humble housing was free, I collected my food on alms round, and instead of buying textbooks, I borrowed them from friends and copied the material by hand. I simply trusted that I would have whatever I needed to finish my education. I had a lot of confidence in myself and also in the Triple Gem—the Buddha, Dhamma, and Sangha.

I felt like the Buddha was alive and walking with me through life, providing me with whatever I needed. I was certain the Dhamma would protect me because I was ardently struggling to learn the Buddha's teachings. And I thought that because I was a member of the Sangha, I would not have any problem getting whatever requisites I'd need. Even today, so many decades later, it feels as though the Triple Gem continues to provide for me. All satisfaction of my material needs seems to manifest eventually, without any struggle.

One day an older monk asked me to shave his head. That was a common practice in the monastery, but I had never shaved anyone's head, not even my own. I told him this, but he insisted. "It's time you learned," he said.

Head-shaving is an important part of the Buddhist monastic discipline. Both monks and nuns do it. A shaved head promotes cleanliness and humility and it avoids the problem of having to kill head lice! It is also a symbol of renunciation and is intended to decrease monks' and nuns' attachment to physical beauty. If monks and nuns don't have to spend time washing, combing, and fixing their hair, they're free to spend more time on spiritual pursuits.

The Vinaya, or monastic code of conduct, says that monks and nuns can keep their hair as long as two inches. Some shave their heads only once a month, usually right before the full-moon day. Others shave once a week, or even every day.

The ritual is so important that a straight razor is one of eight items included in a bundle of possessions (usually called requisites) that a monastic receives at his or her ordination. (The others are an undergarment robe; a robe that wraps around the body; an outer robe that doubles as a blanket; a cloth belt; a water strainer; a sewing kit; and an alms bowl.)

When the older monk insisted that I shave his head, I bowed and agreed, as tradition demanded. I wet his head, slathered soap on it, and took hold of the razor. Standing behind him, I dragged the blade against his scalp and an inch-long flap of skin lifted away from his skull! In the next instant there was blood everywhere. I was so scared I started to shake.

"Venerable Sir, please forgive me," I said, and then ran to find another monk, who brought cool water to wash the wound. While I watched in shame and panic, that monk shaved the rest of the unfortunate fellow's head. We of course had no Band-Aids in those days, so the wounded monk went on alms round with a large dab of herbal salve on his head.

Because of my photographic memory, I sped through my studies. Sinhalese, Pali, and Sanskrit were mandatory subjects. Tamil, Hindi, and English were optional. Without much effort, I mastered them all. As a reward, I was finally allowed to live in the dormitory with the other students despite my continued inability to pay the lodging fee. I was assigned to a room with another novice monk.

Unfortunately, my roommate was jealous of me. One day I went to pull out a thin English textbook I had borrowed from someone and found it ripped in two. I was worried about how I would pay for replacing the book and started to cry. A monk in the next room heard me sniffling and offered to help by buying another book.

A couple of days later, my roommate confessed that he had torn up the book because he was jealous of my popularity and of how well I did in school. We cleared the air between us that evening and eventually became good friends.

Eventually, the date of my higher ordination was set. It would take place June 25, 1947. I was very excited and happy. Finally I would become a full bhikkhu, my goal at long last coming true. Before a solemn assemblage of senior monks, I would pledge a new and deeper commitment. Instead of being a novice monk following ten precepts, I would now agree to follow 227 precepts—the code of conduct that governs full-fledged Theravada Buddhist monks.

I could hardly wait.

Sadly, right from the beginning, there was a shadow over the proceedings. The problem was not my eligibility to become a monk, but rather the politics of the Buddhist Sangha in Ceylon. Those politics threatened to derail the dream I had held all my life.

CHAPTER SIX

Higher Ordination

In Sri Lanka, there are three major sects of Theravada Buddhism. The oldest and largest, to which I belong, is Siyam Nikaya. This sect has more monks and temples than the other sects. It also has the most ancient temples in the country. Its name, Siyam, dates back to a time when the Sangha, or order of monks, had dwindled to its lowest numbers due to British rule in Ceylon, and because of Dutch and Portuguese missionaries. There were many novices, but not a single bhikkhu left who had received higher ordination and was observing the 227 precepts—and thus could ordain others.

A novice Ceylonese monk traveled to Siam, as Thailand was then called (or "Siyama" in Pali), to receive higher ordination as a full bhikkhu. Then he returned to Ceylon and reestablished the order of monks in 1753.

Only the highest caste members of society in Ceylon, called Goyigama, were allowed full ordination into the Siyam Nikaya order. My family, though poor, belonged to this caste. In Ceylon, caste was not based on wealth but on family lineage. Years later, a group of non-Goyigama novice monks traveled to Amarapura, in Burma, and received full ordination there. That group returned to Ceylon and founded the Amarapura Nikaya sect in 1800. A third sect, founded in 1810 by monks who went to the Ramanna district of Burma, became the Ramanna Nikaya sect.

Originally there was a great deal of rivalry between the sects. Each one thought the others were not strict enough in their interpretation of the Vinaya, or code of conduct for sangha members. Siyam Nikaya monks, for example, shaved their eyebrows as well as their heads. Members of the other sects did not. On the other hand, when leaving their temples, Siyam Nikaya monks were allowed to leave one shoulder bare when they draped their robes around them. Monks of the other sects covered both shoulders.

My teacher, Venerable Sonuttara, belonged to the Siyam Nikaya sect. His teacher was a disciple of the sect's supreme patriarch, Most Venerable Pahamune Sumangala.

In 1911, when he was twenty-five years old, my teacher was sent to open a temple in Malandeniya village. Immediately there was trouble with the head monk at the temple in the next village, Kebilitigoda. The temple in Kebilitigoda had already existed for ten years before my teacher arrived in Malandeniya. Even so, the head monk became jealous of my teacher, so he made a legal claim to the new temple's property. As a result, my teacher had to pay tribute to the monk in Kebilitigoda and visit every day to pay respects.

As it turns out, that monk in Kebilitigoda was Venerable Sumanatissa, who had given me novice vows when I was thirteen. He could have "claimed" me then as his student, but he didn't. I guess I didn't seem like a particularly promising monk at that point.

Over the years, animosity festered between the two temples. And when time came for my higher ordination in 1947, I ran headlong into the dispute.

According to tradition, when a novice monk is about to receive higher ordination, an announcement of the ceremony is sent to friends, relatives, temple attendees, and all other temples where that novice has lived. It is printed on cheap paper and is mailed or delivered by hand.

The principal of the monks' school wrote my announcement, and according to tradition, I took it to my teacher to have him sign it. For some reason, Venerable Sonuttara was reluctant to sign his name as head of the temple in Malandeniya.

"But you started this temple in 1911," I said to him. "You built it and you have always been the only monk living here. Who else could be head of the temple?"

Venerable Sonuttara said nothing and finally signed the paper. I made copies and hand-delivered the first one to Venerable Sumanatissa, my original preceptor, at the temple in the neighboring village. As soon as he saw my teacher's signature as head monk of the other temple, he became enraged.

"Venerable Sonuttara is not head monk at that temple," he thundered. "I am! And I am not even listed here as one of your teachers."

He immediately went to the Siyam Nikaya headquarters in Kandy and requested that my ordination be canceled. My teacher and I were dismayed, but we continued to get ready for the ceremony, hoping the dispute would somehow be resolved.

On the night before my ordination, as was custom, the people of Malandeniya had arranged a large procession and reception at the temple in my honor. Even though Venerable Sumanatissa was threatening to stop the procession, it went ahead without a problem.

The next day, June 25, we went to Kandy. The ordination ritual would take place in the *sima*, a consecrated building on the grounds of the Siyam Nikaya headquarters. On that day, twenty-six novices, including me, were scheduled to receive higher ordination. Our relatives, friends, and well-wishers had already gathered in the sima.

As I had feared, Venerable Sumanatissa wasn't going to let this pass. He entered a formal complaint against my ordination because he, not my teacher, was the head of the temple in Malandeniya. Therefore, my teacher had no right to sign his name in the ordination register as "head monk." Venerable Sumanatissa insisted my teacher sign his name only as "resident monk."

My teacher, Venerable Sonuttara, was an uneducated man and was not clever with words. He was afraid to oppose any monk who was his senior. But most of all, he didn't want this dispute to ruin my chances of being ordained. I was angry at Venerable Sumanatissa, both for

being harsh with my teacher and for trying to spoil the most important day of my life. I found the politics of the whole thing appalling,
but there was nothing I could do about it.

Without a word of argument, my teacher signed the register as
Venerable Sumanatissa demanded, with the words "resident monk"
beside his name.

A few hours before the ceremony, two senior monks dressed me
all in white, with a crown-like headdress. If a candidate has wealthy
relatives or supporters, he might ride on an elephant, the symbol of
majesty and status. He might also have hundreds of people following,
beating drums, blowing conchs and flutes, and dancing. Because my
family was not wealthy, my ceremony was more humble.

While I was being dressed, my relatives and teachers had prepared
trays of gifts for members of the ordination committee. Each tray contained betel and areca nuts for chewing, tobacco for smoking, a towel,
a bar of soap, toothpaste, a toothbrush made from a small twig, and
a box of cookies.

There were twenty dignitaries in attendance: the supreme patriarch
of the Siyam Nikaya sect; his two assistants, who were also very senior
and respected; a secretary monk, who maintained all records for the
sect; and sixteen others. Following a strict hierarchy, I was to go to
each monk at his kuti, in turn, and present him with a gift tray. This
ritual took about an hour.

Even though it might seem redundant, every candidate for higher
ordination is reordained as a novice and dressed in a new, bright yellow robe in the last hours before he becomes a bhikkhu. This reminds
the aspirant, once again, of Siddhattha's renunciation of his princely
life, wrapping himself in a yellow cloth when he took up the life of a
mendicant. It also serves to "wipe clean the slate," in case the aspiring
monk had broken any precepts during his novicehood and had failed
to confess them to his teacher.

At 6 P.M. the ceremony began.

A rope divided the sima in half—one side for monks, the other for
laypeople. The laypeople's side was packed with hundreds of noisy

guests. Children played with one another, babies cried, and adults chatted and laughed.

At the far end of the assembly hall was a large Buddha statue. It sat on a dark wooden altar with peeling paint that was crowded with devotional candles and small earthen lamps, smoking incense burners, vases of flowers, and small cups filled with fruit juice, tea, or water. A flat tray held the traditional betel chewing mixture. A pair of large brass oil lamps flanked the altar, casting a sputtering light against the serene face of the Buddha.

At the right of the statue sat the supreme patriarch, flanked by his two assistants. The remaining monks on the ordination committee sat on the wooden floor, in lines facing each other.

We novices were asked to sit on the floor according to our ages. At six months shy of twenty, I was the youngest. Twenty is the minimum age at which a novice may take higher ordination, but because I had completed all other requirements, I was allowed to ordain six months early.

The first order of business was an oral examination in which a senior monk would ask the novices, one by one, to recite stanzas and answer questions. The examiner that evening was the second-ranking monk, a man known to be very strict. His method was to recite the first line of a stanza from the Buddhist texts, then ask the candidate to finish it.

Most of the other novices had memorized the minimum number of stanzas required. I, with my photographic memory and eagerness to excel, had memorized many more. Even so, I was nervous in front of the large crowd.

Finally, after twenty-five other novices, my turn came. The examiner had been at work for an hour and a half and he looked exhausted.

He asked me to recite a stanza from the Dhammapada. I took a deep breath, closed my eyes, and recited eight stanzas without stopping.

"That is enough," the examiner said. "You have studied well."

Next, each of the novices had to be formally accepted as candidates for ordination. Like the others before me, I got up and stood in front of one of the committee monks. Methodically, he questioned me: my name; my gender; my parents' names; my teacher's name; whether I had any contagious diseases; whether I was a soldier or a free man; and even a question about whether I was human or demon.

While mostly a formality, these questions were intended to confirm that I was not a criminal trying to escape the law by hiding in the robe. The question about contagious diseases was to make sure that I had no illness that might sweep through the community of monks. The other questions, more quaint, were traditional queries dating back to the time of the Buddha.

After I answered all his questions, this monk announced to the supreme patriarch that I was a suitable candidate for ordination. I knelt before the patriarch and bowed, touching my head to the floor in front of him three times. Again I answered the series of questions, this time with the patriarch listening.

Then I was told to sit with my fellow novices. Two monks lectured us on the importance of the 227 disciplinary rules we would have to follow after our ordination, emphasizing the four main rules: not to have sexual intercourse; not to take anything not explicitly given to us; not to kill; and not to boast of supernatural attainments. There was also a reminder about cultivating nonattachment to the four requisites provided by laypeople: robes, food, lodging, and medicine. All this advice came from the original words of the Buddha to his disciples.

Finally, with our new alms bowls hanging from cords around our necks, we bowed before each of the committee members, starting with the patriarch. Then we sat down in long rows, and all the laypeople filed by to present us with gifts. This is a very joyous part of the ceremony. It emphasizes the interdependent relationship between the monastic Sangha and laypeople. Many people cried as they bowed and laid their gifts before us.

This presentation of offerings is one of the most beautiful aspects of Buddhism and is sometimes misunderstood by outside observers who conclude that bhikkhus are lazy beggars, supported by a gullible populace. In fact, it is quite the opposite: The givers receive as much, if not more, than the recipients because they are practicing dana, or generosity.

Anyone who gives gifts is practicing generosity. The Buddha found this practice to be a good method for removing greed and attachment. In many of his discourses, he urged Buddhists to practice dana whenever and wherever possible:

> Just as a pot filled with water,
> If overturned by anyone,
> Pours out all its water
> And does not hold any back.
> Even so, when you see those in need,
> Whether low, middle, or high,
> Then give like the overturned pot,
> Holding nothing back.

In another sermon, the Buddha taught that there are three ways of making merit. Those three ways are virtuous behavior, meditation, and generosity.

The expression of generosity between laypeople and monastics is very much a reciprocal arrangement. The laypeople offer requisites that allow the bhikkhus to walk their spiritual path without having to worry about mundane necessities. In return, the monastics offer blessings, as well as teachings—the gift of the Dhamma.

During my ordination, as the gifts slowly piled up on the floor before me, I sat there and thought of my mother. How I wished she could have witnessed this ceremony! I knew how much it would have meant to her, how much it would have meant to me to have her there. But because of her back injury, she couldn't walk the nine miles from our village, and there was no other way for her to make the trip. If she had been there that day in Kandy, she would have surely shed tears of joy, seeing her youngest son at last become a fully ordained monk.

CHAPTER SEVEN

The Final Cure: Meditation

A FEW DAYS after my higher ordination, I eagerly took on one of the privileges of a full monk, to participate in a seven-day chanting. This ritual, called *paritta* in Pali, is designed to drive away evil spirits—another example of how folk beliefs and Buddhism often coexist. If someone is sick or a village is suffering from famine or drought (misfortunes that potentially could be the doing of evil spirits), people ask monks to perform this special chanting. For an entire week, pairs of monks chant nonstop. Each pair chants for an hour at a time and is then relieved by another pair. The chanting is energetic, more like shouting than singing. Only monks with strong chanting voices are selected, and they are held in high esteem for their efforts. Young monks impatiently wait their turn to join the chanting teams.

One of my friends from monks' school was as eager as I to participate in a chanting. He was ordained the day before I was, so we became eligible at the same time. Soon, we wrangled an invitation to participate in a chant from a friend of ours who was head monk at a temple nearby.

We were young and enthusiastic, and since this was our first seven-day chanting, we wanted more than just one turn. So my friend and I begged some of the older monks to give us their slots. They had already done many parittas and were happy to oblige, so we ended up chanting most of the time. Our only breaks were for eating and answering the call of nature. We didn't sleep at all!

Each day at 6 A.M., 11 A.M., and 6 P.M., drummers would announce the start of devotional services by beating on drums. They had to beat loudly to be heard over our chanting. To prove our zeal, my friend and I chanted even louder. Trying to drown out the drums, we were eventually shouting at the top of our lungs.

After three days my friend passed out. Some of the laypeople at the temple took him to a bedroom and laid him on a bed to sleep. By evening he recovered and joined me again in the chanting.

By the end of the week, we were both in bad shape. Even though we desperately needed rest, we couldn't sleep. We couldn't eat, either, and both of us had severe headaches. We couldn't stand to be around anyone else, and I think we must have been suffering some kind of nervous breakdown.

Worst of all, I lost my memory, and not just my photographic memory, but everything! I couldn't recognize any alphabet—Sinhalese, Sanskrit, Tamil, or English. I would open a book and be unable to make any sense of what was on the page. If I met someone and then saw him five minutes later, I couldn't remember his name. I was upset and humbled by what had happened to me. All my pride in my academic achievements was gone.

Back at school, I failed my final exams. The principal, puzzled that his star pupil had done so miserably, called me into his office. I told him about the seven-day chanting and how my memory had disappeared. He told me to go back to my temple to rest and get some treatment.

For most of the next year I subjected myself to all kinds of treatments, in a desperate search for a "cure." First, my teacher made a medicinal paste from plants and applied it to my forehead every morning. After a month I was no better, but I yearned to return to school nonetheless. My glory days were over. I now had to struggle to learn even the simplest things.

Not only was my photographic memory gone, but I had to struggle to read sentence by sentence, word by word, sometimes even letter by letter. Some nights, while reading a textbook, it felt like insects were running all over my scalp. I was in agony and began to entertain thoughts of suicide. I didn't want to live in that condition at all. I had heard that the fabric mantels in kerosene lamps were poisonous if you ate them, so I started collecting them and hiding them in a box. Luckily, my friends got wind of my plan and threw the box away.

Some people suggested I go see an Ayurvedic doctor who advertised in the newspaper. I went to him and told him my problem, but said I had no money. He was a kind man; he gave me a very expensive medicine for free. Every day, as he recommended, I applied some of the oil to my head, sniffed it, and even drank a few drops of it. It helped clear my sinuses, but brought back only a little of my memory; I was still a long way from recovery.

Then my teacher suggested that my affliction was the work of some evil spirit. "We'll do an all-night chanting for you," he said. At the time, this suggestion didn't strike me as ironic. While I lay on the floor, eight monks chanted suttas in Pali all night long. The next morning I felt no different.

My parents agreed that an evil spirit might have possessed me, so they called in an exorcist. I met the man at my parents' house. He asked my father to get seven lemons and then had me sit on a chair, while he held a lemon and a pair of scissors over my head, chanting a mantra in some language I think he made up on the spot. As he chanted, he cut the lemon with the scissors and let the juice drip onto my head. He repeated the ritual with all seven lemons. Then, as a finale, he tied a cotton thread around my neck.

My parents were sure this would do the trick. It didn't, so they invited another exorcist, supposedly one with more power.

This one came to the house with an entourage of six people. He asked my father to gather a long list of things: coconuts and coconut oil, areca nuts, red hibiscus flowers, and several dry sticks wrapped in cloth to serve as torches. Meanwhile, the exorcist was carving a clay statue to represent me. It was round and plump, like a terracotta snowman. When it was finished, the exorcist and his attendants put on white sarongs and turbans. They led me to a small shed and sat me down in front of the clay statue they had made. Other family members were allowed to sit nearby, on mats on the ground. After chewing betel, the men started chanting in a strange language. It was neither Sinhalese nor Pali nor Sanskrit. I had never heard anything like it. It was just a jumble of sounds. While chanting, they held the lit torches and threw powdered incense into them to make their flames brighter.

Each time the torches flared, two of the attendants sitting on either side of me would yell in Sinhalese, "Ayu bova!" (May you live long!)

The ritual continued the entire night, until the torches were burned down. At dawn, the men skewered some spikes into the head of the statue, evidently to free me from my affliction. Then they tied a thread around my neck, just as the first exorcist had done.

Again, there were no results.

My parents were all out of ideas, but my teacher offered one more: He gave me a talisman made of copper sheeting that had been rolled into a two-inch tube about the size of a ballpoint pen. It was a traditional Ceylonese talisman called a *ratana yantra,* or jewel talisman. Selected stanzas of the Ratana Sutta are engraved on it. The Sinhalese believe that if this type of talisman is worn around the neck or waist, it will keep evil spirits at bay. My teacher hung it around my neck.

I was very grateful to my parents, my teacher, and the healers who tried to help me. Unfortunately, their efforts were all in vain. Nothing worked. My superb memory was gone forever.

At this point of utter desperation, a very unusual thought occurred to me: Perhaps meditation would help. When my friends heard that plan, they burst out laughing. The practice of meditation was hardly a common thing to do in those days, even for a bhikkhu.

"Are you crazy?" one friend said. "Meditation is only for old people who can't do anything else anymore. You're still young, too young to meditate. Don't be foolish."

Although I was well-versed in the theory of meditation and knew the four foundations of mindfulness by heart, I had never actually meditated, believe it or not. Very few monks did in those days. They were too busy preaching Dhamma, chanting, and performing blessing ceremonies. There was much talk about meditation, of course, but very little practice. Some people actually believed that if a person meditated too much, it would cause mental disturbance.

Well, I figured, I already had a mental disturbance. What did I have to lose?

Secretly I began to meditate—sometimes late at night, sometimes early in the morning. Whenever I could steal a few minutes alone, I meditated, sitting in a dark corner of the shrine room where I hoped nobody would notice me. I knew I was trying to instill a new mental habit, and in order to be successful, I had to set aside time every day to do it. It was like a workout for the mind, trying to flex muscles that were weak from lack of training.

At first, I simply tried to calm my mind by recalling mundane things—names of my friends or temples I had visited, titles of books I'd read. It wasn't easy; there were big gaps in my memory. But I tried not to panic.

Then, drawing on my scriptural training in the four foundations of mindfulness, I began to watch the flow of breath, of bodily sensations, feelings, and thoughts that moved through me.

That watchful observance gradually led to a very peaceful feeling inside. Occasionally I even experienced spontaneous flashes of joy. Those brief moments, of course, made meditation enjoyable and encouraged me to keep going.

Eventually things I had studied in the past started coming back to me. I began to recognize letters and numbers. Unexpectedly, my temper, too, began to improve. After a couple of months of steady practice, I was able to read again and to remember what I had read. I was elated, and so relieved that I had found a "cure."

Meditation did what all the incantations and medicinal oils and talismans hadn't been able to do.

It brought peace to my mind.

CHAPTER EIGHT

The Struggle to Stay in School

THANKS TO MEDITATION, my two-year nightmare of losing my memory finally ended. Once I started meditating, my brain seemed to heal from the trauma inflicted by the seven-day chanting. But although I was now able to remember things roughly as well as anyone else, my photographic memory never returned.

Two years later, in 1949, I was able to resume my studies. That made me very happy. At the end of that academic year I took the first public school examination, which was known as the Senior School Certificate Examination, similar to final exams in high school. I was tested in eight subjects (Sinhalese, Tamil, Pali, Sinhalese literature, Ceylonese history, arithmetic, health science, and Buddhism) and passed them all.

I was proud of my record, because just a few months before, I had been unable to read or recall anything.

That same year, however, my eagerness to master English got me into trouble. I took an examination at the monks' school where I had been a student for several years, and my grades for English were much higher than for Sanskrit.

The principal of the school called me into his office. His face was stern. "Gunaratana," he said, "You must understand that the Buddha's dispensation has been handed down for the last twenty-five hundred years not in English, but in Pali and Sanskrit. I advise you to pay more attention to those languages." In 1950 I was admitted to Vidyalankara

Pirivena, a college for monks near the capital city of Colombo, and one of the two most prestigious colleges in Ceylon. It had a faculty of about ten men—wonderfully religious, humble teachers who were experts in Dhamma, Buddhist history, Pali, Sanskrit, Sinhalese, Tamil, and Hindi.

I was thrilled to be admitted, but again I couldn't afford to pay boarding fees. I had no place to live, so I spent a couple of weeks visiting nearby temples, looking for lodging. Finally, I found a temple on the banks of the Kelaniya River, and the head monk gave me permission to move in. I resumed the duties of a temple-dwelling monk. Collecting alms in the nearest village was less than fruitful. Usually, I received only rice in my bowl, without vegetables or anything else. I would go back to the temple, put plenty of salt on the rice, and eat it.

My commute to school from the temple was long and complicated. First, I rode across the river in a small boat owned by Jinadasa, a man who lived at the temple. Every day after lunch, he would be waiting in his boat to take me across the river.

Often during those daily boat rides, I would think about the Alagaddupama Sutta, often referred to as "The Simile of the Raft" because, in that discourse, the Buddha compares the Dhamma to a raft: We can use the Dhamma to cross the raging river of life, he says, but once we've reached the opposite shore, we should leave the boat behind. Grasping and clinging to anything, even good things, can weigh us down.

After crossing the river each day, I walked to a bus station where I would catch a bus to the college on the Kandy-Colombo road. Of course, I had no money for bus fare, but the owner of the bus company kindly allowed me to ride for free.

On weekends, I went to Yakkala, a village nearby, to teach Dhamma Sunday school. I also gave regular sermons on full-moon days at the temple where I was staying. Despite my age, people seemed to respect me, and they wanted to hear my teachings.

Sometimes I preached on important subjects such as kamma, rebirth, and dependent origination, but I'm not sure that I myself understood what I was talking about back then. Often I just memorized passages I had read in books and repeated them.

I also told stories based on Buddhist folklore. A favorite of mine was one of the many stories about the Buddha and Devadatta, a monk who was always plotting to kill him. They had been enemies in many previous lives, and there were numerous stories about their clashes. In my favorite one, Buddha has taken birth as a compassionate monkey and Devadatta as a man wandering in the jungle.

While in the jungle, the man falls into an abandoned well, and the monkey, who happens to be nearby, works for hours to pull him out. Exhausted after his feat, the monkey lies down on the ground to rest. The man, also exhausted, and hungry as well, picks up a rock and hits the monkey on the head so that he might have some food to eat.

Because the man is weak, his blow doesn't kill the monkey. Bleeding, the monkey scrambles up a tree and sits awhile to think. "Although he just tried to kill me, if I run away and abandon this foolish man here," thinks the monkey, "he might starve to death. He'll never find his way out of this dense jungle. I need to lead him to the nearest village."

So the monkey begins jumping from tree to tree, crashing around as if he's hurt. The man, thinking the monkey might fall dead at any moment, follows along. When they reach the edge of a village, the man forgets about the monkey and walks on to get food and water, and the monkey returns to the jungle.

That story demonstrates the admirable qualities of the Buddha, even before he was in a human form or fully enlightened, and it never failed to delight my Sunday school audiences.

One day Jinadasa said he would like to offer me something as a gift the next time I gave a talk. He asked me what I would like, but I didn't answer him because I knew he was quite poor and couldn't really afford to buy a gift.

Even so, on the next full-moon day, he offered me a flashlight. Little did either of us know what a portent this was.

One evening, I gave a Dhamma talk in the new dining hall at the college. It was a big occasion; all my teachers, classmates, and hundreds of laypeople came to hear me speak. My sermon was about the Culamalunkyaputta Sutta from the Majjhima Nikaya, which warns people not to waste time on unimportant things. The Buddha says that we should feel an urgency to work toward attaining liberation from suffering.

By the time my sermon was over and everyone had finished asking questions, it was almost midnight. I had missed the last bus, so I walked the six miles to the river, where I hoped Jinadasa would ferry me across.

The river, swollen by rain, was running very fast. It was almost 2 A.M. and I knew Jinadasa would be asleep. I lit the flashlight he had given me, shone it across the river, and called his name as loudly as I could. After some time, he appeared on the opposite bank and got in the boat. He was furious at being woken up.

As he rowed across, I could hear the curses coming out of his mouth. He was calling me names, hurling insults of all kinds. Evidently he thought I had been in town doing something unseemly for a monk, carousing or carrying on with women or some such thing. He didn't know that I had been giving a Dhamma sermon.

I got in the boat and apologized for disturbing him in the middle of the night. I tried to explain why I was so late, but he wouldn't listen. He continued to shower me with filthy words, accusing me of doing all kinds of things I never would have dreamed of doing. Then he handed me an oar and demanded that I row.

I had never rowed a boat before, and certainly not in a strong current. I put my oar in the water, and as soon as I did, the boat started to tip over. I was petrified. All of my near-drowning experiences flashed before my eyes.

Jinadasa, spewing more curses, snatched the oar from me. He started rowing against the raging current, grumbling and cursing the whole time. Normally the trip took only ten minutes, but that night it was nearly two hours. They were the longest two hours of my life.

The next morning, after a couple of hours of sleep, I woke up and resolved that I would leave the temple where I was living because I simply couldn't bear any more harrowing river crossings with Jinadasa.

After alms round, I packed my few books in a bag and walked to the riverbank. Jinadasa was there, looking sullen.

"Why is your bag full today?" he asked me.

"Because I'm leaving this temple," I answered.

He asked me why, and I let him know how much his insults had hurt me the night before. I told him I'd had a good reason for being late, but he had refused to listen to me. I told him that I had nearly drowned several times, that I was afraid of water, and that his cursing at me only made me feel worse.

Jinadasa was in tears. With eyes downcast, he begged me to stay, but I was adamant.

"I want to find a place where I don't have to cross a river every day to go to college," I told him.

And so, once again, I was looking for a place to live.

Eventually, I ended up at a temple about eight miles from the college. The monk there told me I could stay in a little kuti on the temple grounds that had been empty for years, empty except for about fifty bats! Sometimes, the rank odor was so strong that I couldn't sleep.

In the afternoons, after alms round, I rode the bus to the college. After classes, when I was ready to come home, it was evening rush hour and the buses were full—no room for people like me who couldn't pay—so I had to walk the eight miles home from school every day.

I would arrive at my kuti about nine or nine-thirty at night, and would light the kerosene lamp. Nearby lived a merchant named Albert. He was Sinhalese, but like many of my countrymen, he had a British first name. Some Sinhalese gave their children British or Dutch or Portuguese names, depending on which country was in possession of Ceylon at the time, because they hoped this would help their children get into a prestigious Catholic school, or later, a government job.

Albert was a generous man. Each night, when he saw the light come on in my kuti, he would send over his servant with a cup of hot tea for me. Even though it was only plain tea, that warm drink always tasted wonderful after a long day. I would study until midnight, then go to bed.

Albert took an interest in me and in my desire to finish college. He offered to bring me food every day, so I would not have to go on alms rounds. And he offered to pay for my schoolbooks. I would have preferred being independent, but as a monk with no material wealth, I was supposed to accept any support laypeople gave me. So I said yes to his kindness.

Unfortunately, Albert's support eventually got me in trouble. About a month after I moved in, Albert told the head monk at the temple that he thought I was a wonderful young monk who gave excellent Dhamma sermons.

The head monk immediately became suspicious and concluded I was plotting to take over his temple, so he sent one of his pupils to tell me I had to leave. He forced me to go right then, and I didn't even have time to tell Albert goodbye. I was sent to live in a vacant kuti at a temple nearby, but a month later, I was told to depart from there, too. I guess the suspicious monk wanted me out of the area entirely.

Luckily, I found a new home, a kuti that was close to the Kandy-Colombo road, with an easy walk to the bus stop. This kuti had been financed by a wealthy woman who wished to provide it for monks studying at the college. It seemed perfect. I began giving Dhamma sermons again, and the local people came to hear them. They seemed pleased with me and even offered me a gas stove for boiling water.

Sadly, trouble found me there, too. The head monk who had considered me such a threat sent his pupil to roust me again. This time, he claimed that two other student-monks needed to live in the kuti, and there wouldn't be sufficient food for all three of us. Therefore, he said, I would have to leave. The head monk of a local temple had a great deal of authority over such matters.

I pleaded for mercy. "I come from a poor family," I said, "and I can't afford the ten rupees a month to board at the college. I'm going to graduate in only six months—just let me stay here until then."

Nonetheless, he insisted that I leave.

I took my books and went back to Yakkala, where I had been warmly received the year before. This time, I was given a room in the temple.

Unfortunately, even with this warm reception, all the previous struggles over housing weighed on me. "Why should I work so hard to stay in college?" I asked myself. "These subjects are not going to be useful in a monk's life. Why am I trying so hard to achieve this goal?"

I was also ashamed of always borrowing money. I couldn't afford my books, so I had to beg other students to lend me theirs. Then I would have to return the books before I was finished reading them. When I needed a few rupees for exam fees, I had to go to my mother or my original teacher, my preceptor, to beg for a few coins. It was embarrassing and I hated to ask people who already had so little themselves.

So, in 1952, I decided to leave school, even though all I had to complete before graduation were the final exams. The exam fee was fifteen rupees, about $4.50, and I didn't have the money. So I dropped out.

CHAPTER NINE

Missionary Monk

EVEN THOUGH I dropped out of college just before taking final exams, my boyhood urge to teach the Dhamma in English remained as strong as ever. I don't know exactly where this urge came from. Maybe part of it was because English was spoken among the Sinhalese elite, a cultural leftover from British occupation. I had dreams of going to India or Malaysia, where English was spoken even more widely. Maybe, if I was very lucky, I might even teach in England, the source of my country's British heritage.

Never in my wildest dreams did I imagine teaching in America; that was the end of the earth to a young man in Ceylon.

After monks' college, I continued taking English classes wherever I could find them, sometimes traveling for many miles just to be able to sit in a classroom where English was spoken. Most people pooh-poohed my interest in learning such an obscure language.

"Little monk," they would say, "why do you insist on learning English? Only laypeople use English, and very few at that. You need to settle down at a temple and fulfill your duties there."

"But I might go abroad someday," I would protest. "I might need to know English."

They would look at me like I was crazy.

For at least six years, I taught Dhamma Sunday school at the temple in Yakkala. There were hundreds of Sunday schools in Ceylon and this one was comparatively small. On any given Sunday, there might be about two hundred students, most of whom were younger than eighteen. I covered the basics: the precepts, the noble eightfold path, the life of the Buddha, and the history of Buddhism. At that time, the school didn't offer meditation instruction, which is what I primarily teach nowadays, nor back then did I suggest they should.

Fortunately, the head monk at the Yakkala temple, Venerable Candajoti Thera, supported my goal of learning English. He, too, thought it was an important language to learn and held a junior high school certificate in English.

Eventually, with Venerable Candajoti's help, my brother and I opened a small English school at the temple in Kebilitigoda. Because my brother knew English so well, having lived in Colombo for several years and studying it there, he was the main teacher at our little school. We borrowed desks, chairs, and a chalkboard from another temple. Then we put up a sign, and lo and behold, twenty students showed up! They were mostly children of poor families, however, and had no money for tuition. This was a problem because my brother needed to be able to pay for his food and lodging. I, of course, was supported by the temple.

Venerable Candajoti managed to raise one thousand rupees (roughly $300), which was enough to run the school for three months. At the end of that time, despite our best efforts, no one else came forward with donations. So we reluctantly closed the little school and returned the furniture we had borrowed.

And so my itinerant life continued. For a while I continued to live at the Yakkala temple, where Venerable Candajoti treated me like a brother. Because he supported my English studies, he was kind enough to provide me with food since I didn't have time to go on alms round while in school. (At that time, I was studying at Vidyasekhara English School, an institution started at the Vidyasekhara Pirivena, where I had studied in the late 1940s as a novice monk. Because there was no good bus connection between the English school and the Yakkala temple, I moved into a temple in a village called Udugampola. From there I still had to walk a mile and a half to catch a bus to school.)

One weekend in 1953, I went to visit old schoolmates at the Vidyasekhara Pirivena. While there, I was mending one of my robes one evening in the dormitory when I overheard two monks having a conversation in the hallway. They were discussing a message that one of them had received from the Buddhist Missionary School in Colombo. The school was looking for a promising new student to replace a monk who had been dismissed for a behavioral offense.

The Buddhist Missionary School, true to its name, trains Buddhist monks to travel abroad and teach the Dhamma. It was started by a Buddhist philanthropic organization called the Mahabodhi Society, which dates back to the late 1800s.

This school was quite small and very exclusive. There were a few students from other countries—Vietnam, Cambodia, Thailand, and China—but only ten monks were from Ceylon. The school's principal, Venerable Paravahera Vajiranana Nayaka Mahathera, had been educated in the West, and also was well-versed in the theory and practice of Buddhist meditation. He was a great inspiration for me.

The idea of a missionary school might seem odd to those who know of Buddhism as a nonproselytizing religion. However, the Buddha himself was actually a missionary. Within three months after his enlightenment, the Buddha had sixty disciples gathered around him. He then sent these disciples out to "spread the seed of Dhamma," asking them to walk in sixty different directions.

The Buddha made it clear that his disciples should not try to convert people. He told them simply to teach the Dhamma, and that those who have "only a little dust in their eyes," those who are ready to hear, will understand. This instruction highlights an important aspect of the Buddhist doctrine. In one famous sermon, the Buddha described the Dhamma as self-evident. He said that if people "come and see," they can judge for themselves. By that he didn't mean a literal invitation to come somewhere and listen to a discourse. He meant that the Dhamma is available for a wise individual who wishes to examine it.

The Buddha wanted people to apply his teachings to their own lives to see if they make sense. This way, people may come to accept his teachings based on their own experience, rather than blind faith. Describing the Dhamma as something you can "come and see" is based on an understanding that conversion takes place from within and cannot be forced upon an individual from the outside.

When I heard the two monks discussing the vacancy at the missionary school, even though I had never before heard of such a place, I immediately knew this was something I wanted to do. I dropped the robe I was mending and dashed out into the hallway.

"Venerable Sir," I said to one of the monks, "I would like to apply for that opening."

"When will you be free to see the school's director?" he asked.

"Tomorrow," I said.

The next day, I told the director, Venerable Paravahera Vajiranana Nayaka Mahathera, why the missionary school seemed perfect for me. Impressed with my conviction (and maybe my boldness!), he offered me admission. Unfortunately, the students were already halfway through their three-year program, so I would have to struggle to catch up, especially without my photographic memory. "This is a difficult program," Venerable Vajiranana warned me, "and you're coming from behind. You'll have to work especially hard to catch up."

He reminded me what the Buddha had said about hard work: "This Dhamma is for one who makes relentless effort, not for one who is lazy." The director said that if I wanted to be a good missionary monk, I'd need to commit myself to practicing the *parami* (perfection) of effort. That is how the Buddha attained enlightenment, he noted, by perfecting his effort to the highest degree.

So I threw myself into my schoolwork and soon caught up with my classmates. Luckily, the curriculum at the missionary school was similar to that at the monks' college. We studied Pali texts and Buddhist philosophy, as well as Hindi, English, and Tamil. After graduation, most students were sent to live abroad in India, so there were also classes designed to educate us in what we'd need to know while living there. We learned about Indian history, Hinduism, and Jainism.

Because the missionary school had monks from several other Southeast Asian countries, I suggested that we start an International Buddhist Students Association. We conducted all of our activities in English so that we could practice our language skills.

I have one particularly vivid memory from my time at the missionary school. Hunupitiya, a Colombo suburb a couple of miles from our school, had an *uposatha* house—a place consecrated for special religious ceremonies. Every two weeks, on full-moon and new-moon days, we went to the uposatha house to recite the Vinaya, the 227 rules that govern monastic life. This ceremony can be done on any consecrated (that is to say, specially dedicated) ground and is attended only by monks; no laypeople are allowed.

That particular uposatha house was 150 years old. It sat in the middle of a lake, on top of wooden pillars. It had half walls made of brick, with strong beams that supported a tile roof. To get there, we monks walked across a small, wooden bridge and removed the bridge after we were all in the house, an action that symbolized our separation from lay life.

As we approached the uposatha house on one occasion, some children warned us that several of the floorboards had been stolen, probably for firewood. "It's not safe," the children said. "Don't go in."

"Never mind," said an elderly monk. "Keep walking."

We all obediently followed his orders and continued to walk silently in a single-file line.

When we got into the uposatha house, we saw that the children were right: Half of the floor was missing. Normally we spaced ourselves evenly across the floor, to distribute our weight along the aging pillars that supported the building. With half the floor gone, though, all fourteen of us were forced to sit on one side.

We began chanting, and in the middle of the ceremony, we heard a loud cracking sound. Several monks looked around in alarm, but the senior monk chanted more loudly, compelling all of us to follow his example.

Suddenly everything gave way beneath us. It was chaos. Some monks jumped into the lake. Others fell, along with the collapsing building, into the water. I tried to heave myself over the half wall and ended up half in the building and half out when the roof fell on me.

Immediately laypeople came to our rescue. Some jumped into the lake, swam out to us, and brought us back to shore. Several monks had broken bones; one of my ribs, near my heart, was poking out of my chest. At first, it didn't hurt much, but as my adrenaline subsided, my chest started to throb. Ironically, the head monk, the one who had prodded us all to keep going, didn't have a scratch on him. The pinnacle of the roof had come down right where he was sitting and had protected him.

The rest of us were taken to a hospital. The next day I was released, with bandages wrapped around my midsection. My chest felt sore for weeks afterward.

Toward the end of 1954, it was time for final exams. Although I had joined the missionary school late, I had worked very hard to catch up. This effort paid off, and I scored well on my exams.

Then it was time for our overseas assignments. Our missionary careers were about to begin. The head of the school called me in and told me he would like to send me to Tanzania.

"Tanzania!" I thought. "Africa! That's half a world away." I wasn't sure I was ready for such a journey. I was only twenty-seven and had never been out of Ceylon.

"I'd rather stay closer to home," I said to him. "How about India?" He nodded.

I was certainly ready to go somewhere. Now that I had finished my studies, I knew I couldn't go back to the temple where I was ordained. Because of the dispute between my teacher and Venerable Sumanatissa, I knew that when my teacher died, Venerable Sumanatissa would contest my claim to inherit the leadership of that temple.

I had nowhere else to go, and I still had this burning desire to teach Dhamma in English someday, somewhere. To do that, I would have to leave the country where I was born. India, it seemed, was as good a start as any, and more appealing than Africa!

The trip from Ceylon to India was only twenty-two miles across the Indian Ocean, a simple ferry ride, but for me it was a grand journey and the inauguration of my world travels.

CHAPTER TEN

Crossing the Ocean to India

As I PREPARED to leave Ceylon for the first time in my life, I needed two things: money and a passport.

But because I was a monk, with no documented income, I couldn't get a passport. Only those who paid income taxes could apply for one on their own, so the head of the missionary school asked a rich supporter, a man who paid plenty of income tax, to be my sponsor. He signed the necessary documents and I was issued what was called an emergency certificate. This permitted me to come and go from Ceylon for two years.

I knew the Mahabodhi Society would pay my fare to India. Though that was wonderful, I felt that I should also have a little money once I arrived in the country, so I could have some independence. But it seemed unworthy for a monk to ask people for cash, so I went to the Yakkala temple, where I had lived for some time, and asked Venerable Candajoti for advice.

"Gune," he said, using a term of endearment, "don't be foolish. You're a monk. Everybody knows you have no money, and everybody knows you need a little money for this trip."

He helped me write a general letter that described my trip and what I would need for it. He got seven hundred copies printed. I distributed some by hand and sent many by mail.

When all was said and done, I received 200 rupees (about sixty dollars), which was an amazing amount at that time. My mother donated one rupee, and my father gave five. My younger sister gave two rupees, and my preceptor, the monk who originally ordained me, sent five rupees from donations he had received from laypeople at his temple.

My journey began at the Colombo train station on January 15, 1955. None of my family members were able to travel the eighty miles to see me off, but my preceptor rode on the train as far as Colombo with me. After we parted, I was all alone. Yet I wasn't scared; I was excited to be entering a new phase of my life. At long last my horizons were broadening. Though I could scarcely have imagined it then, by the age of seventy-five I would have taught Dhamma on six continents.

In Colombo I met my traveling companions, a group of Buddhist pilgrims on their way to Buddhist holy sites in India. We took an overnight train to a town called Talaimanner, at the northern tip of Ceylon. There we boarded a ferry for the twenty-two-mile sea passage.

That was my first time on a large boat, and despite my past near-drowning experiences, I wasn't nervous at all. In one hour we were in India.

The ship docked at Mandapam, a city on the southern edge of the Indian peninsula. That part of India looked like a desert; there were no trees, only dry sand and blazing sunlight. We boarded another train.

On the train, we had snacks of sweet rice wrapped in banana leaves. When we threw our banana leaves out the train windows, beggars would run to pick them up from the ground and lick the last grains of rice off them. Although the small villages in Ceylon could certainly not be said to be rich, this was clearly a much worse poverty than any I had seen.

By the next afternoon we were in Madras, on the east coast of India. My plan was to rest for a week and get acquainted with India before reporting to my assigned temple.

Venerable Batuvangala Jinananda Thera, head of the Madras Mahabodhi Society, met me at the train station. He and his fellow monks spoke Tamil, so we were able to communicate. I spent a relaxing week visiting temples and spending time at the Theosophical Society, a nonsectarian center devoted to the study of various religious teachings.

Soon it was time to leave for Sanchi, my first assignment. Sanchi is in the Indian state of Bhopal, midway between Delhi and Bombay. At seven in the evening, I boarded a train in Madras. More than twenty-four hours later, after riding halfway across the Indian subcontinent, I alighted in Sanchi. I was the only person to get off the train at that tiny dot on the map. The station had no platform; I stepped off the train and my feet landed directly onto the ground next to the rails. As the train chugged away, a man in a uniform approached me. I assumed he was the stationmaster.

It was nearly midnight, very cold and pitch dark. For the first time since I left Ceylon, I was scared to death. I did not understand anything the stationmaster said. Although I had studied Hindi for three years in Ceylon, this was the first time I'd heard somebody speaking Hindi whose mother tongue was Hindi.

Finally, in broken English, which I hoped the stationmaster might understand, I told him I was coming to live at the temple in Sanchi. This seemed to register with him. In equally broken English, he told me the temple was about a mile away, high on a hill, and that it was foolish to try to walk there in the dark. He suggested I spend the night in the train station and set out in the morning.

That night, I was cold for the first time in my life, a totally new experience for a young man who had spent his entire life in tropical Ceylon. But January in central India was hardly tropical!

Luckily, the monks in Madras had given me a thin sleeping bag. I spread it out on the cement floor of the train station and crawled inside. I don't think I slept at all that night, partly out of nervousness but mostly because of the bone-chilling cold.

The next morning, a porter assigned to me by the stationmaster carried my luggage as we set out for the temple. We walked almost a mile, then started to climb a large hill. The climb was about thirty minutes, along a winding dirt footpath. At the top of the hill, we came to the temple compound, which was surrounded by a three-foot-high stone wall. Spaced along the wall, every ten feet or so, were concrete pillars with round disks on top that looked like umbrellas, recalling the ornamental umbrellas atop a pagoda.

Inside the compound was a handsome mosaic stone patio. A short stairway led into the main hall, where two rooms faced each other. The hall was cool and windowless, with a smooth terrazzo floor. At the far end, I could see an altar with a serene Buddha statue in seated meditation posture. It was made of white limestone, and a single white candle burned at its feet.

I was overwhelmingly happy to be here; my life as a Buddhist missionary was beginning in a very auspicious place. The site of the temple at Sanchi dates back to the third century B.C.E., when King Ashoka, a devout Indian Buddhist, sent his son and daughter, Mahinda and Sanghamitta, as missionaries to carry the Dhamma to Ceylon. Before they left India, Mahinda and Sanghamitta visited their mother, who was living in a Buddhist nunnery at the site of the Sanchi temple.

In the late nineteenth century, British archaeologists excavated the Sanchi site and opened several of the stupas, the ornamental buildings that house the remains of the dead, mostly charred bone left after cremation. Inscriptions on the stupas said they were relics of the Buddha and two of his main disciples, Sariputta and Mahamogallana. Until 1941, these relics, appropriated by the British government, were displayed at the Victoria and Albert Museum in London. When the British were prevailed upon to return these treasures, the relics were divided into thirds. One-third was given to Burma, one-third went to Vidyalankara Pirivena, the monks' college I had attended, and the last third went back to Sanchi. There, the Mahabodhi Society built a temple to enshrine these holy relics. The temple was completed in 1954, and Venerable Hedigalle Pannatissa was selected to be its abbot.

The next year, 1955, I was sent to assist Venerable Pannatissa at Sanchi. I was to be his secretary for the next five years and I could not have asked for a better assignment.

CHAPTER ELEVEN

The Relics and the Dalai Lama

As soon as I arrived at the Sanchi temple, I paid my respects to Venerable Pannatissa. I had many gifts to give him, things I had carried from his friends in Ceylon and from the Mahabodhi Society. I also showed him a manual typewriter someone had donated, so I could do secretarial work and type letters in English for him.

Venerable Pannatissa was quite pleased, but what he didn't know was that my English was still shaky and that I had never used a typewriter.

Life at Sanchi was pleasant and peaceful. Not too many people made the climb up the hill, so it was a much quieter place than the village temples I was used to. Because there were no villagers nearby to offer us food, the Mahabodhi Society paid for a cook to prepare meals for Venerable Pannatissa and me. There was also a man who cleaned and brought water for us. He had to carry buckets of water from a well at the bottom of the hill.

Because of the holy relics enshrined at Sanchi, the Indian government stationed a police officer there twenty-four hours a day. The guards worked in eight-hour shifts, sitting and talking with visitors, or with us, when we had time.

In the summer Sanchi was a hot place, so hot you almost couldn't breathe. During the day the temperature reached 120 degrees Fahrenheit. I usually spent most of the day meditating in the inner hall, sitting on a wet towel spread on the cement floor. At 7 p.m. I brought my bed outside into the open air. It was a simple wooden frame, called a *carpai* (literally, "four legs") with ropes woven across the frame and a thin mat laid on top.

I spent several hours sitting on the bed, meditating in the cooler evening air, practicing mindfulness of breathing, as I had before sleep ever since I'd begun meditating. Then I would go to sleep in the open air.

The shrine room that housed the relics was beneath the main altar. A small door to the right of the altar led down a narrow stairway to a dark chamber, maybe ten feet square. On one wall was a door leading to an even smaller chamber, something like a tomb. A large steel cabinet stood in the center of that room. It had three drawers, one for each set of relics. The drawers were lined in white linen and had glass lids. Inside, the relics themselves were in small, round silver cups. The cup for the Buddha's relics was larger than the cups for the relics of his two disciples.

The drawers were double-locked, as were the doors leading to the relic chamber. Three people held the keys—the general secretary of the Mahabodhi Society, the governor of Bhopal, and the head monk of the temple. But none of these three had a complete set of keys for all the locks. Therefore, to completely open the doors to the relics, all three people had to be present. Two police officers were always there as well. Once a year, on the Buddha's birthday during the full moon of May, the relic display cases were opened and brought upstairs into the main hall. Religious pilgrims were allowed to file past the cases. Many prostrated before the relics.

Even though he was head monk at Sanchi, Venerable Pannatissa lived there only between the months of November and February. He spent the rest of the year in Ceylon, and while he was gone, I was in charge. My duties included greeting visitors, conducting morning and evening devotional services, paying the workers, and typing reports to the Mahabodhi Society in Ceylon.

I had taught myself to type using a written manual somebody lent me. I thought I was pretty good, until one day Venerable Pannatissa asked me to type an important letter to the secretary of the Mahabodhi

Society. He dictated in Sinhalese, and I translated it into my fledgling English.

With that translation propped next to the typewriter, I typed the letter, not even looking at the keyboard. I was young and overconfident. I finished the letter, still not really looking at it, and presented it to Venerable Pannatissa for his signature. He glanced at the foreign script, presuming it to contain what he had dictated, signed at the bottom, and the letter was mailed.

Three weeks later we got a note from the secretary in Colombo. He enclosed my letter, which, once I looked carefully at it, appeared as gobbledygook even to me. "I can't understand a word in this letter," he wrote in Sinhalese to Venerable Pannatissa. "What are you talking about?"

Venerable Pannatissa was quite peeved. Red-faced, I retyped the original letter, this time carefully watching my fingers on the keyboard and proofreading the finished product. I wasn't quite so cocky about my typing after that, although there was another time my youthful arrogance got me in trouble.

The general secretary of the Mahabodhi Society came to visit Sanchi. Two days after he left, I got a message from the principal of a nearby college. Apparently, the general secretary had visited the college after leaving Sanchi and left a parcel there, requesting the college principal to ask me to come get the parcel and mail it to Calcutta.

I was appalled. Was I supposed to hike all the way down the hill to pick up this parcel and mail it for the secretary? Why hadn't he done that himself? I fired off an angry letter to the college principal. "Since he left the package with you, why don't you mail it?" I wrote. "There's a post office just down the road from the college. It's much easier for you to get there than me!"

In ten days the principal sent me another message repeating his request. I ignored it, and ten days later, there came a third message. Finally I hiked down the hill, grumbling all the way, and picked up the parcel. When I mailed it, I saved the receipt, which the secretary would need to claim it.

After the packaged arrived in the Calcutta post office, he wrote me, asking for the receipt. I sent it to him along with an angry note.

When the secretary finally opened the box, a month after he had packed it, a horrible stink poured out. The package had contained food, and because of all my delays, the food had rotted. Now it was his turn to send me a fiery letter.

"You got so angry over a simple errand I asked you to do," he wrote. "And then you sent me a nasty letter on top of it. If you want to keep working for the Mahabodhi Society, I advise you to keep your temper under control."

Anger is one of the most difficult defilements to overcome; I know this from firsthand experience. When I was a young monk in Ceylon, I gave many sermons on anger and how to control it even as my own anger caused me to lose my temper repeatedly. I'm calling it "my" anger, but that isn't quite right. Anger would invade my mind and overwhelm me and I let it do that, despite the fact that inevitably it made me feel miserable. When I was angry, I felt pain in my chest and burning in my stomach. My eyesight blurred, my reasoning was unclear, and ugly, harsh words came out of my mouth.

After I calmed down, always feeling ashamed and foolish, I would reflect on the Buddha's words about anger: "One should give up anger, renounce pride, and overcome all fetters. Suffering never befalls him who clings not to mind and body and is detached. One who checks rising anger as a charioteer checks a rolling chariot, him I call a true charioteer."

There's a well-known story from the Buddhist canon that illustrates the Buddha's skill at dealing with anger. One day, a Brahmin, a person of high rank and authority, came to see the Buddha. This Brahmin had a foul temper and quarreled frequently with everyone. He would even get mad if someone else was wronged and that person didn't get angry in response. So, when he heard that the Buddha never got angry, he decided to test him.

The Brahmin went to the Buddha and showered him with insults. The Buddha listened patiently and quietly. When the Brahmin finally stopped and was waiting for the Buddha's reaction, the Buddha calmly asked him, "Do you have any family or friends?"

"Of course," answered the Brahmin. "Why?"

"Do you visit them periodically?" said the Buddha.

"Yes," snapped the Brahmin.

"Do you take gifts to them when you visit?"

"Of course I do!" the Brahmin snarled.

"What if they didn't want to accept one of your gifts?" the Buddha asked. "What would you do with it?"

"I'd take it home and enjoy it with my family," the Brahmin said.

"Well, then," said the Buddha, "friend, you brought me a gift of your angry insults. I don't wish to accept it. I give it back to you. Take it home to enjoy with your family."

If only I could have lived the wisdom of those words as a young man.

Pilgrims often came to Sanchi to pay their respects to the relics and to see the great gateways built by King Ashoka. There were four of them, built in the third century B.C.E. Each gateway was composed of two stone pillars, over twenty feet high, with crossbars between them. They were carved all over with panels depicting scenes from the Buddha's previous lives. The inscriptions accompanying the carvings were in an ancient language similar to Sanskrit and Pali.

Many times the pilgrims arrived with a tour guide who would interpret the inscriptions for them. But sometimes the guide was not with them, so the visitors asked me to explain. At first I simply told them I didn't know and left it at that. But eventually this display of my ignorance embarrassed me. I realized that, after all, for much of the year while Venerable Pannatissa was gone, I was the sole resident monk; I really should have been able to answer questions about the place.

So I asked one of the local tour guides to teach me about the stone pillars. He graciously complied, and after that, I was able to help visitors interpret the panels. Eventually, I wrote a pocket guide to Sanchi that included explanations of the pillars and their panels.

One panel, for example, showed the Buddha's birth, with Queen Mahamaya, his mother, in labor under a sal tree in the forest, as her attendants held a curtain around her, and celestial beings called devas poured water for bathing the baby. Another scene showed the Buddha's enlightenment, which also took place under a tree. As Siddhattha Gotama sat serenely beneath the Bodhi tree, dozens of demons representing the mental defilements threatened him with upraised swords, daggers, bows, and arrows. In another panel, the Buddha descended from heaven after teaching Dhamma to his mother, who had died seven days after his birth.

Another panel showed a monkey and a pair of elephants bowing down to the Buddha, who was spending the rainy season in Parileyya. Apparently, after he was unable to settle a dispute between two quarrelling groups of monks, the Buddha spent the rainy season living alone in the forest of Parileyya. According to the legend, the monkey brought him honeycombs to eat every day and the elephants heated water on a fire to provide warm baths for him.

All the scenes on the pillars, of course, inspired great devotion from the pilgrims who came to visit them.

In April 1956, we started planning a special Buddha Jayanti (celebration) at Sanchi for the Buddha's birthday in May. We decided to invite the prime minister of India, Jawarharl Nehru. Venerable Pannatissa and I traveled to Delhi to deliver the invitation in person.

When we arrived at Nehru's office, having made an appointment by mail, the place was crowded with foreign dignitaries, including several ambassadors from other Asian countries.

For a political leader, Nehru had a very peaceful expression and gentle demeanor. He was medium height, with graying hair, and was dressed in the traditional Indian costume: loose white pants, long-sleeved, baggy white tunic, and simple rope sandals.

Nehru greeted us with a soft voice and a friendly manner. Even though he was in the middle of a lengthy discussion with the visiting dignitaries, he ushered Venerable Pannatissa and me into his office. The three of us talked for about twenty minutes. Nehru said he was sorry, but he couldn't attend our celebration because it conflicted with an upcoming political conference in Indonesia. The prime minister spoke in smooth, fluid Hindi. I worked hard translating his words into Sinhalese for Venerable Pannatissa.

Finally, Nehru wished us the best and stood up to signify the end of the meeting. He posed with us for a quick picture, then bowed good-bye, his palms pressed together.

In addition to that brief encounter with Prime Minister Nehru, I was fortunate enough to meet other dignitaries as well. In November 1956, the king of Nepal was scheduled to visit Sanchi. I wanted to decorate the temple for his arrival, and I decided to hang some Buddhist flags, striped with several different colors, which are said to represent the aura that emanated from the Buddha after his enlightenment. Another interpretation is that the flags represent the Buddha's body: white signifies his bones and teeth, red his blood, yellow his bile, blue his hair, and orange his skin.

I climbed the rock wall on the edge of the compound in order to tie a string along the top of the wall where the flags would hang. As I pulled the string tight, it broke, and my own momentum threw me backward. I fell on the rocky ground and broke my wrist. When the Nepali king arrived, I was in the hospital. He heard about my mishap and came to visit me there.

Kings and prime ministers notwithstanding, late in 1956, we had a very different kind of distinguished guest: the Dalai Lama. As it happened, he came to visit on my birthday. I was the only monk there to welcome him.

At that time the Dalai Lama was only nineteen years old, younger than I was but already the boy-ruler of a Himalayan kingdom recently invaded by the Chinese. I had no idea what an eminent figure he was.

He arrived at Sanchi unannounced, without the police or other guards that surround him when he travels now. He did, however, have several monks attending him. They were very reverent toward him, making sure his robes didn't drag in the dust, and deferentially ushering him where he needed to go. When he took off his shoes to enter the temple, they helped him, then they laid their own rosaries inside his empty shoes, as an act of piety.

The Dalai Lama had a serene face that frequently broke into a radiant smile. He wore small, wire-rimmed glasses and was extremely handsome. His smooth complexion made him look even younger than his years.

He bowed toward me slightly with hands folded and said in English, "This is a beautiful, peaceful place. Quite cool. Are you comfortable here?"

"Yes," I told him, bowing in return. "I am very comfortable. And I'm pleased to welcome you to this holy place."

He seemed a very humble man. We walked together to the shrine room, where suddenly we were joined by the governor of Bhopal state and the general secretary of the Mahabodhi Society. As I found out later, they had been informed ahead of time about the Dalai Lama's visit to Sanchi and his desire to see the Buddha relics. They knew they would have to bring their sets of keys so we could unlock the relics cases in the dark chamber beneath the altar.

After the Dalai Lama's attendants laid a clean, white cloth on the floor before the Buddha image, he prostrated three times, touching his head to the cloth. Then he put flowers on the altar, offered three sticks of incense, and lit three candles. We all went downstairs to the relics chamber and unlocked the cases. When the Dalai Lama saw the holy relics, he prostrated again three times.

Then he presented me with a gift for the temple: a solid gold oil-burning lamp, about twelve inches high. We put the golden lamp in the underground chamber along with the relics.

Three years later, the Dalai Lama and a handful of his attendants rode horses across a mountain pass to escape the Chinese occupation of Tibet. He went into exile in northern India and the sad story of Tibet's subjugation began to spread around the world.

But of course I never would have imagined this as he and I stood side by side at Sanchi.

CHAPTER TWELVE

Among the Untouchables

ALTHOUGH I LOVED living at the hilltop temple in Sanchi, there always seemed to be problems, problems severe enough, eventually, that I started to think about leaving.

One night our cook, Anuruddha, came to me and said, "Swamiji Gunaratana, I asked Swamiji Pannatissa for a loan of twenty-five rupees. He said he didn't have any money because you didn't pay him your share of the food expense last month."

I was astounded. Every month, when I received my seventy-five-rupee stipend from the Mahabodhi Society, the first thing I did was pay Venerable Pannatissa forty rupees for food. Unfortunately, I never asked for a receipt. Given the monks' code of discipline, that would have been an insult. We were supposed to trust each other's word, and now Venerable Pannatissa had flat-out lied to the cook.

That evening, at teatime, Venerable Pannatissa and I gathered in the kitchen, as usual. I sat next to him on a low bench, and Anuruddha was on the floor about four feet away from us, preparing our tea. I turned to Venerable Pannatissa.

"Venerable Sir, is it true you told Anuruddha that I didn't pay you for last month's food? You know I paid you. Why do you try to make him believe I'm dishonest? Even if I didn't pay you, you should have discussed it with me. We are the only bhikkhus in this place. We should be able to discuss anything, as friends."

Venerable Pannatissa's face turned crimson. He stood up, kicked the bench where I sat, and stormed out of the room.

I also had trouble with one of the Indian policemen who worked at the temple as a guard. One day, I was hosting some visitors in the shrine room, when I remembered something I needed from my living quarters. I walked into my room, and there was the policeman bent over a drawer where we kept the cash from sales in our little bookstore.

As soon as the policeman saw me, he yanked his hand out of the drawer, holding a fistful of money! Truly I was more embarrassed for him than angry. I didn't know what to do or say, so I turned and rushed out of the room.

As soon as my visitors left, I sent a note to the police inspector in the village at the bottom of the hill, asking him to come and see me.

Within an hour, he arrived. I told him what had happened and asked him to transfer that officer somewhere else.

After the police inspector left, the corrupt police officer came and knelt at my feet, crying. He begged me to forgive him.

"You're supposed to protect us here," I said. "Instead, I find you stealing our book money. Why would you do such a foolish thing?"

The next day the police inspector general came all the way from Bhopal. He asked what happened, and I told him. He was very angry and said he would fire the officer.

"Please don't do that," I said. "He's a poor man, and he has several children to support. Don't fire him; just transfer him somewhere else. I don't want to see him here again."

Those were the kinds of troubles that made me fantasize about leaving Sanchi.

Also prodding me to move on was the fact that I was itching to resume my studies, and when a professor from the Benares Hindu University came to visit Sanchi, I saw my opportunity. Venerable Dr. Hammalawa Saddhatissa taught Pali at the university and had written books on Dhamma in Hindi, Sinhalese, and English. In 1956, I had heard him deliver an excellent speech about Vesak (the Buddha's birthday). His calm personality and deep knowledge of Dhamma impressed me enormously. I looked at him and saw what I hoped to become in a few years.

When he came to Sanchi, I asked Venerable Saddhatissa for help. I told him I had been studying English for a long time, but it was hard to find good teachers.

"Let me send you an application to the university," he said.

I was thrilled. In the meantime, I thought I should prepare. It had been some time since I was in a classroom. I decided to visit a small college about a quarter-mile from Sanchi, and ask for a tutor. By eating frugally, I had saved part of my monthly stipend, which I could spend on tutoring.

The principal of the college agreed to tutor me. But after a few sessions he began to question my motivation for studying English. "You are a priest," he abruptly remarked one day. "Why do you want to learn English?"

His tone was sarcastic and scornful, as if to say, "Who do you think you are—some high-caste Brahmin who's going to earn a university degree?" I could tell he thought I had no business aspiring to academic achievements.

"I am not one of those Indian beggars who goes around naked with ashes all over their faces, chanting the names of Hindu deities!" I said. "I'm a Buddhist monk, and Buddhist monks can learn any subject they wish. I'm also a missionary, so I want to learn English and teach the Buddhadhamma in other countries. Whether you're willing to teach me or not, I'm going to learn."

That evening, the principal and vice principal appeared at the temple in Sanchi. I made tea for them, and we sat down to talk. The principal apologized for criticizing me that morning. He said that from then on I could have private tutoring sessions for free.

The university entrance exam was in March of 1956. I took leave from my post at Sanchi in February and traveled to Benares for the first time.

Benares was, and is, one of India's most overcrowded cities. It's also one of its holiest places. Many Hindus come to Benares in their last years and live on the west bank of the sacred Ganges River. They bathe in the river and drink its water, even though it's filthy. They believe that if they die there, facing east, they will go straight to heaven.

All along the banks of the Ganges are open-air crematoriums called *ghats,* where the dead are burned. It is a primitive process, not at all like modern cremation. First, the body is placed atop a few pieces of firewood on an iron grill. Then patties of dried cow dung, looking like brown tortillas, are laid directly on the body. Ghee (clarified butter) is poured over the body and the firewood, then it's set aflame, usually by the deceased person's eldest son. When the body has been mostly consumed and the fire has cooled, the ashes and other remains are thrown in the river.

The rest of Benares is dusty and chaotic. The narrow, potholed streets are choked with bicycles, motorcycles, buses, trucks, rickshaws, and open-air, three-wheeled taxis. Beside the roads, people squat in the open to go to the toilet. Religious mystics, people the Indians would label holy men, roll about naked in the dust, chanting the names of God. Beggars, both elderly people and children, walk around with their hands outstretched.

Stray dogs, emaciated and hairless, wander the streets, as do cows. Because Hindus consider the cow sacred, it is allowed to roam freely. Sometimes cows walk right into food stalls to munch on raw vegetables and fruit. Dogs, on the other hand, are ignored or kicked out of the way.

As soon as I arrived in Benares, I started looking for a place to live near the university. Luckily, I met a monk while touring the campus. He said I could stay in his room with him, even though we had just met. By coincidence he had the same second name as I: Gunaratana. He had something else I considered very precious: a Pali textbook. For days, we pored over that book together. I couldn't believe my luck.

Then, two days before the entrance exams began, my friend abruptly announced he was going to stay somewhere else. Our brief stint as roommates was over, and I had nowhere to go. In desperation I visited the Benares office of the Mahabodhi Society. The monk there kindly found me a room in a Burmese temple close to the university. From the temple, it was only a short walk to the examination hall.

I was to take exams in several subjects: Hindi, Sanskrit, Pali, Indian history, and Hinduism. Luckily, I had had some exposure to Hinduism during my studies at the Vidyalankara monks' school.

Each exam was held on a separate day. The day before the Pali exam, I found my friend Gunaratana and asked to borrow his Pali textbook for a couple of hours.

"Do you know the five precepts?" he asked. "The eight precepts? The ten precepts? That's all you need, because that's all they're going to ask you. Anyway, I no longer have the Pali book."

It was only a few hours before the exam and I desperately needed that textbook, so I went to Venerable Saddhatissa and asked his help. He gave me a Pali text, and as he handed it to me, he said, "Last week I gave a copy of this book to the other Gunaratana. You could have borrowed his for a few hours."

I studied the Pali book all night. The next morning, as we entered the examination hall, a monitor told us to leave our cloth shoulder bags on a table in the hallway. As I started back out the door, Gunaratana thrust his bag in my hand and asked me to put it on the table with the others.

Of course, as soon as I got out in the hallway, I peeked in Gunaratana's bag. As I expected, there was the Pali book he'd said he didn't have. That wasn't the first time or the last that I discovered a fellow monk breaking a precept. It always makes me sad, because monks are supposed to be role models for laypeople. Laypeople trust us. We administer the precepts to them, and if we ourselves aren't following those precepts, we're hypocrites.

When even one monk is caught lying, it damages people's trust in the Sangha. People start to generalize that perhaps all monks are liars. So the honest monks have to work harder to earn trust and respect.

I feel sad whenever I see anyone lie, because I know what unwholesome kamma it engenders. I know firsthand. When I was a boy and I lied, I'd do anything to cover up those lies. I told one lie to hide

another, and another to hide that one. Eventually, I was awash in lies
and felt miserably guilty. It took a long time, probably not until after
I had my higher ordination, for me to realize how hypocritical I was
being and how painful it was to be dishonest. I finally understood the
Buddha's words on lying, in the Dhammapada: "For a liar who has
violated the one law (of truthfulness), who holds in scorn the hereafter,
there is no evil that he cannot do."

Later that year, I had my first contact with a group of people
who would become an important part of my missionary work: the
Untouchables. This group of people is the lowest of the low in India's
rigid social hierarchy, the caste system.

The caste system is as old as Hinduism, more than three thousand
years old, and just as firmly entrenched. Hindus believe that a person
is born into a particular caste, be it high or low, according to the wish
of the Creator. There are four basic groups.

Brahmins, the highest caste, are supposedly born from the mouth
of Brahma. Their duties are to learn the Veda (the Hindu scriptures),
teach other Brahmins, preach, perform religious rituals, and serve the
king and advise his administrators on how to run the country.

The second highest caste, the Kshatriyas (which means "rulers"),
are thought to be born from the arms of Brahma. The Kshatriyas are
warriors and kings, and thus are allowed to use weapons in enforcing
the law and defending the country.

The Vaisyas are the third caste. They supposedly are born from the
stomach of Brahma. Their duty is to feed the populace. So they hold
a variety of professions: farmers, merchants, traders. They also engage
in commerce as bankers, brokers, moneylenders, and businesspeople.

The fourth caste is the Sudras, born of the feet of Brahma. They
hold low-ranking jobs, such as cleaning the houses of the higher castes
and scavenging for scrap metal or other reusable materials.

The Untouchables are so far beneath the Sudras that they're not
considered to even have a caste. They are forced to perform the most
menial and disgusting jobs: cleaning sewage pits, hauling garbage,
removing dead animals from public roadways, and collecting cow dung

for fuel. When I was in India, the Untouchables were not allowed to attend school, or go to cinemas, restaurants, and public parks, because they might "contaminate" people of higher caste. When they were out in the streets, they were required to wear a bell around their neck, so others could hear them coming and get out of the way. Untouchables were not allowed to drink from public wells; their drinking water came from open drains.

When the British colonized India, they passed laws against discrimination based on caste. In 1947, a new constitution in India formally abolished the caste system, but it nonetheless persists to this day. The idea of castes is so intertwined with the Hindu faith, and so supported by the privileged classes, that it would be nearly impossible to eradicate. Inter-caste marriages are almost nonexistent, and politicians exploit caste for their own gains.

It's very much like the racial discrimination I have seen in the United States, which, though officially illegal, is still going on in a subtle way and is difficult to prosecute.

The Buddha spoke vehemently against class distinctions, most notably in the Dhammapada:

Not by matted hair, nor by lineage, nor by birth does one become a holy man. But he in whom truth and righteousness exist, he is pure, he is a holy man. What is the use of your matted hair, O witless man? What of your garment of antelope's hide? Within you is the tangle (of passion); only outwardly do you cleanse yourself.

I do not call him a holy man because of his lineage or high-born mother. If he is full of impeding attachments, he is just a supercilious man. But he who is free from impediments and clinging, him do I call a holy man.

And in the Vasala Sutta from the Khuddaka Nikaya, the Buddha talks about the true definition of an outcaste, or one who is expelled from the caste system: "By birth is one not an outcaste. By birth is one not a Brahmin. By action is one an outcaste. By action is one a Brahmin."

In other words, a Brahmin can become an Untouchable and an Untouchable can become a Brahmin, depending on his actions and his attachments. It's not to whom we were born that determines our status, it's what we do as we move through life. This is one of the fundamental ways in which the Buddhist view differs from the Hindu.

When I was in India in the 1950s, there were 80 million Untouchables. In October of 1956, Dr. Bhimarao Ambedkar, the charismatic leader of the movement to improve the lives of Untouchables, converted to Buddhism, a religion he had discovered, ironically, while studying in England. Buddhism, to Ambedkar, offered a path of compassion and an escape from the rigid caste system that Hinduism supports.

To the Untouchables, Dr. Ambedkar's life story is an inspiration. As a child he listened to lectures from outside the open-air schoolrooms he was barred from entering because of his caste. One day, when no one else in the classroom could solve a math problem, the teacher actually invited Ambedkar inside to try it on the chalkboard. He solved the problem, but the other children then threw their lunch bags in the trash because his shadow had fallen on them.

Prodded by his father, Ambedkar kept at his education. In high school, he took his exams sitting outside. He scored so well that the governor of his state took an interest in the young man, and saw that he got sent to New York, and later London, for college. There, in a casteless world, Ambedkar flourished. He earned a law degree and two PhDs, in philosophy and economics.

The first time he walked into an Indian courtroom as a lawyer, however, everyone in the room—the judge, the other lawyers, the jury, and the audience members—walked out. The outlawed caste system was still strong.

So Ambedkar took up politics. He easily won a seat in Parliament because all the Untouchables in Maharashtra state voted for him. When India was ready to declare independence from Britain in 1947, Ambedkar was chairman of the committee that drafted the country's new constitution. It included several clauses to address the misery of Untouchables and lower castes, giving them scholarships for vocational training, low-cost housing, tax deductions, and other financial rewards.

Ambedkar was a hero to the Untouchables. He was their beloved leader for ten years, and when he converted to Buddhism, a half million Untouchables followed his example. Sadly, he died only two months after that, in December 1956.

Because I spoke Hindi well, I was frequently asked to minister to Untouchables who were Buddhist converts, especially after Ambedkar died. In December 1956, soon after Ambedkar's death, Venerable Pannatissa came to me at 4:30 one morning. He had two poor people, dressed in tattered clothing, with him. "These are Untouchables," Venerable Pannatissa told me. "Today Ambedkar's ashes are going to be taken to Nagpur and enshrined in a memorial. And thousands of Untouchables are waiting there to accept Buddhism. They need a monk to administer the three refuges and the five precepts. Can you go?"

"Yes," I said, without hesitation. "Of course."

The train trip took most of the day. We arrived in Nagpur at about 3 P.M. Then we rode a bus about sixty miles to Amarawati, which took another five hours.

When we got to Amarawati I was astonished to see thousands of people gathered on an open plain next to high-rise apartment buildings the government had built for Untouchables. People milled all over the site, standing or sitting on the bare dirt. Children, cows, dogs, and chickens wandered freely.

As soon as they saw me in my saffron robes, a great chant in Marathi rose from the crowd: "*Bhagavan Buddhanca jayaho! Mahaparinirvanprapta parama pujya baba saheb doctor. Ambedkar yanca jayaho!*" (Hail to the exalted Buddha! Hail to the master doctor Ambedkar, who is worthy of greatest respect and has attained final emancipation!)

The sound of one hundred thousand voices praising the Buddha and praising their deceased leader was awe-inspiring, and nearly deafening.

I climbed three steps onto a small wooden platform, and a man waved his arms, signaling the crowd to be silent.

I took the microphone and administered the three refuges and five precepts, in Pali. The crowd shouted enthusiastically, repeating the ancient phrases after I said them. Never before and never since have I given the precepts to such a massive crowd. It was exhilarating. Tears of joy stung my eyes.

After we finished the refuges and precepts, I was asked to give a talk. Because this trip was so spur-of-the-moment, I hadn't prepared anything. Even so, I managed to speak for thirty minutes in Hindi about the significance of taking the refuges and precepts, and about becoming a Buddhist through one's own free choice. The next day my extemporaneous talk was summarized in the newspaper.

For the next four days, I ministered to groups of Untouchables from all over that part of India. People shuttled me from meeting to meeting, starting at 7 A.M. and sometimes continuing into the wee hours of the night. The Untouchables seemed very hungry for spiritual nourishment.

On the twenty-fourth of December, we went to Wardha, a Hindu stronghold where Mahatma Gandhi had his famous ashram. It was the first time a public Buddhist meeting had ever been held there.

At ten o'clock that night I went to bed, exhausted from the incessant schedule of the past few days.

Soon after I was settled in bed, a man ran into my room, handed me a letter, and ran out. The letter was written in English. "Don't attend tomorrow's meeting," it warned, "or someone will try to kill you."

I called for my host, and showed him the letter. He frowned with concern.

"Who gave you this?" he asked.

I described the man who had barged into my room. My host listened carefully, then went and rounded up several men to guard my door for the rest of the night.

I tried to sleep. About a half hour later, I heard a commotion in the hallway.

"We want to talk to Swamiji," I heard several voices say in unison. They were using the typical Indian form of respectful address for a monastic. It means "dear master."

"You can't," replied my host. "He is tired. He's been teaching non-stop for several days and he needs his rest. Nobody gets to talk to him tonight."

They protested, "Swamiji doesn't only belong to you. He belongs to us, too. Let us see him."

"No! He's resting. Go away."

"We're not going anywhere until we get to talk to him."

The arguing went on for a while, but finally the visitors agreed to leave, as long as they were given an appointment to see me the next day.

My host later apologized for the disturbance.

"Swamiji, this is a very strong Hindu area," he said. "There are religious and racist fanatics here. They don't like that you're teaching the Buddhadhamma. The idea of so many Untouchables converting to Buddhism is dangerous. If anyone invites you to a meeting tomorrow, please don't go. It's not safe."

But the next day there was already another meeting scheduled at 4 P.M., in a city called Goregaong, next to another Untouchable housing project. I was supposed to administer the three refuges and five precepts to another huge crowd and give a Dhamma talk. As I was driven there, we passed throngs of people heading to the site in jubilant procession.

At the entrance there was a commotion—shoving, pushing, and angry shouting. I was asked to stay in the car for my own safety.

Finally things seemed to calm down, and I was escorted to a makeshift stage. The organizer told me that several thugs had been trying to force their way into the meeting. The thugs demanded that I go with them instead of giving my speech, and they started fighting with the organizers, who refused to turn me over. One man's leg was broken in the melee, and his companions ran away.

I was later told that I narrowly escaped being kidnapped.

CHAPTER THIRTEEN

Under the Great Bodhi Tree

BY THE SUMMER OF 1956, I was actively plotting my escape from Sanchi. Although I loved the temple itself, and my work there, I had had enough of Venerable Pannatissa's mistreatment. My original assignment from the Mahabodhi Society was for five years, though, and I still had three to go.

One day we had a group of eminent visitors, including Venerable Narada Mahathera and Venerable K. Dhammananda Thera. At that time, Venerable Narada was the most popular preacher of Dhamma in Ceylon because he could deliver sermons in both Sinhalese and English, and Venerable Dhammananda was the head of the Buddhist Sangha in Malaysia.

I knew Venerable Dhammananda had a large temple in Kuala Lumpur. Boldly, I went up to him and asked if he might have need for a young monk in Malaysia.

"Of course," he said. "If you'd like to come to Malaysia, I will help you. Let me know when you're ready to come."

A few minutes later, Venerable Narada suddenly said to me: "Gunaratana, your knowledge of Sanchi and your explanation of the gateways is very good. Since you speak English, I can arrange for you to come to Malaysia, if you'd like."

Two exciting invitations in five minutes—I had struck gold! I told both monks that I was bound by a five-year agreement to serve the Mahabodhi Society, but that I would see if I could wiggle out of it somehow.

What I didn't mention to them was that I had received another invitation a couple of months earlier, when Devapriya, the general secretary of the Mahabodhi Society, was staying at Sanchi. After I confronted Venerable Pannatissa about lying to our cook, he complained to Devapriya that he didn't want "a monk like Gunaratana" around his temple anymore.

Devapriya said nothing in response, but the next morning he invited me to accompany him to Bhopal. He wanted to talk privately with me, and on the train, he told me bluntly that he knew Venerable Pannatissa was a liar.

"I'd like you to go to Calcutta or Bodhgaya," he said. "I will send you a new appointment letter."

While I waited for that letter, I wrote a letter of my own to the Ceylon high commissioner in New Delhi. My emergency passport certificate, issued when I left Ceylon to go to India, would expire in a few months and needed to be renewed.

By December 1956 I hadn't heard back from him and I was getting worried. My certificate was going to expire at the end of January, so I wrote a more urgent letter.

On the fifth of January, with less than three weeks left on my passport, I received a reply. The high commissioner sent me an application for a new emergency certificate, and said if I returned it with the endorsement of a prominent doctor or lawyer in Ceylon, my application would be approved. Once again, because I had no income, I'd need a sponsor.

Luckily, a Ceylonese doctor came to visit Sanchi a couple of days later. When I asked him to sign my visa application, though, he refused because he felt he didn't know me well enough. A few days later, a lawyer came to Sanchi. He asked if I would join him on a pilgrimage to visit the four Buddhist sacred places in India. I figured that if I went with this man, he might help me, and I had always longed to see the pilgrimage places.

We left the next day, bound for New Delhi. The following morning we toured the magnificent Taj Mahal at Agra. Then, after we arrived in New Delhi, I asked the lawyer if he would be willing to sign my emergency certificate application. He said he would be happy to.

I went to the office of the high commissioner, and came face-to-face with the man who had ignored my letter seven months earlier.

"Sir," I said, "I sent you an application seven months ago. Did you receive it?"

"Don't ask me anything about that," the commissioner snapped.

"Why not?" I asked.

"I can't answer that question, either."

I was exasperated, and my youthful arrogance reared its head. I was angry that as a monk, I was so easily dismissed. I was also angry that I had to bring along someone else to vouch for me.

"Sir, I have come four hundred fifty miles to renew my emergency certificate with you. You represent my country here in India. I have a right to ask you these simple questions."

Suddenly the lawyer spoke up.

"I came here to help this monk, but now I feel like speaking against him. He seems to think he knows everything."

"I don't think I know everything," I protested. "But I do know I have a right to ask this man a reasonable question."

The lawyer leaned over and whispered in my ear. "Don't worry. I agree with you. The commissioner is an arrogant fool, but he has the power to refuse to issue your emergency certificate, so it's best to be patient with him."

Of course, he was right. It's never a good idea to argue with bureaucrats who are drunk on their own power. I didn't say another word and the commissioner, with a sour smile, said he would send my new passport to Sanchi in three days. We thanked him profusely, bowed over and over, and left.

Our pilgrimage began at Kushinagar, where the Buddha passed away, in north India. There was a small golden pagoda there, inhabited by a single elderly monk. He was very friendly and showed us around the grounds. I felt overwhelmed with joy to be in a place where the

Buddha had been. The old monk and I recited some parts of the Mahaparinibbana Sutta, which contains the words the Buddha spoke just before he died: "Work out your salvation with diligence. Do not be negligent."

Those two simple sentences summarize the whole of the Buddha's forty-five years of teaching. What he means is that the spiritual practitioner must not waste one moment. We have to make constant effort to be mindful, with the intention of understanding the truth of life, so that we may attain liberation from suffering. Here is another way the Buddha described this sentiment to his disciples:

> Let not a person revive the past
> Or on the future build his hopes;
> For the past has been left behind
> And the future has not been reached.
> Instead with insight let him see
> Each presently arisen state;
> Let him know that and be sure of it,
> Invincibly, unshakably
> Today the effort must be made;
> Tomorrow Death may come, who knows?
> No bargain with Mortality
> Can keep him and his hordes away,
> But one who dwells thus ardently,
> Relentlessly, by day, by night
> It is he, the Peaceful Sage has said,
> Who has one fortunate attachment.

After our time in Kushinagar we went by taxi to Lumbini, the birthplace of the Buddha, just over the border into Nepal.

Lumbini was very run down, with overgrown grass and cows roaming freely. Only a small shrine marked the spot where Prince Siddhattha's mother, Queen Mahamaya, labored in a grove of trees. A stone pillar, erected by King Ashoka, announced that this was the place where Siddhattha Gotama was born. Nearby, inside a hut barely big enough to turn around in, was a stone altar with an engraving of Mahamaya holding on to a tree branch as her female attendants held a curtain around her. The altar was crammed full of fresh flowers, candles, and incense.

We spent some time there, sitting and meditating. It was a wonderful place, but I felt sad to see such a sacred spot not well cared for.

(Nowadays, Lumbini is in much better shape. The country of Nepal, though officially Hindu, has allowed Buddhists to preserve the Buddha's birthplace. Several countries, including Sri Lanka and Burma, have temples there, and a large international "peace pagoda" has been erected.)

The next day we went to Sarnath, in north India, where the Buddha delivered his first sermon, in the famous Deer Park. While walking around the quiet grove of mango, teak, and other tropical trees, I ran into a friend of mine, Ponnamperuma, who worked at the Mahabodhi Society's Sarnath office.

"Did you get your letter?" he asked me right away.

"No," I said.

"There was a registered letter that came to our office from the University at Benares. It was addressed only to Venerable Gunaratana, so I took it to the monk at Benares by that name. He opened it and said it was for you, not him, and he said he was going to mail it to you."

Since we were close to Benares, I went to the temple and found Potuwila Gunaratana. This was the monk I had lived with briefly, right before taking the university entrance exams. He had refused to share his textbooks with me, and he had lied to me. I knew he was not my friend.

"I mailed your letter to you a while ago," he told me. "Maybe the postal service lost it."

I suspected he was lying, but I was most concerned with what the letter said.

"You opened it," I said. "What did it say?"

"I don't know, I didn't read it carefully," he said. "Something about your application. It might have been rejected."

He was smirking. He seemed to be enjoying this.

I wasn't able to get anything useful out of him, so I went to see Venerable Hammalawa Saddhatissa, the Benares professor who had originally suggested I apply to the university. I had indeed been rejected, he told me, but he helped to track down the reason why: I had forgotten to sign the photograph of myself that I submitted with my application, and so the application had been voided!

There were five days left before the deadline and Venerable Saddhatissa suggested I submit a new application. I told my lawyer friend that I needed to stay in Benares for a few days and that he should continue his pilgrimage without me. Then I started the whirlwind of trying to get everything ready for my application.

First I had new photographs taken, and I begged the photographer to hurry the developing. Then I couldn't find an application form—the university seemed to be out of them. Someone suggested that Potuwila Gunaratana might have some, so I went again to his room, accompanied by Ponnamperuma, my friend from the Mahabodhi Society. Standing in his doorway, Gunaratana said he didn't have any more application forms, so we turned to walk away.

"Ponnamperuma, why did you come here with that wretched man?" the monk called out. He was referring, of course, to me. "If you had come alone, I would have given you an application form. But since you're with him…forget it!"

Again I appealed to Venerable Saddhatissa for help. Together, we walked all over the university until we found someone who had an extra application form. By then it was 9:30 P.M., the night before the applications were due. The days had flown by and time was running out.

I sat down to fill out the form. The very first line asked for proof that I had already submitted the fifteen-rupee application fee with my first application. They wanted the number on the money order I had sent, and of course I couldn't possibly remember that detail.

So, after all that frantic work, I was at a dead end. I couldn't submit my application. At that time, before computers became universal, a simple snafu like this could completely derail a person's application, and because of it I wouldn't be attending the university.

To ease my disappointment, I decided to continue my pilgrimage. I gathered a few friends to travel with me, and we went to Bodhgaya.

Once there, at the spot where the Buddha achieved enlightenment while sitting under a tree, I felt reborn. I was filled with an upsurge of devotion and happiness when I saw the great, spreading Bodhi tree.

That tree, by the way, is not the original *Ficus religiosa* that grew there in the time of the Buddha. The original tree was killed—burned and poisoned—by the wife of King Ashoka in the third century B.C., because she was jealous of her husband spending so much time at the temple in Bodhgaya. Later, the devout king planted a new Bodhi tree on the site. According to legend, the Buddha had asked his attendant, Ananda, to take a branch from the original Bodhi tree and plant it near Jetavana, a place where the Buddha often delivered sermons. So Ashoka's new tree in Bodhgaya, grafted from that so-called Ananda Bodhi tree, was a descendant of the original one destroyed by his wife.

Today the area is a magnet for Buddhist pilgrims. People circumambulate the ancient tree, over and over, chanting "*Sadhu, Sadhu, Sadhu.*" The air is filled with the musky smoke of incense. Earthen lamps sputter at the base of the tree, surrounded by piles of flowers, fruit, and candles. Saffron cloths are draped around the tree's trunk. Tibetan monks and nuns prostrate face-down as they make their bows.

I felt that I could sit under that tree meditating for hours. I sensed the presence of the Buddha, making his final, heroic push into liberation. I imagined the Evil One, Mara the Deceiver, sending his daughters—Greed, Hatred, and Delusion—in a last-ditch effort to tempt the Buddha.

Standing there in the immense shadow of the Bodhi tree, I almost heard the Buddha's voice as he touched the earth with the fingertips of one hand, calling it to witness his right to attain enlightenment.

CHAPTER FOURTEEN

A Trip Back Home

As soon as I returned from my pilgrimage, I sent a letter to Devapriya, the general secretary of the Mahabodhi Society, who said he'd give me a new assignment so I could leave Sanchi. When we had spoken earlier, he had mentioned he might send me to Calcutta or Bodhgaya, but when he answered my letter, he had a different assignment in mind: New Delhi. Apparently there was a Bengali monk, Venerable Ariyawansa, who could use my help. I gladly accepted the new assignment and then found another monk to replace me at Sanchi. I told Venerable Pannatissa that I was leaving. His reaction was what I expected: He was glad to get rid of me because I was disobedient.

The only thing Venerable Pannatissa wanted from me before I left was the manuscript I had written explaining the panels on the Sanchi gateways. I had been trying to find someone to publish the booklet in English, so we could give it to tourists who came to visit the temple. I hesitated, because I knew Venerable Pannatissa wouldn't publish the manuscript but would probably ignore it, or even destroy it, and all my work would go down the drain. I was sure that this was precisely why he wanted it. I knew, though, that if I refused, he would never let me leave in peace. So I took a deep breath, handed over the handwritten manuscript, and, carrying my one suitcase, walked down the hill for the last time. I never looked back.

On February 1, 1957, I arrived in New Delhi, ready to go to work at the Mahabodhi Society office on Reading Road. I lived at a small Buddhist temple with a Bengali monk who had been educated in Ceylon. He spoke fluent Sinhalese and welcomed me warmly.

Immediately I wrote to Mr. Moonasinghe, secretary of the Mahabodhi Society in Ceylon. I told him I had been transferred to New Delhi and to please send my monthly stipend there. His answer came within a few days. "Who permitted you to go to New Delhi?" he wrote. "That office is owned by the *Indian* Mahabodhi Society! We can't pay you as long as you're living there. If you want your seventy-five rupees from us, you'll have to go back to Sanchi. We own that temple."

I was flabbergasted. I hadn't known the Mahabodhi societies in Ceylon and India were separate entities. I appealed to Devapriya for help. "How can I live without this stipend?" I asked him. "There are few Buddhist supporters here, and I can't go on alms round in Delhi because the streets are already clogged with beggars."

Devapriya wrote a letter to Moonasinghe, explaining that he was general secretary of the Mahabodhi Society in both India and Ceylon. As such, he had the authority to appoint, dismiss, or transfer any monk, and he wanted me in New Delhi.

From then on, Devapriya made sure my monthly stipend arrived from Calcutta with no problem.

My work in New Delhi was among the Untouchables who had converted to Buddhism. Every Sunday I went to their meeting hall and gave a Dhamma talk. I also visited Untouchable communities on the outskirts of the city. One time I went to Beerat, which is believed to be the place where the Buddha delivered the famous Mahasatipatthana Sutta, the Discourse on the Four Foundations of Mindfulness.

I also found a nearby school, Das Gupta College, where I could take classes in English and other secular subjects. The principal, a generous and compassionate man, waived my tuition. Das Gupta wasn't Benares University by a long shot, but at least I was doing some learning, and that made me happy. The only problem was, from my first day there, the other students verbally harassed me. I think they thought I was an Untouchable because I spent so much time in Untouchable areas.

All monks employed by the Mahabodhi Society were granted a leave every two years. By that time, I had been in India more than two years, so I was eligible and, in fact, overdue for a leave. I had gotten letters from my family telling me that my father was ill and asking me to come to Ceylon and perform a chanting ceremony for him. I wrote them that I would leave on the twentieth of March.

My application for a leave was quickly granted, but I didn't expect things to go entirely smoothly. Although transportation costs were supposed to be included in the leave, the society office did not send me a train ticket.

By the time March 20 approached, I was still anxiously awaiting my ticket. Then, out of the blue, I met a monk who had just given away a first-class train ticket to Bombay. He said he wasn't going to use it and had given it to another monk, who probably wasn't going to use it either. By 10:30 A.M. on the twentieth, I tracked down that second monk. He said he had had a tentative trip planned, but had just canceled it, so he gave me the ticket. The train was scheduled to leave for Bombay at 5:30 P.M.

I quickly packed my belongings, and because I only had three rupees on me, I hired a three-wheeled taxi, an oversize tricycle—with the taxi man pedaling in the front, and the passengers on a seat in the back—to take me to the train station. My first-class ticket to Bombay allowed me to get on and off the train as I wished, so I did a little sightseeing. Along the way, I stopped at several temples, staying one or two nights at each. And I also visited the famous Buddhist caves at Ajanta and Allora. By the time I arrived in Bombay, it was early April.

I got off the train, unsure what to do. I was only partway home and out of money. Luckily, I ran into a group of twenty or so Sinhalese. They had been on pilgrimage in India, and they were returning home to Ceylon. They said they had a reserved railway compartment and that there was plenty of room for me to join them, so I did.

That night, I kept my briefcase under my pillow as I slept. Thievery was common aboard trains and you had to be careful. That briefcase had all my travel documents in it, including my hard-won emergency certificate.

In the morning, I woke to find the briefcase gone. Someone had slipped it from beneath the pillow as I slept! I desperately looked everywhere, but couldn't find it. I knew I couldn't travel back and forth between India and Ceylon without that certificate. I needed to get another one, and the closest place was Madras. So I handed my suitcase to one of my fellow Sinhalese travelers. I asked him to hand my things to whomever came to meet me at my destination. "No," said the pilgrim. "Just come with us to Mandapam, the passport checkpoint, and tell your story to the immigration officer. Hopefully he'll give you a note explaining everything to the Ceylonese officials. If he doesn't believe you, then you can go back to Madras and get a new emergency certificate."

I wasn't so sure about that idea. If I ended up needing to go back to Madras once I was in Mandapam, my trip would be even more delayed. But they talked me into it.

Standing in the immigration line at Mandapam, I worried. "I should have gone back to Madras earlier," I thought. I had an unsettling vision that I couldn't get out of my mind: a vision of my father's funeral. I saw my mother, sisters, and brothers crying as they stood around his coffin.

I was also thinking, "What if I have to return to that same high commissioner in New Delhi who gave me such a hard time with my first certificate?"

But when my turn came, I explained to the immigration officer that my briefcase had been stolen. Luckily, he believed me and promptly gave me a letter to show to Ceylon immigration at the border. I was so relieved.

The other travelers, meanwhile, had taken up a little collection for me because they felt sorry about my briefcase. They secretly slid the money into my shoulder bag.

At 5:00 the next morning, April 6, 1957, I was back in Ceylon.

When my train pulled into Kurunegala, I looked around for familiar faces but saw none. I felt exactly the same as when I had left home for the first time—all alone.

Using the money the Sinhalese pilgrims had collected for me, I hired a taxi. It took me through the coconut estates near Malandeniya, until the road ran out. I walked the rest of the way, through the same rice paddies I had sneaked across years ago when Gunawardhena and I had run away.

When I got to the temple, it was completely silent. My teacher was not there, so I asked a group of laypeople if they knew where he was. "He went to pick you up at the train station," one person told me. "He's gone out," said another. They were all nervously whispering to one another and looking at me sideways. Something was definitely wrong. Finally, at about 10 A.M., my teacher walked into the temple compound. I bowed at his feet.

"I have just been at your family's house," he told me. "Your father died last night."

1954. At age twenty-seven, as a student at the Buddhist
Missionary School in Colombo, just before leaving
Ceylon for the first time to go to India.

1956. At age twenty-nine, with His Holiness the Dalai Lama (nineteen at the time) in Sanchi, India. Also pictured are Devapriya (general secretary of the Mahabodhi Society) and Opanayaka (manager of the Mahabodhi Society bookstore).

1975. Working in the Vietnamese refugee camp, Eglin Air Force Base, Florida.

1980. Outside the Washington Buddhist Vihara.

2002. At the foot of Mount Kinabalu in Malaysia before dressing for the climb.

2002. Summiting Mount Kinabalu (13,435 ft.) at age seventy-four.

CHAPTER FIFTEEN

My Father's Funeral

I WAS STUNNED. I had arrived home in Ceylon just a few hours too late. My father was dead at age seventy-nine. I had not gotten there in time to perform the chanting ceremony I promised my family. I knew how upset my mother would be.

I hired another taxi and rode to Henepola. As soon as my mother saw me standing in the yard of her little house, she burst into tears.

"You were supposed to perform an offering ceremony for him," she sobbed. "Look what happened so suddenly! He's gone."

Tears slid down my cheeks.

For two days my father's body lay on the bed where he died, on the front veranda of the house, dressed in a white shirt and sarong. To mask the odor, we burned incense and citrus leaves. Kerosene lamps flickered at the head and foot of the bed. Our first task was to invite the monk at the village temple to come and conduct a funeral ceremony. He, in turn, would invite as many other monks as possible, walking from temple to temple to spread the word. Funerals in Ceylon were not held in temples; they took place at the home of the deceased, if it had a large yard where a crowd could mill around outside. If there wasn't enough room at the house, the monks would come to the cemetery and do their chanting there, in a graveside ceremony.

Even though everyone in the village already knew my father was dead, we were expected to formally invite each household to attend.

This was done by my brother, Rambanda. Normally Tikiribanda, who was the eldest son, would have done this, but he was traveling and my mother didn't know how to reach him. He didn't even know our father had died.

According to Sinhalese tradition, betel leaves are used for invitations of all kinds. At each house, you hold three leaves in your hand, and when the head of the household answers the door, you hand him the leaves. Just by the way the leaves are arranged, that person can guess what event you're inviting them to.

For happy occasions—weddings, housewarmings, naming ceremonies for new children—the leaves are turned with their stem ends toward the guest. When it's a funeral, the tips of the leaves point toward the guest. This is an important ritual and we could not leave anyone out or they would have been highly offended. In Ceylon, everyone in a village attended a funeral, whether or not they were friends of the deceased. It would be considered very rude to miss such a ceremony, for any reason.

During the two days before the funeral, many friends and neighbors came to our house to offer their condolences. Because a bereaved family does not cook, the visitors brought us food. All pictures and mirrors in the house were turned backward, facing the wall. My mother and sisters spent a lot of time crying.

Rambanda and I walked three miles to a shop and bought a length of white cloth to be used in the funeral. Normally, that cloth is about twenty yards long but we could only afford eight yards.

Meanwhile, family friends collected scrap lumber to build my father's coffin. Others went to the cemetery to dig the grave, a task that took a whole day.

On the day of the funeral, my family and I moved our father's body to his coffin while neighbors lit firecrackers in the yard, according to custom. The lid was left partially open so that his face and chest could be viewed. Villagers kept arriving, until there were probably four hundred people milling around.

That afternoon, ten monks appeared at our house. After viewing the body, they sat on chairs we had covered in cloth. The most senior monk administered the refuges and precepts to everyone. Then Rambanda unfolded the long, white cloth we had bought and handed it to the senior monk. He in turn passed it down the row of monks, so that each could hold a part of the cloth.

In unison, they chanted the ancient Buddhist verse on impermanence. Their words were Pali, of course, but in English the verse means this:

> Impermanent are all conditioned things, subject to rise and fall away. Having arisen they then must cease. Blissful is it when they subside.

These notions of impermanence and death are some of the most difficult parts of Dhamma to teach. People chafe when hearing things like, "We're all dying, moment by moment," or "Everything is impermanent; we can hold on to nothing." But it's only because of our attachment to changing things, things we'll inevitably lose, that we suffer.

But if we really look directly at change, we start to see that it has an upside, as well. We can count on the fact that whatever the conditions that exist in our lives, they will inevitably change. Things may get worse, but they may also improve. Because of impermanence, we have the opportunity to learn, develop, grow, teach, and make other positive changes, including practicing the Buddha's path. If everything in our world were set in concrete, none of those changes would be possible. The uneducated would stay uneducated; the poor and hungry would stay poor and hungry. We would have no chance to overcome hatred, greed, and delusion, and their negative consequences.

As for the inevitability of death, we have to remember that it's not just the body that grows old, decays, and dies. Our feelings and mental states do the same thing. If you close your eyes for just one minute, you can experience how a feeling or emotion is born, grows old, and passes away. It's like a wave, rising to a peak and then breaking apart. In the same way, our perceptions grow old and die. Our thoughts grow old and die. Our consciousness grows old and dies. This is the nature of our existence, and it's happening every moment.

The simple ceremony to mark my father's death closed with a transference of merit. My mother, brother, and sisters knelt on the floor and poured water from a pitcher into a cup while reciting the traditional sharing of merit.

> Let this merit go to our relatives.
> May our relatives be happy.

As they continued pouring the water, the monks chanted wishes for our father's rebirth:

> As the rivers full of water go to make the ocean full, so may that which is given here go to the benefit of the departed. As water fallen on the highlands flows down to the plains below, so may that which is given here go to the benefit of the departed. By this may you achieve longevity, good health, a rebirth in the heavens, and the attainment of nibbana. May all your hopes and wishes succeed, may all your desires be fulfilled, as if by the wish-fulfilling gem or like the moon on the full-moon day.

Those sweet words about a rebirth in the heavens illustrate the one part of Buddhist teaching that must be taken on faith by the believer. Buddhist cosmology describes thirty-one planes of existence. There are hell realms, the realm of hungry ghosts, the animal realm, the human realm, and many celestial realms. Beings are born into these states, which vary in pleasantness, according to their kamma. It is the law of cause and effect that drives the whole process.

Faith might seem problematic in a teaching that emphasizes personal effort and responsibility. But the fact is, we don't know what happens after we die, so we must decide if we want to accept the Buddha's words on faith alone. Sometimes it is wise to do that. Say, for example, a doctor gives you a medicine and says it will cure whatever problem you're having. You don't know that it will cure you; you must have faith in the doctor's knowledge and experience.

Still, someone whose faith isn't strong might think, "I'm not worried about some future lifetime. I just want what I can gain from this life." The Buddha advised us to consider another possibility.

Even if there is no future life, he said, doing wholesome things will bring you happiness and a clear conscience in this life. If it turns out that there *is* a future life beyond death, then the wholesome person will be doubly rewarded—now, and in the next life.

On the other hand, let's say you choose the path of unwholesomeness. Even if there is no future life, you will still feel miserable and guilty in this life. And if it turns out that there really is a future life beyond death, you will suffer again later.

So whether rebirth is a reality or not, letting go of unwholesomeness and cultivating wholesomeness guarantees our happiness.

At my father's funeral, the head monk spoke about some of these things. Then several of our friends and relatives stood, one by one, and gave short speeches about my father.

Finally, it was my turn to thank everyone for coming. Until that point, I had been able to control my emotions. But as I began to speak, I broke down and cried. It was all I could do to get out the words of thanks.

After my father's funeral, I stayed a couple of days at my mother's house, then I left for Colombo. I wanted to visit the Buddhist Missionary School and pay my respects to Venerable Paravahera Vajiranana Nayaka Thera.

What a rude awakening waited for me there!

"What are you doing here?" was Venerable Vajiranana's less-than-warm greeting to me. "We trained you, then you left us and joined the Indian Mahabodhi Society! Now you want to come back and stay here and eat our food? You have no right to come here. We don't want anything to do with you anymore."

This was my second lesson in the deep divisions between the Sinhalese and Indian branches of the Mahabodhi Society. They were apparently bitter rivals, and Venerable Paravahera Vajiranana Nayaka Mahathera was furious with me for trying to serve both.

Not only did he seem to have forgotten the letter I wrote him explaining why I left Sanchi, he still didn't want to hear my story. He didn't ask me a single question about the situation in Sanchi, nor did he give me a chance to speak.

When I went to visit Moonasinghe, he also was angry. He remained seated in his chair, even though laypeople usually greet a monk and then sit on the floor to show respect. He wouldn't talk to me, or even look at me.

That's the way it has been for generations in Sinhalese culture. Young people are simply not allowed to express their opinions. Nowadays, many young monks disrobe and leave the temples out of frustration over such treatment. A few old monks are left to struggle along and keep the temples going, all because of the wrong kind of management style, not giving fair treatment to both young and old.

When I was a boy, we could never talk back to our parents. Never. We were supposed to keep our mouths shut out of respect for our elders. Not once in my whole childhood did I dare to disagree with my father, or even speak strongly to him. It was the same at school; the teachers knew everything. They dispensed the knowledge, and we weren't allowed to question or debate any of it.

So all during my childhood, I was dutifully quiet. I hardly spoke around adults. And that conditioning persists, believe it or not, seventy years later. Sometimes I have a dream in which I'm sitting with my father or my teacher, and I'm afraid to speak. The fear is deeply rooted in my subconscious.

On May 6, 1957, a month after my father's death, I returned to India. I spent a month in Madras, visiting friends, then I went back to New Delhi. There I resumed my duties at the temple and my classes at Das Gupta College.

When Devapriya, the Mahabodhi Society secretary, heard that I was attending college classes, he got angry. He tried to convince me to go to Bodhgaya, to replace a monk there who, he said, had gotten "an ill reputation"—a euphemism indicating the monk had probably broken a major precept.

It was early July, the beginning of the rainy season when monks traditionally stay in one monastery for three months, to honor the time when the Buddha and his disciples observed the "rains" retreat. So I told Devapriya I couldn't go anywhere right away.

In October, as soon as the rains retreat ended, Devapriya was at me again. He sent another letter, this time instructing me to go to Bombay.

"If you don't go, we might lose our center there," he wrote. "Please leave immediately."

That temple no longer had a resident monk, I learned, and the Mahabodhi Society officials were concerned that some of Bombay's millions of homeless people would move into the empty buildings and claim squatters' rights. Such a thing was not unheard of in those days.

So I went to Bombay. The center there was called Ananda Vihara; *vihara* is a Pali word that literally means "dwelling place of the Buddha"; nowadays vihara is used more broadly to describe the living quarters of any monk, as well as the shrine room, meditation hall, and other spaces that collectively make up a Buddhist temple or meditation center.

The Ananda Vihara was located on Lamington Road, in the middle of a hospital compound. It was built through the donation of a doctor who worked in the hospital. On the ground floor, we had a library. Upstairs was a shrine room, bathroom, bedroom, and what was to be my office.

Opposite the office was the hospital's maternity ward. Day or night, whenever I sat at my desk, I could hear the screams and moans of women giving birth. Much of the time during my stay in Bombay, however, I was out visiting the Untouchable communities surrounding the city. There was another monk in the temple, but he didn't speak Hindi or English, so the Untouchables preferred me. I gave refuge and precept ceremonies, taught Pali, chanted suttas for the sick, performed funerals, and held Dhamma classes. I also visited patients in the hospital.

Every Sunday at least five hundred people came to the temple for services. This was a great improvement from the center's past, when it had served more as a social club where people gathered to smoke and drink. We also started a small library and bookstore. For the first anniversary of Dr. Ambedkar's death, we organized a grand ceremony that was attended by the governor of Bombay state.

Sometimes I would minister to the Untouchables for a week or two at a time, and would simply go from one village to the next without returning to my temple. These people lived in very poor homes— most of them were one-room shanties with mud walls, grass roofs, and floors covered in cow dung. When I entered a home, the family would spread a straw mat on the floor for me to sit on. Then they'd serve me food, what little they had. Usually someone sat next to me and flapped a cloth in the air to keep flies away.

Outside, the yard would be full of stagnant puddles, human and chicken excrement, broken pots, and other trash. Insects swarmed all over. I knew that eating food in such unhygienic conditions was going to make me sick, and it did, over and over. But I never said no to their invitations; I couldn't refuse the Untouchables' heartfelt hospitality.

When my teacher came to visit in 1958, he was surprised to see how thin and weak I had become. Visiting the Untouchable villages was taking a toll on my immune system. I think my teacher must have reported this to the Mahabodhi Society.

In September I got a letter from Venerable Dhammananda, whom I had met at Sanchi. He sent me a visa application form and asked me to fill it out and return it to him. He wanted me to go to Malaysia.

And so, on the first of October, after eighteen months in Bombay, I was again moving to a new temple. Before leaving, I made a quick visit to my home village to say goodbye to my mother and relatives. Then I boarded a ship in Madras. The ship was bound for Japan, but would stop in Malaysia, which is where I would disembark—and begin the next chapter of my missionary career.

CHAPTER SIXTEEN

Malaysia

ON NOVEMBER 5, 1958, my ship docked in Penang, the second largest city in Malaysia. Malaysia had just won its independence from Britain the year before, so it still had a pleasant colonial flavor. It was so much cleaner, and more modern, than India. The roads were in good repair, and poverty seemed nonexistent. There were no beggars, and people in the streets were well-dressed. There were many beautiful Chinese temples with enormous Buddha statues. These temples were always full of devotees offering fruit and flowers, and burning incense. At the marketplace, there were Chinese signboards in front of almost every store.

It was a beautiful country that reminded me of Ceylon—mountains, rainforests, rice paddies, coconut and rubber estates—and it had much of the same tropical vegetation. Because of the rich soil and warm climate, a wide variety of crops could be grown: In addition to rice, rubber, and tea, the farmers of Malaysia also grew papaya, mango, rambutan, tapioca, sweet potatoes, jackfruit, and citrus.

I spent a week at the Mahindaram Buddhist Temple, as a guest of the Venerable Kamburupitiye Gunaratana. (He was one of several monks named Gunaratana whom I've met in my life. None of us are related. We simply were given the same Pali last name at our ordinations. Only our first names—usually the name of our home villages—differ.) He was an elderly monk, the highest-ranking Buddhist bhikkhu in Malaysia.

Every day at mealtime, Chinese devotees clustered around him as he was served a special plate of food. When Venerable Kamburupitiye finished, he mixed the leftovers together—rice, meat, vegetables, fruit, and sweets. Then the devotees lined up to receive a small morsel of that food, which for them contained the Venerable's blessings.

After he died several years later, some said he was a fully enlightened arahant.

When Kamburupitiye saw me for the first time, he looked bemused.

"I don't think you should stay in the robe," he said. "You can't be more than eighteen years old. You're too young to be a fully ordained monk."

I laughed. I was thirty years old at the time, but I still looked like a novice.

When I arrived in Kuala Lumpur, I was welcomed by the eminent monk who had invited me to Malaysia: Venerable Dhammananda Thera. The temple where I was to live consisted of two bedrooms, a kitchen and dining room, two bathrooms, a shrine room, and a larger preaching hall that would accommodate about forty people.

The temple served mainly the fifty or so Sinhalese families living in Kuala Lumpur. A few Chinese Buddhists visited, too. It offered regular devotional services, Dhamma classes, and Sunday school.

Very quickly I realized that I needed to improve my English if I was going to be an effective teacher there. The Sinhalese parents wanted us to teach Dhamma to their children in Sinhalese, but the children, growing up in Malaysia, spoke mostly Malay or English. When their parents brought them to the temple, they were shy around the monks who spoke to them in Sinhalese.

So I decided to start conducting most of the Sunday school classes in English, to make the children more comfortable and willing to listen. I began by telling Dhamma stories.

Some of the Sinhalese criticized me for teaching in English, but the more educated ones supported me. They saw the value of their children learning English.

One day, a Chinese man came to drive us to someone's home to conduct a funeral. On the way, he asked if the temple needed anything. We told him our Sunday school enrollment was growing, and we needed a bigger building to accommodate all the children. The man thought a moment, then he told us something very interesting.

He said he was a member of the Malaysian Lottery Board, and that every once in a while, people who won the lottery didn't claim their prize. When that happened, the money was donated to charity.

"Next time, I will propose to the board that we donate the unclaimed money to your temple," the man said.

A few months later, he suddenly appeared with a check for the equivalent of about forty thousand US dollars. We built a beautiful new Sunday school building with the money.

Nearly a year after I arrived in Malaysia, in late September 1959, the prime minister of Ceylon was shot and killed at his home in Colombo. The gunman was wearing monk's robes. The next day I organized a memorial service at our temple.

When people began arriving that evening, we sat on the porch to discuss the tragedy. All of a sudden I heard a commotion. Mr. K. A. Albert, a leader of the Sinhalese community in Kuala Lumpur, strode onto the porch, visibly angry.

In very abusive language, he began to yell at me. He was irate that a Buddhist monk would assassinate the prime minister, and he started shouting insults about the Sangha.

"Mister Albert," I said, "It's not fair to condemn all monks, just because one man wearing robes did something wrong. That man probably wasn't even a monk. He probably wore the robe as a disguise, so he could get close to the prime minister."

For some reason that seemed to make Mr. Albert even madder. He sprang at me, fists swinging. The Sinhalese ambassador, who had been sitting on the porch with me, jumped between us to stop him. Mr. Albert eventually calmed down and went home. He refused to stay for the memorial service.

Later that night, one of his relatives called to tell me that Mr. Albert was very sick, with a high fever, vomiting, and diarrhea. They asked me to come to their house and chant for him.

I went, but found him lying in bed, facing the wall, his back to me. He would not speak to or even look at me. Nevertheless, I did the chanting and tied a traditional blessing string around his wrist. He didn't resist, but he never said a word.

A few days later, Mr. Albert's physical and mental condition had improved. Moved by my kindness or perhaps having recovered from the effects of his fever, he phoned and invited me to lunch at his house. I think that was his way of apologizing and also testing me to see if I was angry at him. When I accepted his invitation, he knew I wasn't going to hold anything against him. He served me lunch himself, with great affection.

My days at the Kuala Lumpur temple were quite busy. I gave Dhamma sermons in both English and Sinhalese every full-moon day and every Sunday. I also taught Sunday school for the children and conducted a Buddhist correspondence course for people who wanted to study by mail.

The course had twelve beginner's lessons and twelve advanced lessons, all of them about the life of the Buddha and the contents of his teachings. I had an assistant who helped me mail out the packets. Reproducing them was tedious; we had to cut stencils on a manual typewriter by typing on a thin, waxed film and then use that film to crank out blurry copies on a hand-turned printing machine that had a barrel spread with ink.

Each lesson ended with a series of questions for the student to answer. When those answers came back in the mail, I corrected them and sent the material back to the student.

Years later, when I went to the United States, I met people whose first introduction to Buddhism had been through that correspondence course.

The desire to improve my English burned in me like an eternal flame. First, I took afternoon classes at a school run by a Hindu organization, then at a private high school where the principal allowed me to attend tuition-free. Later, I went to another private school closer to the temple, and there, a temple supporter paid my tuition.

In 1960 I decided to take the University of Cambridge's external examinations, which were administered by the Malaysian education department. This was a vestige of the British influence in that part of the world.

There were several levels, all conducted in English. The lowest level, called the qualifying test, was equivalent to ninth grade. The next level, the Senior Cambridge exam, equaled tenth grade. The last, the Cambridge High School Certificate exam, was something like a modern-day college entrance exam. It was geared toward students on a twelfth-grade level. People who passed that exam could enter either Cambridge University or the University of Malaysia.

I hoped to get into the University of Malaysia. I thought a college degree would be the talisman that would earn me respect among people of all educational levels. I figured the more education I had, the more people would be willing to listen to my Dhamma sermons.

When I signed up to take the qualifying test, it included only English. Then, while I was preparing, they changed the requirements. From then on, students would be tested on mathematics as well.

I had only eight months to prepare, so I borrowed a set of math textbooks from a teacher and got to work. I studied with a young Chinese man who visited our temple and was also taking the test. When exam time came, I passed.

One year later, I took the senior examination and passed that one, too. Two years after that, I took the Cambridge High School Certificate exam. On that one, I didn't fare so well. I had to take it twice more before I passed. By 1964 I had passed two subjects with distinction and the other two with ordinary marks. I thought that would be good enough to get me admitted to the University of Malaysia, but when I applied, I was rejected. It was a crushing disappointment for me.

Meanwhile, more and more Chinese people were coming to our temple. In 1961 Venerable Dhammananda invited several prominent Chinese Buddhists to join him in starting the Buddhist Missionary Society. It was a way to honor their many contributions to the temple.

As soon as the society was formed, even more Chinese people came to the temple, bringing more money. Venerable Dhammananda started printing Buddhist books to distribute all over the world. He traveled across Malaysia giving Dhamma talks and forming more Buddhist groups. He also published a magazine called *Voice of Buddhism.*

That same year we added a day school for girls at the temple. Almost two hundred students enrolled. In addition to my other activities, I began to teach there as well. Late in 1961 I was invited to accompany another monk to Thailand. It was going to be my first time there, and I asked a lay supporter, Mr. R. A. Janis, to go with me. On the way, we stopped at a temple in Penang. and while we were there, I started feeling pain in one of my kidneys. For several days, there was blood in my urine, and finally I ended up in the hospital. The doctor diagnosed a kidney stone and prescribed antibiotics. Although I recovered, I never did pass the stone.

After I had lived at the temple in Kuala Lumpur for two years, I earned a vacation. The society that supported the temple gave me a ticket to return home to Ceylon for a visit. In December 1962, just a day or two before my thirty-fifth birthday, I left for Singapore, where I planned to spend a few days visiting temples before my ship sailed toward home.

On December 14, I sent my luggage to the port so it would be there when we embarked two days later. That afternoon, while talking to some people after lunch, I suddenly felt severe pain in my chest. I excused myself and went to lie down. I was sweating profusely. Eventually, the pain got so bad that I passed out.

My host, the head monk of the temple I was visiting, called an ambulance. During the ride to the hospital, the pain was unbearable.

It felt as though a giant hand was squeezing my heart. It was so hard to breathe, I thought I was going to die before we reached the hospital.

But I made it and before long found myself in a private room with a "No Visitors" sign on the door. The doctor said I had had a mild heart attack, but he didn't give me any medicine; he just told me to rest.

Two days later, I felt immensely better. When I woke up in the morning, the pain was gone and I felt normal again. I realized it was now December 16 and my ship was about to sail with my bags on it. I called a nurse and told her I needed to check out of the hospital. She called a doctor.

"Are you crazy?" the doctor said when he arrived at my bedside. "The day before yesterday you had a heart attack and now you want to leave?"

"I feel fine," I protested. "I don't have any pain or weakness. I have to go."

"I can't release you," he said sternly.

We argued back and forth for several minutes. I explained that my luggage was on a boat that was leaving soon, that I had written ahead to tell my relatives when I would arrive in Ceylon.

Finally the doctor relented, but he made me sign a paper saying that I was leaving the hospital against his advice. I went straight to the dock, boarded the ship, and seven days later, I was in Ceylon.

Although the heart attack was a hint that I might have cardiac trouble much later in life, at that time I felt strong and healthy. I was in the physical prime of my life. Even so, I continued a daily practice I had done since age twenty: contemplation of my own death.

Every night when I lie in bed, just before sleep, I think, "I could die tonight. I might never see tomorrow." When I go for my daily walk, I think, "I could be hit by a car." When I fly, I think, "This plane could crash." When I ride in a car, I think, "We could have an accident."

Maybe it is because I had several near-drowning experiences as a young person that the thought of death persistently hovers around me. It has been there for as long as I can remember, but it's certainly not a morbid obsession. It is something much more precious—an opportunity, and a reminder, to practice Dhamma diligently.

We never know how much time we have left.

CHAPTER SEVENTEEN

An Invitation to the West

Venerable Dhammananda had originally invited me to Malaysia, I assume, because he respected me. Eventually, though, our friendship wore thin. I'm not sure exactly why.

Maybe it was my insistence on teaching so much in English. Maybe it was my youth. Maybe it was the extra classes I took that kept me away from the temple and my duties there.

I know I ruffled feathers among some members of the Sasana Abhiwurdhiwardhana Society, the group that supported and operated the temple. Some of them were annoyed that I continued to teach Dhamma to the children in English. Because it was considered fashionable and progressive among the upper middle class to speak English, these kids heard English at home. They also heard it at school and on the radio and television. But their parents wanted us, the monks, to speak Sinhalese to the children when they came to the temple.

I knew it would be better to use English, a language the kids were comfortable with. Dhamma concepts are hard enough for young children to grasp, and if I taught in a language they couldn't understand well, they would be frustrated and not want to come to the temple at all.

I had many conversations with the parents about this.

"We rely on you to help us preserve our language and culture," they said. "We invited you here to teach our children in Sinhalese. Instead, you carry on in English all the time."

"That's not true," I responded. "I give Dhamma sermons in both Sinhalese and English. I also found volunteers to teach Sinhalese in the Sunday school. But I teach Dhamma in English. That's the best way."

Unfortunately, they weren't convinced.

Meanwhile, the immigration authorities of Malaysia had informed me that they couldn't extend my visa anymore. Nine years in a row, they had renewed it each time I applied. But that was evidently their limit. They warned me that they couldn't renew it a tenth time. I would have to leave the country for good by the end of 1968.

So I began to consider my options. I sent queries to temples in Hong Kong, Korea, Indonesia, and Canada. Most of them responded positively, with invitations to live and teach there. It was simply a matter of choosing where I wanted to go next.

In 1967 I took a wonderful trip all over Asia, courtesy of the Sasana Abhiwurdhiwardhana Society. During a period of six months, I visited ten countries: Thailand, Cambodia, Laos, Vietnam, Korea, Japan, Taiwan, the Philippines, and Indonesia, as well as Hong Kong. It was an amazing adventure for a young monk, and really the first "vacation" I had ever taken. I didn't have to teach classes or study. I just stayed in temples and visited local religious sites, wherever I went.

Vietnam was particularly interesting. Despite the war beginning to rage in their country, the Vietnamese people were very kind to me. They took me to visit temples and organized talks for me everywhere I went. Hundreds of people would come and listen; someone always translated my speech from English to Vietnamese.

At one Vietnamese city, Danang, United States B-52 bombers were dropping bombs in the DMZ every few minutes. The entire building where I was staying would shake with each bomb.

In Laos, I visited the cities of Luong Prabang and Vientiane. Since there were no civilian airplanes available, a highly respected Laotian monk arranged for me to go by military plane. My fellow passengers were soldiers.

In Cambodia I climbed the steep stone steps of Angkor Wat, the famous twelfth-century temple complex that stretches through the jungle for miles.

In Japan, I met another Sinhalese monk, Venerable Ratmalane Sivali, who also was traveling through Southeast Asia. I mentioned to him that my visa in Malaysia was due to expire. He told me that a Sinhalese temple had been established in Washington, DC, the first Sinhalese temple in the United States. He said they were looking for an English-speaking monk with missionary experience to assist the monk who was already there. Venerable Ratmalane Sivali gave me the address of the temple and the name of the monk living there. He suggested that I also write to the Sasanasevaka Society in Ceylon and express my interest in going to Washington.

At the end of my six-month tour of Asia, I went home to Ceylon.

I spent about a month visiting all my relatives. I also met Venerable Madihe Pannasiha Nayaka Thera, the patron of the Sasanasevaka Society, who had already answered my letter about the opening in Washington. After a short interview, he said he would tell the society members about me, and they would let me know of their decision.

One day near the end of my time in Ceylon, I had lunch at my brother Rambanda's house. Then I went to stay at the Yakkala temple, about seventy miles from my village of Henepola. The next day, a message arrived from my younger sister.

"Rambanda has died," it said. "You must come right away."

What?! It was impossible. He was fine at lunch just the day before. Rambanda was young, only forty-five, and perfectly healthy.

I showed the note to Venerable Candajoti. "This must be a mistake," I said. "Or some kind of cruel joke."

"No," he replied. "I don't think it's a joke. Death can visit anyone at any time. You'd better go."

I hired a taxi and rode to my brother's house. There was the whole family, in mourning.

I learned that the night before, just a few hours after I had left, Rambanda had taken his oldest son to pick jackfruit for the water buffalo. He had told his son to stay on the ground and that he would throw the big fruits down to him. Rambanda climbed high into the tree, maybe fifty feet.

As he threw the first jackfruit, the branch he was standing on and the branch he was holding with one hand both broke. He came crashing to the ground and broke his neck. He was killed instantly.

The next morning I walked to Galagedara with some relatives to buy the white cloth and other things we needed for my brother's funeral. I was numb. The next few days were a blur.

After the funeral, it was time to go back to Malaysia. I boarded a plane in Colombo, and as I took my seat, my heart was aching for the brother I had lost. We were so close as children, always getting into trouble and having adventures. Memories flooded my mind.

And then I thought of how, every time I left Ceylon, Rambanda was the one who took me to whatever port or station I was leaving from. This time, he wasn't there.

I began to cry.

Quite soon after I got back to Malaysia, I received the letter that would determine the next chapter of my life. It was a formal invitation from the Sasanasevaka Society, asking me to come to Washington, DC, to be a resident teacher at their temple. My assignment was to begin the next year, 1968.

I was forty years old, and finally I was about to do what I'd always wanted—to teach Dhamma in English, in the capital of the foremost English-speaking country in the world.

I was going to the United States.

CHAPTER EIGHTEEN

Coming to America

In 1968, I went on a pilgrimage to all the sacred sites in Ceylon. I was about to embark on a trip to a distant place, America, and none of us knew when I might be able to come home again. It was important to pay my respects at Ceylon's holiest places before I went abroad.

It was a wonderful trip. Most of my relatives and a few good friends went along. We rented a bus. I wish my mother could have gone, too, but she was so crippled by that time that she couldn't have withstood the long bus ride. When my father was still alive, she had been able to get around their house with his help, leaning on a walking stick she held in one hand and with the other hand, holding on to a rope my father strung along the wall for her. But now it was more than ten years after his death, and I was shocked to see how immobile she was, almost bedridden.

Making a pilgrimage to holy places in Ceylon is like going on a picnic in other countries. People rent buses or minivans and decorate them with coconut flowers. They sing songs as they travel, and every so often they stop the bus and get out to sit under shade trees and eat the food they brought with them. It is very relaxed and joyful.

Our group visited several ancient monasteries and temple ruins. We paid homage at an ancient Bodhi tree and visited the mountain-top palace of King Kassapa the fifth, where beautiful frescoes of celestial nymphs holding lotus flowers adorned the walls. In Kandy, we visited the Temple of the Tooth, where a relic of the Buddha is enshrined. It is considered one of my country's most sacred spots. Our folklore says that when the prince Danta Kumara and his sister, Hemamala, brought the relic to the island, she twisted her hair into a knot and hid the tooth in it so that it wouldn't be stolen. A beautiful temple was built to enshrine the relic.

According to Sri Lankan history, each king must promise to protect the Temple of the Tooth if he wants to remain in power. If he does not honor the relic, he'll be overthrown. And so the temple has always been protected. Even the British respected the temple when they captured Sri Lanka and turned it into a colony called Ceylon.

Today, politicians usually pay an honorary visit to the Temple of the Tooth after winning an election. And there's a huge procession every year in Kandy to honor the relic.

Unfortunately, the temple was damaged in a terrorist bombing in 1998, another casualty of our long civil war. The beautiful front facade was badly damaged in the blast. For several years, large barricades around the temple prevented anyone from driving near it, but those were removed in 2002 as a show of good faith during peace talks between the government and the Tamil rebels.

During that trip home, I also went to the US embassy in Colombo to apply for a visa. The immigration officer gave me two interviews, on two separate days. Then I was asked to have a medical exam. As it turns out, the doctor who performed the exam remembered my visiting his parents' house years before, on alms round, when I was a student at the Vidyasekhara Pirivena in Gampaha. He was amazed to see me again and wished me luck on my journey.

In those days air travel was easier to book than it is today. No cancellation penalties, no extra fees for stopping over somewhere. You could choose any itinerary you liked, with as many stops as you liked, as long as you ended up at your final destination.

Since I was going so far, I decided to make it an adventure, to stop along the way and see places I had never seen. I made a list of countries

I wanted to visit and wrote to the Ceylon embassy in each of them, asking someone to help me find a place to stay for a couple of days.

These were my stops: India, Pakistan, Afghanistan, Iran, Iraq, Turkey, Egypt, Greece, Italy, France, Germany, Switzerland, Belgium, Holland, and England.

In Rome, I was met at the airport by a representative of the Ceylonese ambassador. He drove me to a beautiful hotel, and as soon as I checked in, I told the desk clerk I wanted to take a guided tour of the Vatican. There was a tour leaving right away, so I put my luggage in my room and left immediately, aboard a bus with several other tourists. We were divided into groups according to what language we spoke. I joined the English-speaking group. When the tour leader came around to collect our tickets, I couldn't find mine, even though I remembered the desk clerk giving it to me. The guide said, "Sir, it's all right. I know you came from a hotel. Just give me the name of your hotel."

I swallowed hard. I didn't know the name of where I was staying. I had just been dropped off there, and I hadn't looked at the name. I didn't have a receipt to show him, either.

Still, he was unruffled.

"Don't worry, sir. Just enjoy your visit to the Vatican, and the bus will come back at 5 P.M. to pick you up. Hopefully you will remember the name of your hotel by then."

The tour of the Vatican was wonderful, but the whole time, I was distracted, trying to think of the name of my hotel. My unmindfulness in neglecting to note something as simple as the name on a building had robbed me of the chance to be in the present moment and fully enjoy the beauty of the Vatican.

When the bus returned at 5 P.M., I still had no idea where I was staying. I was so embarrassed. I told the guide that my hotel might be near the Ceylonese embassy.

"Ceylonese embassy. And where is that?" he asked.

I had no clue.

Now the guide was losing patience. It was past dinnertime. He said his work day was over; he had to go home. He said he was sorry but they would have to just drop me off right where we were, and I would have to find my own way to my hotel or the embassy.

For several hours I wandered the streets of Rome. It was a chilly, rainy night. I asked everyone I met if they knew where the Ceylonese embassy was. All I got in response were quizzical looks. I walked into shops, clubs, bars, restaurants—anywhere there were people.

Finally, about 10:30 P.M., I walked into a gas station and asked the attendant if he knew where the Ceylonese embassy was. Miraculously, he understood me.

Even more miraculously, he went into his office and emerged a couple of minutes later holding a letter from the Ceylonese embassy, complete with its address and phone number. The gas station had that letter on file because the Italian government had exempted the embassy from sales tax when buying gasoline.

The final miracle was that someone actually answered the phone at the embassy! An hour later, much relieved, I was back at my hotel.

I still don't know the name of it.

In Brussels I knew no one, and there was no Ceylonese embassy. At the airport, I paid about ten dollars for a visa, then I took a taxi into the city. I looked in the telephone book, found a Sinhalese name, and called the number. That family came and picked me up. I stayed with them several days, and we visited several local sites of interest, including Waterloo, the infamous battlefield where Napoleon met his fate.

In England, I stayed at the London Buddhist Vihara. One day I made a side trip to Stratford-upon-Avon, Shakespeare's home. While I was there, an American couple struck up a conversation with me. I told them I was a Buddhist monk, on my way to live in the United States.

"Well, when you get to the United States, you'll have to change the clothes you're wearing," the husband said.

"No, he won't," said his wife. "He's a Buddhist monk. He's wearing the robes of a Buddhist monk. Why should he have to give that up? That's the problem with our priests today. There's no outward sign that they're priests. You can't even recognize them. You can't find one to make confession to. We should admire these Buddhist monks' courage to continue their tradition."

Actually, wearing the robe is not just a tradition, or something we do so that people can recognize us as monks. It's more to remind ourselves who we are, what we are supposed to do, and how we should interact with others. It helps us to choose our speech wisely, to avoid overindulgence, and to remember to strive for peace with those around us.

Wearing the robe when we travel makes us self-conscious in a positive sort of way. "Am I doing anything that would offend others?" we ask ourselves. "Is my conduct setting a good example to others? Am I representing the Sangha well?"

All these reflections are inspired by a simple orange cloth.

From Amsterdam, I caught a flight to New York City. It was the final leg of a very long journey, the last piece of a puzzle I started putting together so many years before, when I opened my first English textbook. I was very excited.

At 2 P.M. on September 18, 1968, I landed at John F. Kennedy Airport. I had no idea where to go, so I just followed the other passengers getting off the plane. After immigration and customs, I carried my luggage into a huge arrival hall. There was no one there to meet me.

I was on my own, in the country that was to become my new home.

CHAPTER NINETEEN

Manual Labor Missionary

I ARRIVED IN NEW YORK with only one lead—the address and phone number of a Chinese temple in the Bronx that, years earlier in Malaysia, a visiting monk had given me, inviting me to visit them if I was ever in America.

I wandered around Kennedy Airport until I saw a pay phone.

I walked over to it, took the receiver off the hook, and dialed the number on the temple's business card. I saw the coin slot on the phone, but I had no idea what it was for. And even if I had known, I had no US coins yet, only paper money.

Over and over, for at least forty-five minutes, I dialed the number, with no luck. I couldn't understand why nothing was happening. And I couldn't understand the recorded prompt that kept telling me to insert a dime.

Finally I gave up. I saw a young woman sitting at what looked like an information desk. I approached her and with the best English I could muster, I asked her how to use the telephone.

She didn't answer. She just stared at me. I repeated my question. She looked at me as though she was mesmerized. I thought maybe she hadn't understood me. Or that my accent was too thick.

Then I realized: This young woman had never seen anything like me. A small man with a bald head, swathed in orange robes. Maybe she thought I was some kind of hippie free spirit, wearing Indian clothing—this was the sixties, after all.

I gave up and walked away, lugging my two heavy suitcases. I was tired and jet-lagged. By this time, I had been wandering the airport for at least an hour. In desperation, I started asking people who passed me if they knew how to get to the Chinese temple in the Bronx. I stopped anyone, everyone.

Of course, I learned later, this is something you just don't do in Queens.

People looked at me as if I were crazy. Or they simply ignored me, brushing by without acknowledging my question.

Finally, one man took pity on me. He told me to go out in front of the airport and catch a taxi to the Bronx.

I did as he told me, and soon I was standing in a long line with other people, at a taxi stand. When it was my turn, for some reason, the taxi driver refused to let me get in his car. So did the next one, and the next one. None of them wanted to give me a ride.

I was utterly confused. What was so threatening about my appearance? I could speak English, and I had money to pay the fare. But they were not interested in driving me.

Finally, one driver consented to let me in his car. He seemed less than thrilled as he threw my bags in the trunk. We pulled away from the curb and he asked where I was going.

"The Chinese Buddhist temple in the Bronx," I said.

The taxi swerved back to the curb and squealed to a stop. The driver jumped out.

"Get out of the car," he said. "I'm not going to the Bronx."

Dejected and baffled, I took my bags and trudged to the end of the taxi line. Again, the same frustrating scene: When I finally got to the head of the line, driver after driver refused to take me.

By now it was dark, and getting very late. I began to panic. Where was I going to spend the night if I couldn't get a taxi driver to even let me in his car? I had thought America was an open, friendly place, but here I was being treated with such rudeness and suspicion.

(Much later, of course, I understood that going to the Bronx late at night isn't the safest thing in the world. That, coupled with my strange appearance, must have given the taxi drivers the jitters.)

Finally, at about 10:30 P.M., when customers were scarce and drivers more willing to go a bit out of their way, one man finally consented to drive me to the Bronx. I was vastly relieved.

The temple was dark when we arrived but as soon as I rang the bell, a porch light came on. I announced myself, and shortly the door opened, revealing the face of a Chinese monk. He spoke no English, but he recognized my robes and let me in. He gave me a steaming cup of green tea and a comfortable room to sleep in. It was wonderful just to have a place to lay my head, at last.

The next morning, after breakfast, a young American woman appeared. She had dark, short-cropped hair and wore horn-rimmed glasses. She introduced herself as Martha Sentnor and said she was a Buddhist.

When I told her I had come to the United States to live at the Washington Buddhist Vihara, she smiled broadly.

"I'm a member of that vihara," she said. "I've been there many times."

I told Martha about my difficulties at the airport.

"Oh, Bhante," she said, using the term of address that means "venerable sir," "that's normal in a big city like New York. People can be very rude. You were lucky you didn't get mugged."

She had to explain to me what *mugged* meant.

For the next few days, Martha kindly took me around to see the sights of Manhattan: the Statue of Liberty, the Empire State Building, New York Harbor. The size, bustle, and noise of the city overwhelmed me. I had never experienced anything like it. It seemed like the other end of the earth from my little village of Henepola.

A week later, I flew from New York to Washington, the last leg of my journey. I arrived at National Airport on September 26. Two people were there to greet me: Venerable Dickwela Piyananda and Michael Roehm, a young American man who was a supporter of the Washington Buddhist Vihara.

My new home was a run-down three-story brick house on Sixteenth Street Northwest. On one side of it was a Greek Orthodox church, on the other side a private house. Down the street were the Russian and Canadian embassies.

The Washington Buddhist Vihara was the first Theravada Buddhist temple in the United States and was established by the Sasanasevaka Society of Ceylon.

In 1965 a young Sinhalese monk named Venerable Bope Vinita came to America to study at Harvard Divinity School on a scholarship from the Asia Foundation. While living and studying in Boston, Venerable Vinita saw that Americans were interested in Eastern religions. It was the time of Jack Kerouac and the Beat Poets, Alan Watts and Zen, and Richard Alpert, aka Ram Dass.

When Venerable Vinita went back to Ceylon, he reported this interest to Venerable Madihe Pannasiha Mahanayaka Thera, head of the Sasanasevaka Society. Venerable Pannasiha came to the United States himself the following year, 1966, and traveled to many cities. He, too, saw the interest in Buddhism. When he returned to Ceylon, he convinced the Society to raise money to build a temple in the United States.

With $16,500 in hand, Venerable Vinita returned to America in early 1967 and consulted with Oliver Weerasinghe, Ceylon's ambassador to the United States.

"Why not found the new temple right here in Washington?" said Weerasinghe. They discovered a suitable building, the former Thai embassy, that was for sale. While they were negotiating with the Thai government to buy the house, another Sinhalese monk arrived, Venerable Dickwela Piyananda. He and Venerable Vinita lived in a tiny apartment on Harvard Street in Washington.

The negotiations took many months. When it finally looked like the sale would go through, the Thai government allowed Venerable Piyananda to move in, even though the deal wasn't quite closed. Venerable Vinita stayed in the apartment.

And it was right about that time, in the fall of 1968, that I arrived.

My very first evening at the vihara, Venerable Piyananda said to me, "I'm the old grandfather here. But you're young and vigorous and you have lots of experience. This place needs work, and I want you to take on that job. I'll be the figurehead, here to advise you whenever you need help. But I want you to be in charge."

Venerable Piyananda wasn't that old, not even sixty, but I don't think he was used to physical work. The thought of renovating that shabby building was too much for him. So he was glad to have a younger monk on board.

And so I started work by myself. (Venerable Vinita had returned to Ceylon just as I was arriving in America.)

The house was huge: eight bedrooms, four bathrooms, an attic, and a basement. The Thai embassy had housed college students there, and students can be hard on a building. Windows and doors were broken. In many rooms, wallpaper curled off the walls. Plaster sagged from the basement ceiling. Some of the doors didn't have locks. The roof was in bad shape. The yard looked like an overgrown jungle.

The water heater leaked, and so did the toilets. In one of the bathrooms, the shower was only roughed in. When you turned on the water, it would shoot up to the ceiling, so we put a piece of glass up there to deflect the water back down. To take a shower, if that's what you could call it, I would sit underneath this deflected stream.

When it came to renovation, I didn't know what I was doing. I had no construction experience whatsoever, so I walked one mile to the nearest hardware store and started asking questions. For big projects, I had to wait until enough donations came in to pay for our materials. Then I had to carry home any materials I purchased, including lumber.

After a while I had some help from a few Thai people who came to the temple. And eventually, some Burmese and Vietnamese families also joined. Downstairs, we tore out walls and turned several rooms into one large one, to serve as a shrine room for devotional services. Then we went to work making the bedrooms livable.

I hammered and chiseled, put up studs, and blew insulation—all without wearing a mask. I think all the dust and debris I inhaled during those months caused me to develop allergies that persist to this day.

I was also responsible for the other daily tasks at the temple—grocery shopping, cleaning, mowing the lawn, running the office, collecting donations, and teaching Dhamma classes. To attract more members, I decided to print a monthly newsletter. I produced it on a hand-cranked mimeograph machine. The first issue was quite simple: I wrote about my arrival in Washington and about our renovation work. I also made an appeal for financial support to help with the pending purchase of the building.

Most of the time, I was exhausted. My days ran from 5 A.M. to 11 P.M., with nonstop duties. And if visitors came to the temple, I had to drop whatever project I was working on and receive them.

Of course, because we were in America, we could not go on alms round to get food. Begging at people's doors would probably have landed us in jail. Some of the families who belonged to the temple brought meals as an act of *dana,* or generosity, but it certainly didn't happen every day. So I taught myself how to cook.

As a monk living in Asia, I had been waited on much of my life. Never did I expect to come to America and be a manual laborer and a cook and a repairman.

To tell the truth, I was quite angry.

But of course, I couldn't turn around and go back to Asia. There was nowhere to run to, and I had planned on staying in America for good. Luckily, the sheer physical exercise and effort involved in fixing up the house helped me to literally "work out" my anger.

Eventually, I began to enjoy the work. It was interesting to learn so many new skills. And I finally realized that anger was nothing more than a waste of energy—energy I needed to get the drywall hung!

The third week of October, less than a month after my arrival, Venerable Piyananda left for Ceylon for a two-month vacation. Now I was truly in charge, and I was alone.

Around dinnertime on the last day of October, the doorbell rang.

I opened the front door to see a bunch of children standing there, wearing scary masks. Little devils, vampires, and witches were leering at me. Maybe this was one of those "muggings" Martha Sentnor told me about.

"Who are you?" I said, nervously.

"TRICK OR TREAT!" the children shouted.

"Excuse me?" I asked. I had no idea why these children were shouting at me.

One of the older boys, rolling his eyes, explained that they wanted some candy. If I didn't give it to them, he said, they would throw eggs at our house.

I still didn't understand, but I thought I'd better humor the youngsters. I went to the kitchen and found several boxes of cookies left by temple supporters. I went back to the front door and gave one cookie to each child standing there. To my great relief, they took the cookies and ran away.

A few minutes later, the doorbell rang again. I couldn't believe it: More kids, demanding more candy! Again I doled out cookies.

It went on like that all evening. The next day, I told one of our American temple members what had happened. I thought he wouldn't believe my incredible story. He sat down with me and explained about Halloween. We laughed for a long time.

In December, on my forty-first birthday, the sale of the building finally closed. The Washington Buddhist Vihara, sale price $33,000, was officially ours.

CHAPTER TWENTY

Mistaken for a Woman

DURING THOSE FIRST FEW YEARS at the vihara, we always seemed to have just enough money to pay the bills. Our mortgage was $172 a month. Along with utilities—telephone, electric, gas—our expenses added up to $500 or $600 a month. All of it, of course, had to come from donations.

Every time people visited the temple, they would drop a dollar or two into the collection box. When we went to people's houses for chanting, they usually gave us a small donation, maybe ten or fifteen dollars. Each month we took in about $600 or $700.

Somehow, it always came out on the plus side. Just barely.

We started enrolling people as official members of the vihara. We created three types of membership—lifetime, standard, and student— and printed up membership cards. My little newsletter continued to bring in more members, and slowly the vihara grew. Within a couple of years we had finished the major repairs to the building.

Three evenings a week I taught a meditation class. Sunday afternoon was the devotional service. We published a small booklet with Pali chants, called the Vandana, so that people could follow along during the service.

On Buddhist holidays, we had elaborate celebrations, Sinhalese style. On Vesak, we celebrate the Buddha's birth, enlightenment, and death, each of which happened on a full moon in the Indian month of Visakh, around April or May. In preparation for Vesak, people clean and decorate the temple, make lanterns out of bamboo strips and tissue paper, and cook lots of food—usually vegetarian. On the actual day, they wear all white and spend hours at the temple, where they chat, eat, and listen to the monks chant. It is the most festive day of the whole Buddhist year.

Kathina, another popular celebration, marks the end of the traditional "rainy season." For three months (from mid-July to mid-October), monks stay in one temple. This practice began in the Buddha's time, when he and his disciples observed an annual three-month "rains" retreat, during which they stopped roaming around the countryside and stayed in one place until the monsoon flooding ended.

Nowadays, there's a Kathina ceremony each October, during which laypeople formally offer new robes and other necessities to the monks. The pile of gifts that appears in the shrine room includes toothbrushes, mouthwash, shaving cream, soap, and toilet paper.

The most precious gift of all, though, is the Kathina robe. A hand-sewn length of orange cloth is lovingly folded, wrapped in plastic, and then symbolically offered to the entire Sangha. The monks decide among themselves who specifically will receive it. Sometimes it is the most senior monk, or the one with the most tattered, worn-out robes. Or sometimes it will be given to a monk visiting from a remote location where there may not be lay supporters to donate a robe.

Throughout those early years at the Washington Vihara, I was adjusting to life in America, and America was adjusting to me.

I was quite small, five-foot-three, wrapped in robes and with a shaved head. That was beyond the average American's realm of experience in the late 1960s.

Many times, when I asked directions to a public restroom, the person would point to the women's room.

One day I was walking home from the grocery store, my arms full of bags, and I passed a man washing his car in a driveway. His dog rushed at me, barking. The man scolded him: "Don't bother the nice lady!"

Even people who saw me every day mistook me for a woman. During the twenty years I lived in Washington, every day our cheerful mail carrier would greet me: "Here's your mail, ma'am."

One afternoon in February 1969, a man rang the vihara doorbell and politely asked if he could use our library. I was delighted that someone was interested in reading about Buddhism, so of course I said yes.

After that, the man came almost every day, often carrying a baby and bringing a portable crib. While he read books on Buddhism, his child would sleep. He hardly ever said anything to me, so I left him alone.

In May, when we celebrated Vesak, the man joined a small group of people who wore white and spent the day at the temple observing the eight precepts and meditating.

Michael Roehm, one of our American members, saw him.

"What is Dr. Rodier doing here?" he asked me.

"Who's Dr. Rodier?" I said.

Michael told me the man's name was David Rodier and he was a philosophy professor at American University, only a few miles away.

The next day, I could hardly wait for Dr. Rodier to appear for his usual afternoon session in the library. When he did, I approached him.

"Is it true you are a professor at American University?" I asked.

He nodded, smiling.

I told him how much I wanted to continue my studies. I told him about the schools I had attended in Ceylon and India, trying to patch together an education. And I told him about passing the Cambridge external examinations, but then failing to get into the University of Malaysia.

Rodier advised me to have Cambridge send my scores to American University. He also suggested that I sit in on his classes so I could improve my English.

Every day for months, Dr. Rodier picked me up at the vihara and drove me to the university, so I could audit his philosophy courses. It was wonderful to be in a classroom again!

Around that time, I started having pain again in my left kidney. Eventually I went to a doctor, who referred me to a urologist. That doctor, like the one in Malaysia, said I had a kidney stone, but this time I needed surgery.

Luckily, Venerable Piyananda and I were insured through the Ceylon embassy's group policy. I was in the hospital for ten days. Insurance paid 80 percent of the bill and Michael Roehm generously paid the balance.

In 1971, at the age of forty-three, I was admitted to American University as a freshman. Michael Roehm paid my course fees and also donated the money I needed for textbooks. In addition, I was able to save a little of my hundred-dollar-a-month food stipend from the Ceylonese government and used that toward school expenses, as well.

Because of my duties at the vihara, I only had time for two classes a semester. I spent the next couple of years running the vihara, being a university student, and traveling to other universities to give lectures on Buddhism. I went everywhere, from Miami to Saint John's, Newfoundland. Some places heard about me through American University; others saw the small ad we placed in the *Washington Post,* advertising the vihara's services and classes.

In 1972 I started leading a meditation class at American University. More than two dozen students signed up. The university chaplain gave us a large room in the chapel for our meetings. We furnished it with comfortable meditation cushions.

About a week after we started, I arrived early one day and found that someone had slashed every single cushion with a knife. Fluffy white kapok filling was scattered like snow all over the floor. I was so disappointed! The chaplain arranged for us to have a new set of cushions, but the point had been made: Someone wasn't happy with what we were doing.

Also around that time, the vihara needed new letterhead stationery. I went to a printer, showed him our logo, and placed the order. The next week, when I went to pick it up, a different person was working behind the counter—the owner of the print shop.

"Get out!" he shouted, as soon as I mentioned the name of the vihara. "I'm not going to do any job that has the word *Buddhist* in it."

These were some of my earliest tastes of religious discrimination, American style. Before that, I had a storybook vision of the United States as a liberal place founded by courageous patriots who wanted freedom for all. I had read about George Washington and Abraham Lincoln. I knew that US history was all about fighting for equality. I thought that here, anyone was free to practice any religion they liked.

But it wasn't that simple.

In 1973 American University appointed me its Buddhist chaplain, a new position created for me. The university had chaplains of other faiths, but never before a Buddhist. In fact, I think it was the first university in the United States to appoint a Buddhist chaplain. The news was printed in the campus newspaper. Immediately someone wrote to the university's president, demanding to know why he had appointed a "heathen" as chaplain.

For a couple of years, I went once a month to a place in upstate New York called the Missionary Orientation Center. They invited me to speak about Buddhism. Often, I was accompanied by Richard Stoneham, a member of the vihara who lived in New York.

Whenever I spoke there, I was careful not to compare the Buddha with any other religious teacher. I wanted to be respectful. One time, though, a young female student spoke up at the end of my lecture and said, "This is wonderful. I didn't know all these things about the Buddha."

An elderly minister in the audience spoke up. "Still, our Lord Jesus Christ is superior to Buddha," he said firmly.

"In what way?" Richard asked.

The minister stood up.

"I lived in Thailand for eight years," he said. "I saw this Buddha sitting cross-legged in decorated rooms, doing nothing. I saw men in orange robes going out begging in the streets. They do nothing for the world. Jesus Christ sacrificed his entire life for humanity."

Richard and the minister got into a bit of a debate. I kept quiet. Finally, the young female student started crying. She said, "We invited this monk to come all the way from Washington and teach us about Buddhism, to tell us what he believes. Is this how we treat a guest?"

When the afternoon session began, the director of the institute came and asked me if there was any trouble. I told him everything was fine. Then I addressed the elderly minister directly.

"Sir, you said that the Buddha does nothing but sit in a decorated room. What you saw were images of the Buddha, not the real man. The real Buddha was very active. He sacrificed his kingdom, his throne, his wealth, and his family—all to live a very simple life. Even after attaining enlightenment, he slept only two hours a day. He was busy teaching people. He worked for humanity twenty-two hours a day for forty-five years, until he died.

"And those men you saw wearing orange robes and begging, those are monks dedicated to living a simple life, as the Buddha did. They're not beggars like you are imagining; they are respected by people for the spiritual life they lead. Laypeople offer them food, robes, shelter, and medicine. In return, the monks offer spiritual sustenance to the people. They gather their food by collecting only a little from each house. That way, no one person will be burdened."

I probably didn't convince him of anything, but perhaps I was able to dispel some of his misconceptions.

The early '70s were the years of the Vietnam War, flower children, and antiwar protestors.

Many times when I lectured at colleges and universities, students would ask me what Buddhists believed about suicide, because they had heard the news stories about Vietnamese monks who had set themselves on fire to protest the war.

I always answered that suicide was not advocated in the Buddha's teachings. In fact, he was totally against it. The third rule of the

Patimokkha, the guidelines for monastic conduct, says that any monk who kills any human being, or participates in a murder, is automatically expelled from the Sangha. Killing oneself is the same as killing any other human being, which ranks among the top offenses. But when people become desperate in the face of religious discrimination or social injustice, they sometimes abandon their religious principles.

Those in power in Vietnam at that time blatantly abused their authority. The majority of Buddhists were treated inhumanely by the Roman Catholic government of Ngo Dinh Diem. Buddhists were denied the right to hold public meetings or religious processions, and they were labeled Communists, to turn the US government against them. Basically, Diem took advantage of the United States' eagerness to stamp out Communism to help him suppress Buddhism in his country. It was a brilliant, and quite evil, strategy.

In desperation, the Vietnamese monks publicly killed themselves to tell the world what was happening. Their acts had nothing to do with Buddhism and everything to do with nationalism.

In contrast, I tried to help students understand the real meaning of the Buddha's teachings. Buddhism, I told them, is a peaceful religion.

CHAPTER TWENTY-ONE

"Officer Bhante G."

MANY OF THE THINGS I did at the vihara—mowing the lawn, cooking, fixing plumbing, wielding a hammer—monks do not traditionally do. Ours is supposed to be a life of quiet and simplicity. But America was a new world, and I was forced to take on a new role.

Eventually, I even had to learn to drive!

One day, a young American woman and her boyfriend came to the vihara. They were regular visitors. I asked them if they could drive me to the hardware store. It wasn't the first time I'd requested such a favor. Whenever somebody came to the vihara, I usually asked for a ride to the grocery store, the post office, the Laundromat—wherever I needed to go.

It pained me to do that, because Buddhist monks are not supposed to ask laypeople for anything on their own behalf. That would be seen as too grasping, too greedy.

"Bhante," the young woman said, "this is very unfair. We come to the temple to relax, to read and meditate. But as soon as we walk in, you ask us to drive you all over the place."

I felt my face flush with anger.

"Oh, so I'm supposed to work like a slave so you can come here and sit comfortably and relax? All I'm doing is asking for your help. I can't do these errands, otherwise."

She thought a moment.

"What if we teach you how to drive?" she asked. "Then you can go wherever you need to go, anytime."

Now I was really exasperated.

"How can I do that? I don't have a car. And besides, as a monk I can't ask someone to teach me how to drive."

"You're not asking," she pointed out. "I'm offering."

Though most monks don't drive, there actually is no rule forbidding it, although the Buddha told his disciples not to ride animals or in a cart pulled by an animal, out of compassion for other living beings. What he might say about a modern automobile is anyone's guess. In Asia, a monk driving would be frowned upon, but it doesn't seem inappropriate to Westerners. I think the important thing is that we remember our monastic principles of nonharming, nongreed, and nonhatred. If we can use a car for purely practical purposes, without becoming inordinately fond of it or attached to it, then I don't think we have compromised the spirit of our vows.

So, the next day the young woman's boyfriend pulled up in a big Dodge. The Dodge was the young woman's car, but she had designated her boyfriend to teach me how to drive. I had never been behind the wheel of a car in my life, so I excitedly slid into the driver's seat.

After a few instructions I started out on a side street, and was doing all right. Then we went onto Sixteenth Street, a busy thoroughfare. My teacher was trying to get us to another side road along Rock Creek Park, where I could practice without battling traffic. We got to the intersection of Sixteenth and Colorado Avenue, which crosses Sixteenth Street diagonally. I was told to turn left, and while I was concentrating on where I was going, I took the corner at the same speed.

"Slow down!" my teacher yelled. "Slow down!"

But it was too late. I smashed into a blue Saab stopped at the intersection.

I jumped out of the car and went over to the Saab. Much to my relief, the driver, a young woman, seemed to be fine.

Her car, however, wasn't in such great shape. The crash had completely smashed the front end—bumper, fender, lights, everything. And under the crumpled hood, the radiator was spewing water.

I apologized profusely and told the young woman I was a student driver. She smiled.

"Don't worry," she said. "This kind of thing can happen to anyone."

The police arrived, and I got a twenty-five-dollar ticket. I guess I got off easy, considering that I didn't even have a learner's permit to drive.

Back at the temple, I called the woman who owned the Dodge. I felt very bad about her car.

"Please don't worry," she kept saying. "I have insurance, and my parents will take care of this. It's no big deal."

Luckily, my driving teacher didn't give up on me. For the next several weeks, he came to the vihara whenever he had time, and I practiced driving his car. He was quite patient with me.

After one formal lesson at a driving school, I was ready to apply for my driver's license. The first time, I failed the driving test. I passed a truck that had stopped at a green light. The examiner said the light had, in fact, turned red, but I couldn't see it because I am so short and the truck blocked my view.

On my second try, I was more careful and I passed the test. I was the proud possessor of a US driver's license!

But of course we couldn't afford a car for the vihara, so I was still marooned much of the time. In emergencies, I borrowed a car from the Ceylon embassy. To this day, I seldom drive, even though I know how—at least I think I do!

One day in May 1975, American University's head chaplain told me that someone at the State Department had called looking for me. I returned the call and spoke to a man who asked if I'd like to help some refugees from Vietnam who were arriving in the United States. The State Department needed a Buddhist chaplain to minister at one of the refugee camps being set up in Florida.

I had zero experience working with refugees, and I didn't speak Vietnamese or French, but I said yes.

Then I called a friend of mine, one of the American members of the vihara, John Garges. John had worked with refugees, and he spoke a little French. So he volunteered to go with me and translate, if needed.

The next day we reported to Andrews Air Force Base, as instructed. We filled out forms and were interviewed by several officers. Then they told us to go get a hepatitis shot and report back the next day.

We still had no idea how long this assignment might last, or where we'd be staying. I didn't know enough to even ask such questions.

The following day, an air force jet flew us to Eglin Air Force Base, near Pensacola, Florida. We were the only two passengers.

We were given a comfortable bungalow to stay in, and my duties were explained to me. I was there, basically, to console the ten thousand Vietnamese refugees who had already begun arriving. I was told I should visit them daily, perform religious services, and provide whatever spiritual comfort they needed. There were also Catholic and Protestant clergymen at the camp to serve refugees who had converted to those faiths.

That first afternoon, about two hours after we got to the base, a planeload of refugees arrived. John and I went to meet them. They were young and old, male and female. Most of them walked off the plane wearing ragged clothes, carrying little or nothing. They seemed in shock, and many were crying, especially the children. Some were obviously sick or wounded; others appeared to be emotionally disturbed. Too many of them had been separated from their loved ones—parents, siblings, spouses. Some clung to the hands of total strangers.

When they saw me in my orange robes, many of them smiled. Others burst into tears and bowed to me over and over.

Every day we met planeloads of refugees, and every day that scene repeated itself. The familiar sight of a Buddhist monk seemed to be a life preserver for many of the refugees who were scarred by war and now transported to a totally alien land.

After two weeks, John had to go back to his job in Washington, and once again, I was alone and without a car. So I asked my contact at the State Department if someone could pick me up from my bungalow every day and take me to the refugee camp. The next morning an Air Force taxi pulled up in front of my bungalow and the driver got out, looking confused.

"I'm here to pick up Officer Bhante G.," he said, eyeing my orange robe.

"That's me," I replied.

"Then I can't drive you," he said. "Civilians can't ride in this car. It's only for officers."

After that, I was given a State Department vehicle and drove myself. I had a similar problem when I first went to eat lunch in the officers' club. As a base staff member, I was invited to eat there, even though I wasn't in the military. But my "uniform" raised eyebrows. Eventually, though, people at the base grew to recognize me and my robe.

My work with the refugees was very rewarding. I felt I was providing necessary comfort to people at a very difficult time in their lives. That was the easy part of the job.

The hard part was getting along with some of the other clergymen at the camp. Some of them considered this the ideal opportunity to evangelize: There were thousands of souls to save there.

Religious services were held under a large tent, and the different denominations took turns leading them. When I held services, I put a Buddha statue on the altar. When the Catholics or Protestants held their services, they put a cross on the altar.

The tent for services was next to a smaller tent where I had my office. One day, while I was working, I saw about thirty children being herded into the large tent. Most of them looked no older than ten. One of the Protestant ministers, a particularly zealous man, was with them. I heard him start intoning the rites of baptism.

I hurried over there and interrupted the ceremony.

"Joseph, what you're doing is wrong," I said. "I've seen you going all over the camp, talking to these kids' parents, trying to convert them."

He and I both knew that most of the children would wind up Christian, anyway. Every one of the religious organizations sponsoring the refugees was Christian. When they finally left the camp, they would be resettled and compelled to go to Christian churches. But that, at least, would come later. I thought it was wrong to start converting them before they had even left the camp.

"These refugees are like drowning people," I told him. "They'll grasp onto anything you tell them because they're desperate to get out of this camp. Have you seen me trying to convert any of the Christian refugees back to Buddhism?"

I was livid. I went straight to the State Department's office on base and reported what was happening. I told the officer that these kinds of conversions would give a bad name to the entire refugee operation. The next day, in the refugee camp newsletter, there was an article giving strict orders that no one was allowed to convert anyone in the camp to another religion.

Thankfully, most of the other clergy were tolerant of one another. One day, I was talking to two Catholic priests, one Vietnamese and one American. The American priest had two rosaries hanging around his neck, one with a cross on it and the other with a small Buddha figure. He said that that morning they had gotten so intertwined, he could hardly untangle them.

"That shows that the Buddha and the cross should never be mixed," said the Vietnamese priest.

"No, no," I said. "It shows that the Buddha and Jesus love each other so much that you can't separate them."

When I first arrived at the camp, I planned to use our Pali devotional chanting book for the Buddhist services. I assumed most of the Vietnamese Buddhists would be familiar with the Pali. Unfortunately, that was not so.

One day I was walking through the camp, and a young boy greeted me with these words: *"Namo ayidafat."*

"What did you say?" I asked him.

He repeated it: *"Namo ayidafat."*

I asked him what that meant.

"I don't know," he replied. "It's just what we say when we meet Buddhist monks."

When he added that his parents had a book with such sayings written in it, I asked him to take me to meet his parents. When I got to their tent, they offered me a seat. I asked them if I could borrow their Vietnamese devotional book. They were pleased to lend it to me.

I took the book to the base printing shop and asked for two thousand copies. Within a couple of days, I had the booklets, and our services began to be in Vietnamese instead of Pali. I asked an elderly Vietnamese man to lead the chanting, and I followed along as best I could, without knowing the language. Then I would give a Dhamma talk in English, and the old man would translate it into Vietnamese. I could see by their glowing faces that the refugees appreciated this enormously.

I also taught English classes, which was fun both for me and for the children who came to learn. My class always seemed to be full.

Another part of my job was to help locate sponsors—families or individuals who would agree to take a few refugees into their community and help them find housing and jobs. I was given a telephone with which to call potential sponsors anywhere in the United States.

We were supposed to do background checks on the sponsors, but every once in a while someone with bad intentions slipped through the cracks. One day, three men came to the camp and selected three girls who were between fourteen and eighteen years old. The men wanted to sponsor them, they said. They signed the necessary paperwork and started to walk out of the camp with the girls.

As soon as I saw that, I stopped them. These girls can't leave the camp without their parents, I said. If their parents aren't here, then they have to be sponsored along with some Vietnamese adults who'll be responsible for them.

I can't be sure, of course, but I think I might have saved those girls from a life of prostitution, or worse.

Another time a woman living nearby, who had agreed to sponsor a young Vietnamese man, brought him back to the camp saying she wanted to "return" him. She had only taken care of him for a month.

"I thought he was a good Christian," she said, her mouth set in a frown.

"He's not a good Christian?" I asked.

"No, not at all," she said, obviously disappointed.

"What is his religion?"

"He's Buddhist," she snapped. "I just found out."

"Well, what made you think he was a Christian?" I asked.

"Because he's kind and polite. He's very patient and he always treats me respectfully."

I often ran up against that kind of discrimination. Not long after my arrival at the base, a strongly worded editorial appeared in the local newspaper. How could the US government use taxpayers' money to bring a pagan to help the poor Vietnamese refugees at the camp? If those miserable people don't become Christians, the writer declared, then let them go to hell. Just don't use our tax dollars to teach them a satanic religion.

My response to discrimination is usually simple: metta, or loving-friendliness. It is one of the four brahma viharas, or "heavenly abodes," described by the Buddha. It's a pure, unadulterated desire for the well-being of others, a love without attachment or expectation, practiced unconditionally. It's the ultimate underlying principle behind all wholesome thoughts, words, and deeds.

Metta transcends barriers of religion, culture, geography, language, and nationality. It is a universal and ancient law that binds all of us together. We need it in order to live and work together harmoniously. Especially because of our differences, we need loving-friendliness. And when we extend this sentiment toward others, it naturally makes our own lives happier and more peaceful. I used the power of metta every day in that refugee camp. The refugees needed it to help heal their psychological and emotional wounds. I needed it, too, to stay strong enough to work with them in such painful circumstances. And those who opposed what I was doing— well, quite frankly, they needed it, too.

One day there was a Catholic wedding at the refugee camp, officiated at by the Vietnamese Catholic priest. Soon after that, a young couple approached me and asked if I would perform a Buddhist wedding for them. I told them monks are not allowed to officiate at weddings, but if they could find an elder to recite the rites, I would then do a blessing chant for them.

The wedding blessing is like any other, really—the same verses monks would chant for a housewarming, a new baby, a birthday, or any auspicious occasion. The blessing includes the Mangala Sutta ("Blessings Sutta," which lists thirty-eight kinds of blessings); the Ratana Sutta ("Jewels Sutta," which lists the admirable qualities of the Triple Gem); the Karaniyametta Sutta ("Loving-Friendliness Sutta," which extols the virtues of metta); and the Jayamangala Atthagatha ("Eight Great Verses of Joyous Victory," which describes scenes in the Buddha's life during which he vanquished conquerors by using his qualities of generosity, wisdom, patience, truthfulness, and the like).

After a monk performs all these chants for a wedding, he then might sprinkle water on the couple and tie an orange "blessing" thread around each of their wrists.

So, when the refugee couple asked me to perform a ceremony for them, I knew I could handle the blessing part. The other trappings, I left to Mrs. Longacre, a local woman who often volunteered at the camp. She graciously got a wedding gown, a wedding suit, rings, a cake, and soft drinks for a small reception. The couple, who had hoped to have just such an American-style ceremony, were delighted.

After that, wedding fever struck the camp, and I was the only Buddhist monk available. Some days I performed as many as three weddings!

Almost every day, I called Washington to make sure everything was going well at the vihara. Venerable Piyananda talked to me, but reluctantly. His answers were short and abrupt. I suppose he was angry I had gone off to Florida and left him to do all the work at the vihara. But he never said that directly, he just seemed to stew in silence.

One time when I called, my nephew, Upali, answered the phone.

"How is Bhante Piyananda?" I asked him.

"He's getting ready to go to Ceylon," was the answer.

"What?! Let me speak to him."

Venerable Piyananda got on the phone.

"Bhante, is this true? You're going to Ceylon?"

"Yes," he said.

"When are you leaving?"

"Tomorrow."

I couldn't believe it.

"You're the only monk at the vihara," I said. "You can't just leave. Can you wait until I come back?"

"No," he said tersely. "I have to leave now."

"Why are you doing this?" I pleaded. "Why are you leaving the vihara with no monk?"

He said nothing. I held the phone, waiting, but there was only silence. Finally, I hung up.

I then found out that a Sinhalese monk, Venerable Piyadassi, was visiting the vihara in Washington. I called Michael Roehm and asked him to extend an invitation to that monk to stay a little longer than he had planned, until I got back. I also made some calls to other refugee camps and asked if there were any Buddhist monks among the refugees. At Fort Chaffee, Arkansas, there was one monk, a Vietnamese man who had joined the Sangha late in life, after having been married and had children. Amazingly, he spoke fairly good English. So I asked if he'd like to go to Washington and live at the vihara. He said yes.

That patchwork arrangement would have to do until I got home.

In August, the State Department told us to hurry and find sponsors for the remaining refugees. They wanted to dismantle the camp at Eglin before the brunt of hurricane season appeared.

So by the end of August, most of the ten thousand Vietnamese had been transferred, either to homes with sponsors, or to other camps that were out of the path of a hurricane.

I had been away from the vihara for four months. And when I got back, I found trouble waiting for me.

CHAPTER TWENTY-TWO

A Last Visit with My Mother

A LITTLE WAR was brewing at the Washington Buddhist Vihara. As soon as I got home, some members of the board of directors pounced on me. "You've been neglecting the vihara," they said. "We invited you to the United States to work for us, but now you've spent all this time working for the Vietnamese. Don't we come before them?"

"I work for the Buddha, Dhamma, and Sangha," I told them. "As a monk, I work for all living beings. I can't discriminate between Sinhalese and Vietnamese. Those people were in crisis, and I wanted to help."

Although they stopped grumbling, I knew it wasn't the last I would hear about it.

I had returned home in early September, just in time to start a new semester of study at American University. I had a full scholarship to start work toward a master's degree in religious history—what a wonderful gift!

A few months into my studies, I got a letter from my younger sister saying that our mother wasn't well, and that she hardly ate anymore. Tucked into the letter was a note from my mother. It was only a few lines, but at the end of it she said that it had taken her a week to write it. She was so weak she couldn't write more than one or two letters at a time. It was hard even to hold the pen. But she was determined to write me herself. She probably knew it was going to be her last letter to me. "I wish I could see you," she wrote.

"You should come home," said the letter from my sister. "She may not live much longer."

That was in the late fall of 1976. I informed the vihara's board of directors that my mother likely was dying and I needed to go home. They approved the purchase of a ticket for me.

In December I boarded a Pan Am 747 and was headed home to Sri Lanka. (In 1972, the Ceylonese government officially changed the country's name back to the more traditional Sri Lanka, meaning "prospering and beautiful" in Sanskrit.) I sat in a window seat, as I usually choose to do. The plane went first to Honolulu, and then Guam and Singapore.

About an hour after we departed from Honolulu, I looked out the window and saw fire coming from one of the engines. I thought maybe it was excess fuel burning off.

It wasn't.

A few seconds later, the pilot made an announcement that we were returning to Hawaii because one of the engines was on fire. Then the flight attendants did a demonstration of how we would exit the plane after we landed. The evacuation chutes would be used, so that we could get away from the plane as fast as possible. Obviously, everyone was worried that an explosion was imminent.

Parents with children would go first, they instructed. Then pregnant women and older people, then the rest of the passengers. Leave all of your carry-on luggage in the plane, they said.

I noticed some of the passengers making the sign of the cross on their chests. Others were crying, or biting their nails, or whispering to the person next to them. I saw several Bibles open in laps.

"Well," I thought, "I have done what I could do in my life. I taught Dhamma to many people, and I've earned merit. I am on my way to see my mother. If I die now, I'll have a good rebirth."

I didn't really feel scared. I thought if the plane started to nosedive, we would all be unconscious by the time we hit the ground, anyway. It didn't seem like too horrible a way to die.

Then, automatically I started to think about the Buddha's teachings on fear. Fear, he said, arises from clinging to the five aggregates—our body, feelings, perceptions, thoughts, and consciousness. We are attached to those things we identify as "myself." We don't want to lose this "self," so we become afraid if this self is threatened in any way.

"Sorrow springs from craving," says one stanza in the Dhammapada. "Fear springs from craving. There is no sorrow or fear for one who does not have craving."

As that plane dipped down out of the sky, I knew if I could focus my mind on the Triple Gem, I would be peaceful. A mind full of defilements is dominated by fear, worry, tension, and anxiety. But a mind occupied with thoughts of the Buddha, Dhamma, and Sangha is filled with serenity.

In Honolulu, the plane landed jarringly. There were fire trucks lined up on the runway, and as soon as we hit the ground, the trucks started pumping out foam all around the plane.

Everyone jumped up and headed for the exits. We didn't know if the plane was going to burst into flames any second.

I imagine I was the only person on that entire plane who had never slid down a slide as a child. It was a bit embarrassing, of course, with my robes billowing around me, but I have to admit it was also a little fun! When I got to the bottom, I jumped off and ran as fast as I could. That night, we stayed in a luxurious Hawaiian hotel, courtesy of Pan Am.

The next day I continued on to Singapore. When I landed there, I was surprised to be met by several people from the Sri Lankarama Buddhist Temple, a Sinhalese vihara. They asked me to stay a month in their temple. I told them I was going to visit my sick mother, but that I could send a reply-paid telegram to my sister, asking her how my mother was doing. Perhaps I didn't need to rush.

The next day my sister's reply came. She said our mother wasn't so bad at the moment, so I stayed in Singapore for one week. Then I went on to Malaysia and spent a week there. That extra time was good, because it allowed me to put together a wonderful surprise for my mother.

Some friends in Malaysia donated a slide projector, and I also collected an FM radio with a cordless microphone. I had about five hundred color slides of places I had visited all over the world. There were temples, skyscrapers, landscapes, animals, and festivals. I wanted to show my mother where I had been all these years while I was gone from home.

When I arrived in Sri Lanka, we had the slide show at my sister's house. Because there was no electricity there, we had to run extension cords from her neighbor's house. My mother sat, fascinated, as she looked at the slides and listened to my narration. Her eyes were shining.

We started the show at 10 P.M., and it went on until 2 A.M., but my mother never seemed to get tired. When it was over, she asked if there were any more slides. That was our last good time together.

The next day I called her doctor and asked him about her condition. Her heart is weak, he told me. She's eighty-six; she could go at any time. You really ought to have her in a nursing home, where she can be cared for properly.

So my sister, my nephew, and I decided to move her into a nursing home in Kandy. Then I said goodbye to her, and I left for Colombo. They were on their way to the nursing home as I left. The next day, I got a call from my nephew. He was crying.

The nursing home had decided they didn't want my mother after she spent one night there. Who knows why; maybe they thought that if she died soon after arriving there, it would be bad luck for the nursing home. But by then, perhaps because of the long drive to the nursing home, her condition had worsened. My sister and nephew knew she would have to go to a hospital. So they drove back to the nursing home and picked her up—there was no ambulance available.

She insisted on sitting up in the back seat, instead of lying down. And they said she was moaning the whole trip. By the time they got to the hospital, she was silent.

She had died in the back seat of the car, sitting bolt upright.

I thought about how many times my mother had nursed my wounds when I was a child, how she always knew exactly what to do to make me feel better. I remembered how her arms felt, wrapped around me. I thought of that last letter she had written me, just a few lines, so painstakingly.

I was so sorry she had died in pain and regretted that I wasn't there for her.

"To be separated from loved ones is suffering," said the Buddha. Although I had spent years delivering sermons about grief and sorrow, conducting funerals, and consoling people after the death of relatives, I don't think I totally understood those words of the Buddha until I experienced the loss of my mother. When she died, my grief was so intense that my heart felt as though it had been injected with some bitter, painful substance.

All through my monastic career up to that point, I was always striving to please my mother. I wanted to make her happy, more than any other person in the world. She was so proud that I was a monk and that I was teaching Dhamma all over the globe. So every time I achieved something new or did something good, I wrote her a letter about it, not to boast but because I knew how much pleasure it would bring her.

Now that she was gone, whom would I try to please?

I've found that grief really confuses the mind. My attachment to my mother was the strongest fetter I had. When I lost her, I temporarily forgot all of the Buddha's teachings about death and impermanence. I was simply awash in sorrow.

Because both of my older brothers were gone, the funeral arrangements fell to me, the sole surviving son. My sisters and I decided to have her cremated. The ceremony was simple, with monks chanting beside her pyre in the cemetery. Just as I had done at my father's funeral, I gave a little speech thanking everyone for coming. Only this time, it was harder. Much harder.

Even today, I feel great fondness for the memory of my mother.

In 1979 or 1980, I was speaking at an interfaith conference in

Dallas, Texas. Because it was near Thanksgiving, we were asked to speak about gratitude. I decided to speak about my mother.

But when I stood at the podium and tried to say the first words of my speech, I started crying. It was embarrassing. I was sobbing so hard I couldn't speak at all. The audience just sat, watching me. It took me a long time to gain my composure.

All I wanted to say to them was that I would never forget my mother, and that I was grateful for her endless love. Instead, standing there crying before that auditorium full of people, I came to understand one of the Buddha's statements about death and grieving. He said the tears we have shed over the death of our mothers in this earthly plane, samsara—those tears are greater than all the water in all the oceans.

CHAPTER TWENTY-THREE

"Are You Mister Gunaratana?"

I STAYED IN SRI LANKA for about a month after my mother's
funeral.

Seven days after her death, we had a traditional dana ceremony for
her, in which several monks came to the house for chanting and to eat
a meal we offered them on my mother's behalf. The night before, one
monk came to the house and delivered a sermon just for us.

Then I spent a few weeks visiting friends and the old temples where
I had lived.

On my way back to the United States, I added quite a few more
stamps to my passport. I stopped in India, Nepal, the Soviet Union,
Greece, Italy, France, Germany, Belgium, and England.

Of all those places, Russia was perhaps the most interesting. It was
my first visit there.

At the Moscow airport, I was met by Stanley Liyanapatirana, a
Sinhalese man who worked at the Sri Lankan embassy. He had helped
me get a visa to enter the Soviet Union.

The next day I went to the tourist office in my hotel and asked them
how to take a tour to Leningrad. The woman behind the desk asked
me to leave my passport with her and come back the next day.

When I returned the next day, she gave me my passport and told
me to catch a certain taxi outside the hotel. She gave me the taxi's car
number. I found the taxi, but there was no driver in it. So I simply
got in the back seat, thinking I would wait until the driver showed up.

Suddenly a man, a very large man, yanked open the car door. Before I could say anything, he ducked halfway into the back seat and grabbed hold of the strap on my camera bag. I didn't even think, I just reacted instinctively: I grabbed the bag and held on.

"No! No!" I was yelling.

He said nothing, just kept tugging on the bag. He was much bigger than me, and I knew eventually he was going to win if I didn't do something.

Without letting go of the camera bag, I lifted my elbow and rammed it into his nose as hard as I could. I guess my aim was dead-on. He yelped, let go of the strap, and took off running.

Yes, I definitely broke one of the monk's 227 rules of conduct that day. A monk should never resort to physical violence, and there is no exception for acting in self-defense. I should have just let him have the camera, but my attachment to it caused me to be unmindful. There was film in there, shots I had taken all over Europe. I wanted to show them to my friends, and that was all I thought of when I lashed out on instinct.

And as we know, when instinct takes over, mindfulness gets squeezed out.

Just as I was catching my breath from that excitement, the taxi driver appeared.

"Are you Mister Gunaratana?" he asked.

"Yes," I answered.

He got in the car without another word and drove me to the station.

As soon as I got out of the taxi at the train station, a man materialized on the sidewalk next to me.

"Are you Mister Gunaratana?" he asked.

"Yes."

"Please follow me."

He walked me to the door of the train, nodded curtly, then disappeared.

"Are you Mister Gunaratana?" the train conductor asked.

"Yes."

"Please follow me."

The conductor showed me to a compartment with a bed. Of course, being shuttled from one handler to another, all of them unsmiling, was rather comical, but I knew enough, in the Cold War–era Soviet Union, not to try and make jokes about it.

The next morning, we were in Leningrad. When I emerged from my compartment, a young woman was waiting.

"Are you Mister Gunaratana?"

"Yes."

"Please follow me."

She helped me off the train and walked with me to a nearby restaurant. There, she showed me a particular table and slid the chair out for me.

When the waiter came, he had one question: "Are you Mister Gunaratana?"

"Yes."

He brought me a breakfast of two eggs, toast, butter, jam, and tea. I ate alone, and as I finished the meal, another man appeared at my table.

"Are you Mister Gunaratana?"

"Yes."

"Follow me, please."

That man took me to a tour bus waiting outside the restaurant. I boarded, and the bus driver asked: "Are you Mister Gunaratana?"

"Yes."

And at last, I had my guided tour of Leningrad.

After returning home to Washington in the spring of 1977, I resumed classes at American University. I was in my second year of master's studies. Dr. Rodier, my longtime advisor, made it clear he expected me to continue on toward a PhD in philosophy. I was flattered and thrilled. So I applied for another scholarship, and it was granted. My patchwork quilt of an education, which had begun so long ago at a village school in rural Ceylon, had carried me all the way to the highest academic levels of the American education system. I could hardly believe it.

Meanwhile, the vihara was also flourishing. In the nearly ten years since I had come there, our membership had multiplied hundredfold. The devotional services and meditation classes were very popular, with both Americans and Sinhalese attending. I was asked to teach a twice-weekly meditation class for employees at the World Bank.

I also began to receive more and more invitations to teach and lead meditation retreats around the country. It was the late 1970s and meditation centers were beginning to crop up everywhere. One place, in New Mexico, first invited me in 1976. I had never been there and I didn't know the organizers, but I accepted their invitation.

The place was beautiful, high in the mountains. I was given a small, private cabin to stay in, which was accessible only by a hiking trail, and was tucked away from the rest of the buildings. As if to capitalize on the beautiful view of a pond, my cabin's toilet was located outside with no walls around it. I was a little hesitant about this arrangement, but since the cabin was fairly remote, I thought it might be all right.

The next morning, while answering the call of nature, I was shocked to see three young women suddenly appear at the pond for a swim. They were perhaps fifteen yards away from me, directly in my line of sight. However, they did not appear to see me.

Quite unashamedly, they took off all their clothes and stood on a rock to warm themselves in the sun before jumping in the pond. I was horribly embarrassed. I had been a celibate monk since the age of twelve, and I had never seen a naked female in my life!

As soon as I finished my toilet duties, I hurried to see the manager of the retreat center.

"This is entirely inappropriate," I said. "I need to be moved to another cabin immediately."

He apologized profusely. I was given another cabin, this one with a private bathroom.

The next year, when I visited that center to lead another ten-day retreat, my cabin had an outdoor shower next to it. It had black tubes coiled on the top, for solar heating, and a curtain hanging at the entrance. Embarrassed by the toilet incident the year before, the manager knew to take special precautions for my privacy. He asked me what time I would like to take a shower every day, and then he hung a sign on the shower wall, saying "Bhante G. takes his shower at noon. Please do not disturb."

The next day, I was in the shower at 12:00, when all of a sudden, a young woman walked in, totally naked. She said she wanted to ask me a Dhamma question.

I was incensed. I shouted at her, "You can ask Dhamma questions at my evening talk! Not here!"

She scurried away, red-faced.

I certainly hoped that was the last time I'd have to deal with unclothed young women. But it was the era of free love.

The next year, when I returned to the center, the poor manager gave me the most isolated cabin on the property. It took several minutes to walk to it from the main retreat area. No one will bother you there, he assured me.

A few nights later, I was walking back to my cabin at 10 P.M., after the last meditation session of the evening. Ahead of me in the dark forest, I could see a light gleaming in the window of my cabin.

"How nice," I thought. "One of the staff members has lit a candle so I won't have to come into a dark room."

When I got inside the cabin, I saw who had lit the candle. A woman was lying in my bed. She was very young, very attractive, and very naked.

"Get out!" I sputtered.

She didn't say a word, she just lay there smiling. Evidently she thought I was joking.

"I mean it," I said. "If you don't leave right now, I'll have to go get the manager." I turned my back to her.

I guess it dawned on her, then: I wasn't one of "those" kinds of gurus. She jumped up, crying, snatched her clothes, and ran out the door.

In each of those episodes, you might expect that I was overcome by lust, or at the very least felt a bit of sexual excitement. But I can honestly say that I was so embarrassed, and so angry, that those two emotions completely dominated my mind.

It seemed to me that any person who tried to seduce me was disrespecting me as a monk and as a teacher. It was a slap in the face to 2,500 years of tradition and a grave insult to the teachings of the Buddha. Maybe it sounds incredible, but I don't find the vow of celibacy a burden. As a monk, it is my choice to live this way. It has been my life since I was a young boy. I wouldn't think of compromising it.

In 1980 I earned my doctorate in philosophy. On graduation day, I was amazed to see two dozen Sinhalese friends in the audience.

"Bhante," one of them said, "when did you ever find time to earn a PhD?"

I laughed at the truth of his question. When people visited the vihara, they usually saw me mowing the lawn, giving a Dhamma talk, or fixing a leaky faucet. I had a full-time job there.

But my other full-time job was, and always has been, being a student. I don't think we ever "finish" our education, just because we earn academic degrees. I think our learning goes on and on, if we pay attention. We are all learners until we attain enlightenment.

In fact, when compared to the more esoteric levels of spiritual attainment described by the Buddha, we "worldly" learners aren't even qualified to be called learners. We're in preschool, as it were.

A true learner, according to the Buddha, is someone who has earned the designation of stream entry. What is the "stream"? Well, anyone who has studied a bit of Buddhism is familiar with the noble eightfold path: skillful understanding, skillful thought, skillful speech, skillful action, skillful livelihood, skillful effort, skillful mindfulness, and skillful concentration.

The eightfold path is the Buddha's foundation for spiritual practice, something each of us can work on every day. But it's just the beginning, because no matter how hard we work to perfect those different kinds of skillfulness, we're still subject to doubt. We may practice generosity, loving-friendliness, compassion, and truthfulness. We may speak softly and gently. We may be mindful and have good concentration. But all of it is subject to change—doubts can creep in when we're under stress, and at other times as well.

A higher level of the practice is called Supramundane Noble Eightfold Path. This is the "stream" referred to in the phrase stream entry. It is a level where doubts are washed away, where a person knows for certain the truth of the Triple Gem.

At the point of stream entry, a person begins moving along a path that takes him or her to higher and higher levels of attainment. When practitioners finally let go of the belief in a permanent self, they achieve the fruition of stream entry. You might say they've passed the entrance examination to the Supramundane Noble Eightfold Path. They will either reach enlightenment in this lifetime, or they will be reborn not more than seven times, either in this world or in the divine realms.

After doubt is abandoned, the next fetters to be loosed are hatred and grasping for sensual pleasure—in other words, aversion and greed. After the practitioner conquers these, he or she is called a once-returner, someone who will take rebirth only one more time. When the second obstacle falls, he or she becomes a never-returner.

Even then, at that extremely realized stage, there are still five fetters to overcome. They are the desire to exist in a material form, the desire to exist in an immaterial form, conceit, restlessness, and ignorance. The never-returner has reached a high level on the Supramundane Noble Eightfold Path but still hasn't quite earned the spiritual PhD, the ultimate achievement.

That achievement happens when those last five fetters come crashing down. At that point, the practitioner finally reaches the fruition of the entire path: He or she is an *arahant,* a fully enlightened being.

Then, and only then, is learning complete.

As soon as I earned my "worldly" doctorate, I was more in demand as a teacher. Several universities offered me faculty positions: Georgetown University, the University of Maryland, American University, and Bucknell University. I didn't accept any of these offers because my first responsibility was the vihara, but I did teach occasional courses in Buddhism at most of these universities for the next ten years.

Starting in the late 1970s, several more Sinhalese monks arrived to live in Washington, and the big house on Sixteenth Street became quite a lively, busy place. By then we had close to three thousand members, with a good mix of Americans and Asians (Sinhalese, Thai, Burmese, Cambodians, Laotians, and sometimes Koreans, too). The weekly classes and devotional services were full, and people dropped by every day, at all hours, to meditate and visit. The telephone rang constantly.

At about that time, an earnest young man named Matthew Flickstein started coming to the vihara regularly. He was a psychotherapist in Maryland, with a wife and two children. He was also very serious about learning meditation. He asked me many questions. But I was so snowed under by my duties at the vihara that it was hard to find the uninterrupted time Matt craved with me.

So he started taking me to motels, as a way for us to have that sort of time. He would rent a room and we'd spend several hours there, meditating and talking about his practice. We started with *anapanasati,* or mindfulness of breathing.

Every time we breathe in and out, I told Matt, we can experience impermanence. First, we begin to feel the need to breathe in. Subtle tension in our lungs grows and grows, as the amount of oxygen is depleted further and further, until we are forced to inhale. Then there's a moment of rest. But it doesn't last long. Soon the growing discomfort of having full lungs causes us to exhale. It is the pain-and-pleasure spectrum, right there in one cycle of breath. We have no control over it at all.

Seeing that kind of flux is our ticket to freedom. We are ready at any time to accept pleasure or pain, whatever arises. When pleasure inevitably changes, we're not shocked because we know it's impermanent. And when pain arises, we're not depressed because we know that it, too, is impermanent. We can accept both, without being overwhelmed by either one.

I enjoyed the time I spent with Matt, the breaks from the vihara for these impromptu teaching sessions, and he enjoyed the personal instruction. A friendship grew between us.

One day in 1979, I told him, "Matt, I'd like to start a meditation center. Somewhere quiet, out in the country. A forest monastery."

He looked at me with a gleam in his eye.

"Really? Are you serious?"

"Yes, I'm serious. The only problem is, I don't have enough money or people to support that kind of place."

"I can help," Matt said immediately.

We didn't talk about it much more that day. I think we both knew it was a big dream that would take some time to come to fruition. We needed to mull it over a bit more. But Matt is an energetic man, a person who wants things to happen now rather than later. He could only wait so long.

Several months later, he was driving me somewhere one afternoon and he suddenly said, "Bhante, what about that forest monastery? Are you still serious about it?"

"Of course," I answered.

"Then why don't you get going on it?"

"Because we still don't have the basic pieces in place. We don't have enough money or people, and we don't have a place for it, either."

"Bhante," said Matt, impatience in his voice, "now's the time. Life is short, and we need to get going on this."

A sly grin curled the corners of his mouth.

"If you're not ready to build this center, I'm going to have to go find another meditation teacher," he said.

I smiled.

"Okay. Let's start."

CHAPTER TWENTY-FOUR

Breaking Free

WHEN MATT AND I started our land search, I had $50,000 in the bank. I had saved it up over at least ten years. It was the money the State Department paid me for working at the refugee camp in Florida, plus honoraria for speeches I made and classes I taught at universities—anything I had earned on my own, outside of my work at the Washington Buddhist Vihara.

Matt and I started driving around Virginia, looking for pieces of land for sale. One day in 1983 we found a beautiful tract, with 189 acres and twelve buildings. The sale price was $1.5 million. We both thought it was perfect. Matt, charismatic talker that he is, talked the owner down to $700,000. On the spot, we gave them a $2,000 check as "earnest" money, to take the property temporarily off the market. In three months, we would owe a $100,000 down payment.

We got back in the car and I said, "We must be crazy. We don't have that kind of money. And we don't have any way to raise that kind of money in three months."

Matt seemed unperturbed.

"I know a fundraiser," he said, "a guy who will help us get that $100,000."

Several days later, we sat looking at a graphic the fundraiser had drawn for us. It was a pyramid. The people at the bottom of the pyramid were donating ten dollars. There were a lot of them. As the pyramid rose to each successive level, fewer people would donate more: twenty, fifty, one hundred dollars.

When it was all added up, it was more than $1 million.

"It looks very nice," I told Matt. "But this man isn't going to help us get this money for free. He wants $5,000 a month. Where is even that first $5,000 going to come from? And what if he only raises $5,000? We'll be losing money faster than he makes it."

Matt saw how nervous I was. He knew I hated the idea of mortgages and loans, of borrowing money we would be obligated to return with interest.

So he suggested a fundraising road trip. "Let's get in my car," he said, "and let's go visit everybody you know, and everybody I know. And let's ask them if they can help us."

For the next month, we crisscrossed the northeastern United States in Matt's Toyota Cressida. We went to New York, New Jersey, Rhode Island, New Hampshire, and Massachusetts. We crossed into Canada and visited people in Montreal, Ottawa, and Toronto. We even went up into Newfoundland and Nova Scotia.

Sometimes we drove fourteen hours a day. We would arrive at people's houses at midnight. They would give us ten, fifteen, or twenty dollars, sometimes just to get rid of us, I think. Sometimes they felt sorry for us and invited us to spend the night.

Some people were quite generous. One person wrote us a check for five hundred dollars. Another donated one thousand Canadian dollars. Matt's persuasive manner won over many people.

"We are doing something good for the benefit of many," he would say, sitting at someone's kitchen table. "Please help if you can."

At the end of the trip, the odometer in Matt's car had five thousand more miles on it. And we had collected five thousand dollars.

"This seems auspicious," I told him.

We opened a bank account in the name of our new enterprise: Bhavana Society. (The word *Bhavana*—mental cultivation—seemed to summarize our intentions for the forest monastery.)

But it was obvious we couldn't raise $95,000 more in the next two months. We defaulted on the contract for the Virginia land and lost our $2,000 earnest money.

Meanwhile, I had told the monks at the vihara and the board of directors that we were raising funds for a new meditation center outside of Washington somewhere. I never said it would be under the auspices of the Washington Buddhist Vihara, but that is what they assumed.

Later on, after we had acquired enough money to purchase a piece of property, they asked me outright if the new place would be affiliated with the vihara.

"No," I said.

"Why not?" they asked.

"Because that's not the way I want it," I said.

The truth is, I had gotten tired of temple politics. The original founder of the Washington Buddhist Vihara belonged to the Amarapura Nikaya sect of Theravada Buddhism. I belonged to another sect, Siyam. That, unfortunately, created conflict over the years.

One monk, sent in 1980 to live at the vihara, took a disliking to me. He said because I was of the Siyam Nikaya sect, I didn't belong at a temple established in the Amarapura Nikaya sect. He tried to stir up arguments to turn the other monks against me.

By the mid-1980s, I was worn out by the bickering. I felt as though none of the new monks who arrived appreciated all the work I had done over the years to build up the vihara. In 1985 I asked the head of the Amarapura Nikaya sect to come from Sri Lanka and settle the dispute. He came, but nothing was accomplished. He was more interested in visiting his relatives and having a mini-vacation.

I started to think more and more about getting away, about living in a peaceful place where I could simply teach Dhamma and not worry about the politics of running a temple.

By May 1984 we had $18,000 in the Bhavana Society bank account. I suggested to Matt that we start thinking smaller. Let's look for ten or fifteen acres, I said. And let's look in West Virginia. Land is cheaper there.

Matt made an appointment with a Realtor to meet at a café on Route 50, in the hills of eastern West Virginia. When we showed up on the appointed day, the real estate agent wasn't there. Matt asked a few people in the café if they had seen him. One of the customers asked Matt how much land we were looking for.

"About ten to fifteen acres," Matt said.

"I have thirteen acres," the man said. "I want $18,000 for it. You interested?"

Matt and I drove out Back Creek Road, a winding, one-lane strip of blacktop, to see the property. We liked it, and the price was exactly what we could afford. We gave the man an $8,000 check and signed a contract that same day.

In July we had a sort of group pilgrimage to the new land. Everyone who had made a donation for the new meditation center was invited. We left Washington in a caravan of ten cars. Two monks from the vihara accompanied me. Someone brought along a signboard we could erect on the land. It said "Dhamma Village," the name we had decided to give this new place.

The property looked beautiful in the fullness of summer. It was thickly covered with trees, and a small spring-fed creek trickled through it. We sat down on the ground and each of us expressed our gratitude for this place. The other two monks and I chanted suttas.

As soon as word got around that we had bought land, some of the members of the Washington Vihara were up in arms. Some stopped giving donations; others refused to bow to me. Secret meetings were held, to which I was not invited.

Because I had started several meditation groups in Washington and I had other teaching responsibilities there, my idea was to stay there while the West Virginia land was developed. So at least a year and a half went by without much happening at the Dhamma Village site. Some people told me they were worried I had made a mistake.

"Bhante, why did you buy land a hundred miles from Washington?" they said. "Who's ever going to go all the way out there? Who will support you? This was a terrible waste of money."

I used to lie awake at nights, wondering if that was true. It was depressing.

In late 1984 I decided to visit Sri Lanka. I had not been there for nine years, and my family asked me to participate in an offering ceremony for the memory of our mother. I also had several invitations to speak in other countries, and I thought I could combine it all into one trip.

I had lots of adventures on that trip. In Sweden, I opened a new Buddhist temple. In France, I stayed at a Sinhalese temple where, one night, the civil war that was beginning to heat up in Sri Lanka spilled onto the lovely streets of Paris. All the cars parked in front of the Sri Lankan temple had their tires punctured, most likely by Hindu Tamils who knew the temple was visited by Buddhist Sinhalese.

In Malawi, I helped open a new Buddhist temple, next door to a Sikh temple. In Nairobi, I went on safari in the Masai Mara wildlife preserve. And in Australia, I met a Buddhist child prodigy.

I had heard about this child many years before, when someone left a mysterious cassette tape on my desk at the Washington Vihara. When I listened to the tape, I heard the clear, beautiful voice of a child reciting Pali suttas with perfect pronunciation. I did some research and found out who he was. At the time the tape was recorded, he was only four years old. He lived in Sri Lanka. He was said to have chanted these suttas spontaneously, without any guidance or prompting from an adult.

So when I went home in 1984, several years after I had first heard the amazing chanting tape, I decided to try and find the boy. Someone gave me his address in Kandy, but I couldn't find the house, even though I went looking three different times.

After I left Sri Lanka, I went to Malaysia, Singapore, Thailand, and Australia. In Australia, I gave Dhamma talks in Canberra, Perth, and Sydney. At the Sydney train station, a young woman named Elizabeth Gorski met me and drove me to the Thai temple, where I was to stay. She had a dark-haired teenage boy in the car with her. She introduced him as Ruwan.

The next day she picked me up at the temple to take me somewhere else. The boy was in the back seat again, just like the day before.

"Elizabeth," I said, "have you heard of a young boy in Sri Lanka who chants Pali suttas?"

"Bhante, he's sitting right beside you," she said.

I was flabbergasted. I had found this famous Sinhalese boy in Australia. Elizabeth explained that she had met the boy, whose name was Ruwan Seneviratne, in Sri Lanka and was entranced with his chanting. Every summer, while he was on school vacation, she flew him to visit her in Australia, with his stepfather's permission.

"How did you learn chanting?" I asked Ruwan. "Did somebody teach you?"

"No, Bhante," he said. "When I was very young I used to sit on a cushion every morning and just chant. It was like I was doing it from memory."

Elizabeth asked me not to tell anyone I had met Ruwan. If word got out that he was there, people would flock to her house to hear him chant. Based on the boy's own testimony, many people believed that in a previous life in the fifth century c.e., he had been an assistant to the famous scholar Buddhaghosa, and that that was why he could chant Pali so clearly and spontaneously.

Nowadays, whenever I go to Sri Lanka, I see Ruwan. He is married, with two children, and is a devoted Buddhist. In fact, he wants to start a meditation center.

When I got back to Washington in May 1985, the atmosphere at the vihara was icy. While I was away, gossip had started about our new meditation center in West Virginia. Matt and I were starting some kind of business out there, the rumors said.

The board of directors demanded that I meet with them immediately. I hadn't even recovered from jet lag, but I agreed to sit down with them. It was more of an interrogation than a meeting. The questions flew at me like darts.

Why did you start the Bhavana Society?

How is it financed?

Who are the directors?

Why do you have to go all the way out there to teach Dhamma?

I answered their questions as well as I could. "Look," I said, "I'm not starting a brothel out there, or a liquor store, or a casino. It's going to be a meditation center. Why are you so threatened by that?"

Then they got to the crux of the dispute: "Why didn't you affiliate this new place with the Washington Buddhist Vihara?"

"Because I want it to be a monastic meditation center," I said, "not a cultural center. And I don't want Sri Lankan politics to intrude. I want this place to be totally independent."

Sour faces stared back at me.

After that, things went from bad to worse. One night the treasurer of the board suddenly told me there was going to be a meeting at the vihara, and I was expected to attend.

About twenty people appeared that night. As soon as we sat down, a Sinhalese man stood up and started shouting at me.

"You never do anything for this place," he said. "You always just sit around studying. You don't even take care of the cockroaches in the kitchen. You bring your relatives here from Sri Lanka and find jobs for them, but you don't find jobs for anyone else. You should be teaching our children Sinhalese, but you spend all your time traveling and teaching Dhamma to Westerners who aren't even Buddhists."

I was stunned. This man was usually very gentle and calm, and I considered him a friend.

I knew he had been swayed by the people who wanted to expel me from the vihara. And I knew my reaction would be watched carefully. So I didn't answer his accusations. Instead, I simply started administering the three refuges and five precepts to the group, chanting as calmly as I could.

At a later meeting of the board, Matt Flickstein and another friend of mine, Albert Cambarta, were asked to resign. When that happened, I knew the end was in sight.

But there were no buildings on the West Virginia property yet. If I walked out of the vihara for good, I would have nowhere to live. I needed to stay in Washington at least until we got some livable accommodations at the new place.

In fact, I stuck it out for three more years, but it wasn't easy. We continued raising money for Bhavana Society, separate from the Washington Vihara. And this often created an unpleasant and hostile environment.

Finally the board of directors gave me three choices. I could resign from my post as president of the Washington Buddhist Vihara, I could resign from the board of the Bhavana Society, or I could allow Bhavana Society to be absorbed into the vihara.

I gave them an answer on the spot: "I'll resign from the vihara," I said.

I could see from the shocked looks on their faces that they never expected me to call their bluff. I had been there twenty years, on an assignment that was only supposed to last five. I had hand-picked all of them to be on the board. They probably thought I was so attached to my position there that I couldn't bear to leave.

But it was a simple choice, really. If they were bold enough to ask me to resign, why should I want to stay there? And I was excited to think about going to live at Dhamma Village, even though we had only the shell of the first building built.

I immediately sent my letter of resignation to the head of the Amarapura Nikaya sect in Sri Lanka. I asked him to allow Venerable Maharagama Dhammasiri, a visitor at the vihara, to take my place. The answer came back with approval, so I helped Venerable Dhammasiri apply for a permanent visa. He received his green card on the twenty-sixth of May, 1988.

The following day, I handed Venerable Dhammasiri my key ring, with all the keys to the vihara. I told him which bank had the vihara's account and how much money was in it. I told him where all the important legal papers were.

Then I got in a car, by myself, and drove away.

I felt nothing but relief, great, sweeping relief.

CHAPTER TWENTY-FIVE

Building a Monastery

By the time I moved onto our new property, we had already drilled a well for water and there was electricity. But only the skeleton of one long, narrow building rose in the forest.

At first, everything would be in that one building: a kitchen, three bedrooms, and a couple of bathrooms. We turned one of the bedrooms into a shrine room that would hold about ten or twelve people. The dining hall, a large space adjoining the kitchen, had to serve double-duty as the meditation hall.

The kitchen was equipped with a double-burner gas cooker. For water, we toted buckets from our well, or from the springhead that bubbled up at the top of our acreage. We answered the call of nature in a rented Port-o-Let.

Despite these meager accommodations, I was happy. I felt as though I could truly serve the Dhamma at this place, undisturbed by bureaucracy, temple politics, and all the other unpleasantness that had driven me from Washington. Here, in this isolated mountain valley, I could make a place where people would come to experience peace.

I didn't do it to become famous or attract disciples or raise a lot of money. All I wanted was to see monks, nuns, and lay meditators strolling the paths deep in meditation and contemplation of the Dhamma. I hoped that eventually there would be as many of them as there were trees in that forest!

My only companion in those early days was Venerable Yogavacara Rahula, a young American monk who had been wandering around Asia and had ordained in the mid-1970s in Sri Lanka. Venerable Rahula had heard about our plan to build a forest monastery and wrote to me in Washington, asking if he could join us. He had moved onto the land in April 1987, while I was still at the vihara in Washington. He lived in the partially completed building. Bhante Rahula would prove, over the years, to be my right-hand man and the most energetic, dependable bhikkhu I had ever met.

One of the first projects Bhante Rahula took on was clearing a site for a vegetable garden. To do that, he had to pick countless rocks out of the mountain soil. One time when I visited, he was just beginning. When I returned, two weeks later, he had used those rocks to build a handsome retaining wall. I thought: This is the kind of hard worker we need to make this place a reality.

Matthew Flickstein remained a loyal friend, too. In late 1987, he bought ten acres that were for sale near our land and donated it to the Bhavana Society. John Hitchings, another supporter, then bought the two-acre strip that lay between the two tracts, and donated it to the society. That gave us a total of twenty-five acres.

Early on, even before I moved onto the property, we had made a deal with a local builder. Every time we collected enough donations, we would pay him and he would do a little more work on the first building. Luckily, he didn't seem to mind that kind of on-again-off-again schedule.

The foundation for the first building was poured in three stages, as we raised the money. The framing and walls went up the same way. When it was time to put a roof on the building, the builder suggested we build the trusses ourselves, to save money. He said we'd need forty regular trusses and forty scissor trusses. We could build the regular ones, but the scissor ones were more complicated, so he would order those. Then he drew us a design plan for the regular trusses.

So we started recruiting volunteers and asked people to rent power tools and buy lumber and nails. We built those forty trusses in one weekend. Unfortunately, they weren't all even. The builder had to remake many of them.

When the roof was finished, complete with beautiful dark red shingles, a county building inspector came to look at it. He shook his head.

"One snowfall, and that whole roof's gonna cave in," he said.

"What do we do?" I asked.

"You have to take it all off and rebuild it," he said.

I'm sure I must have looked panicked.

"We aren't a wealthy organization," I said. "We don't have the money to do that again."

"Okay," the inspector said. "I'll give you an alternative. Make an A-frame with two-by-ten-by-twenty-twos and bolt that to the trusses. But before you do that, make sure that the frame of the trusses is smooth, by gluing pieces of plywood to them."

Of course, we had to wait until we collected enough money to buy the lumber for those repairs. And then it took us several more months to find someone who had the expertise to build the A-frames.

Meanwhile, I got a letter at the vihara from Russell LaFollette, one of our neighbors in West Virginia. He said he noticed we were storing a lot of lumber in the shell of the main building on our land with no locks or security. "That's not safe," he said. "If you want, I'll keep an eye on your property for three dollars a day." We agreed.

Other neighbors weren't so helpful. Some were downright angry that we were invading their turf.

Soon after we bought the property, we went to introduce ourselves to the nearest neighbor. We stood on one side of the property line. He stood on the other.

"This is Bhante Gunaratana," Matt said. "We just bought this land and we're going to start a meditation center."

The man didn't say a word. He just stood there staring at us, stiff and stern.

"Sir, whenever you have time, you're welcome to come and meditate with us," I said.

"You can do any damn thing you like," the man snapped. "I'm a good Christian."

As soon as we erected a mailbox on the main road, it was torn down. In fact, the mailbox has continued to be a target over the years. It has been shot full of holes, taped shut with duct tape, filled with dog excrement, and stolen. I think we're on our fifth or sixth mailbox these days.

We also put up a sign at the end of our driveway, with an arrow and the words "Dhamma Village." Within a day or two, letters had been selectively blacked out so that the sign read "Dam Village." (Eventually we decided not to use that name anymore and to have our monastery known simply as Bhavana Society.)

Before there were even buildings on the land, we began to hold meditation retreats there. In the beginning, they were one-day retreats. We would sit out under the trees. Later, we invited people to bring tents and stay overnight.

From the very first time meditators started sitting there, we were harassed by the next-door neighbors. The people living there were the man who had given us such an unfriendly greeting, his wife, and their two sons. They would shoot rifles in the air, shout obscenities, and let their dogs howl endlessly. The wife often stood in their yard, singing hymns in a very loud voice. And their sons always seemed to practice their drums during our evening meditation.

We never complained because we didn't want to make things worse, but other neighbors sometimes called the sheriff. He would come, and the noise would stop for a while—but only for a while.

For some time, our cook was an African American man. Every time he walked outside, where the neighbors could see him, the man next door would yell, "Go home, nigger!"

We also had a German nun living at the monastery for a while. She stayed in a one-room kuti in the woods, quite near that family's property. One afternoon she was sitting on the little front porch of her hut, and the pellet of a BB gun came whizzing by her head. It went right through the window and lodged in a wall.

The harassment went on for six or seven years, until the couple divorced and the man moved away. The children, by then, were grown. So only the wife was left living there. Interestingly, just a couple of years ago one of the sons came home to visit. He walked over to our property and greeted Venerable Rahula.

"I've been off in the navy," he said, "and I went to some Buddhist countries. So I understand what you're all about now. I'm sorry we gave you such a hard time. We were just doing what my dad told us to do. He said you were bad people."

Our other neighbors, Bernard and Aveline Denise, were always friendly. They lived behind us and eventually, in 1991, sold us their seven acres. The house they had lived in became our men's dormitory.

On October 2, 1988, we officially opened the main building. There were also three log kutis modeled after the little one-room huts that are a standard feature at monasteries in Asia. By that time, we had electricity and plumbing—the center was up and running.

A month after the opening ceremony, Matt came to me and announced that he'd like to go to Thailand or Sri Lanka and ordain as a monk.

"That's a pretty strange idea," I said.

"Why?" he asked.

"Because I could ordain you right here."

"But I thought you told me you wouldn't ordain me," he said.

"That was ten years ago," I replied. "Your children were young then. They needed you more. It was important for you to stay home with them. Now they're older, and as long as you have your wife's consent, I'll be happy to ordain you here. You can be a monk for a month or two."

Matt beamed.

The idea of being a "temporary" monk isn't as strange as it might sound. In some Buddhist countries, young men are expected to spend a period of time, as long as a year, in the Sangha. Afterward, they disrobe and return to lay life. Sometimes mature men who have wives and families will ordain for a month or two during the rainy season, or maybe just for a couple of weeks, in honor of their dead parents.

But before I could ordain Matt, or anyone else, we had to establish a *sima* at Bhavana Society.

A sima is a consecrated area where special monastic ceremonies are held. It can be a house, a boat, a cave, or even a simple open area marked by boundary lines. The Pali word *sima* means boundary. Monks and nuns meet in the sima twice monthly to confess their transgressions and to recite the monastic rules. Laypeople cannot attend these meetings. On other occasions, such as ordinations, laypeople are invited into the sima to witness what is going on.

The sima is even more sacred than the shrine room. Establishing a new sima is such a holy ceremony that any monk invited to one cannot refuse. If he arrives late, he is not permitted to take part in the ceremony and must wait outside.

The sima is always surrounded by eight stones. There are specific directions for the dimensions of these stones and their placement. Matt took me to a quarry, and I told the stonecutter what we needed: eight stones, each one measuring twelve inches wide, two-and-a-half feet high, and three inches thick.

Because we couldn't afford to construct a new building for the sima, we decided to establish it in my small kuti, which had been built earlier that year, thanks to a donation from Matt.

I thought if we had the sima establishment and his ordination on the same day, it would be particularly auspicious. We set the date for July 22, 1989.

In the meantime, two other ordination candidates appeared at our center: Misha Cowen, a young woman from California who had dreamed of becoming a nun, and Tom West from Vancouver, Canada, who wanted to take vows as a bhikkhu. After observing both of them for several months, I decided they were ready for the homeless life. I would ordain them at the same ceremony as Matt.

We wanted as many monks as possible to attend this grand ceremony. So we invited thirty-five Theravada monks from all over the United

States: Sinhalese, Thai, Laotian, Cambodian, Vietnamese, and Burmese, as well as one Japanese Mahayana monk and two Mahayana nuns.

On the morning the ceremony was to take place, we all assembled on the plywood platform we had erected at the sima site. A photographer from the Smithsonian Institution was there to document the whole day. I asked three people—Matt, John Hitchings, and Daniel Cory—to formally present the deeds for the three pieces of property we owned. Then it was time to dedicate the sima.

The eight stones had been carefully placed in a ring around the sima. One monk stood at each stone.

With great pomp, the senior-most monk, Venerable Dr. Havenpola Ratanasara Mahathera, walked from one stone to the next, starting in the east. As he faced the bhikkhu standing by each stone, that bhikkhu would say, "This is the stone of the east, Venerable Sir." Or "This is the stone of the southeast, Venerable Sir."

After two circuits of the stone circle, the head monk stopped and intoned formally, "This is the boundary line of this sima."

After that, I announced that the ordinations would take place after lunch, at 2 P.M.

During lunch, the visiting Japanese monk approached me and requested that I ordain him, too. He wanted to become a Theravada monk, and I consented.

So we ordained three men and one woman that day. I gave Matt the monastic name of Sumati, which means "Right Wisdom." Tom West became Sona, or "Gold"—the name of a monk sent out by King Ashoka as an early Buddhist missionary. And the young woman from California took the name of Sister Sama, "Peaceful One."

Sumati and Sona took both novice and higher ordination in one day, and the Japanese monk, because he was already in robes, took only higher ordination. Sister Sama, however, was ordained as a novice.

Buddhist tradition requires that at least five other ordained monastics witness any ordination. When the Theravada nuns' order died out in the tenth century C.E., due to lack of support, there were no longer any fully ordained nuns to witness the ordination of new ones. This has been a frustration to modern women wanting to ordain as Theravada nuns. Until recently, they have had to content themselves with a sort of in-between status, as novice nuns who follow the ten precepts. It has been a bone of contention in the Theravada Buddhist community for years.

I knew this question would come up as soon as we started ordaining people at Bhavana Society. Women would want to become full nuns. I had to decide what I would do.

The Buddha laid down detailed instructions for the ordination of nuns, but he never said that only other nuns could perform the ceremony. He also never said that if the nuns' order ever became extinct, it couldn't be restarted. From that, I concluded there was no reason a monk could not ordain a nun.

Also, I knew that Venerable Havenpola Ratanasara Mahathera, the highly revered Sinhalese monk who opened our sima, had ordained a Thai woman in California.

So when Misha Cowen came to Bhavana Society and asked if she could become a nun, I said yes. Because she was new to Buddhism, though, I told her she should first be a novice. I knew I couldn't perform a higher ordination for her without the support of the Sangha, but I was hoping that by the time she was ready to become a full-fledged *bhikkhuni*, someone else would be ordaining women, and I could send her there.

A couple of monks heard what I was planning, and they asked me not to ordain her. I politely said my mind was made up, so she became Sister Sama on that first ordination day at Bhavana Society.

Since then, I have ordained five other women. All of them have received novice status. Several only intended to be nuns temporarily, so they eventually left Bhavana Society. One of them, a German woman who became Sister Sucinta, went on to receive her higher ordination in 1997 at Bodhgaya, India. She took part in a mass ordination ceremony with dozens of other female novices. Both Mahayana and Theravada monks presided over that ordination.

Before our first ordination day at Bhavana, in July 1989, I had ordained only one other person, a fifteen-year-old boy at the Washington Buddhist Vihara who wanted to take on robes for a short period. I had never performed ordinations while I was in Asia.

So this was a big day for all of us. The Bhavana Society had consecrated its sima, and it also had its first monks and nuns.

My dream of a forest monastery was taking shape. I was delighted beyond words.

CHAPTER TWENTY-SIX

No Price Tag

In the late 1980s and early '90s, my travel schedule intensified. I was invited to teach all over the United States, Canada, South America, Scandinavia, Europe, Australia, and Asia. I accepted almost every invitation that came my way—the farther away, the better. I loved to travel.

In many places, a translator would be provided for my Dhamma talks. In other countries, enough of the audience spoke English that I could teach in this language.

Often, after a retreat or a talk, people would approach me with thanks. Sometimes they wanted to shake my hand or hug me. Of course, about half of them were women. This always presented a quandary for me. Theravada monks are not allowed to touch females.

Folding my palms together and smiling, I would say, "I'm sorry. I mean no disrespect, but this is how we Buddhist monks greet someone or express our appreciation."

Some women were confused, and others blushed. Some of them took offense and turned away without saying another word. That always made me sad.

I know that many people think Buddhist monks won't touch women because we think they're "unclean." I've been called a male chauvinist, sexist, prideful, a person with no feeling, and an uptight prude. None of this is true.

I don't avoid touching women because I think they're disgusting, ugly creatures. On the contrary, women are the most beautiful living beings on earth. And that's exactly the problem.

There's a story about the Buddha that explains it well. Once the Buddha's attendant, Ananda, asked him, "Venerable Sir, how should we monks behave toward women?"

"Don't look at them," was the Buddha's reply.

"Sometimes we can't avoid seeing them," said Ananda. "What then?"

"Don't talk to them."

"What if the situation demands that we talk to them?" Ananda persisted. "What then?"

"Say only a few words, mindfully," answered the Buddha.

The Buddha was a man, a flesh-and-blood man. He knew full well that there is no other sight that can grip a man's mind like the sight of a woman. No other voice, no other smell, no other taste. No other thought can fill a man's mind like the thought of a woman, leaving room for nothing else.

It's the same for a woman when she sees a man.

That is why the Buddha laid down strict rules for both monks and nuns. A monk should never physically touch a woman, and a nun should never physically touch a man.

When they ordain, Theravada Buddhist monastics take a vow of celibacy. That commitment is hard enough to maintain, but it is nearly impossible if you start touching members of the opposite sex. A simple hug or kiss can awaken desire and attachment. And those are the very things we're trying to overcome when we take up the life of Dhamma.

At Bhavana Society, we take the monastic discipline very seriously. Visitors and lay residents are asked to observe eight precepts, which are the basic five precepts plus a few monastic-style rules: no eating after noon, no sexual activity, no entertainment such as watching TV or dancing.

The precepts are more of a protection than a restriction. They shelter us by eliminating many of the distractions that would take us away from serious meditation practice.

I have always felt that we don't have to relax our discipline to attract more people to our center. If people feel the precepts are too strict and they don't want to come here, then they won't come and that's fine. There are still enough people who do come. People have a tremendous respect for discipline. When they see how we live here, it inspires them. They take on the precepts willingly, whether it's for a weekend retreat or for a longer stay.

In 1988 we started the tradition of offering laypeople the opportunity to take Eight Lifetime Precepts. They wear white and we have a special ceremony in which each person formally accepts the precepts, then receives a Pali name and a certificate. At first, this was a once-a-year event, held only during a special retreat. Then we expanded it so that anyone attending any retreat of five days or longer can take the Eight Lifetime Precepts if they choose. This includes retreats that I teach in other countries. I'd guess that more than a thousand people around the world have now taken the Eight Lifetime Precepts. We believe this kind of voluntary commitment can create powerful change in people's lives, by giving them a practical way to make the Dhamma a part of their daily behavior.

People also appreciate the fact that we operate Bhavana Society solely on *dana* (donations), instead of dues. We never charge admission for anything—Dhamma talks, retreats, or ceremonies. There is a donation box in the dining hall with a slot in the lid, and a box of envelopes nearby. It is up to each visitor how much, if anything, he or she contributes.

This is a tradition as old as the teachings of the Buddha. *Dana,* loosely translated from Pali, means "generosity." The Dhamma always has been considered priceless, so no price tag can be put on it; it is offered freely.

In America, of course, there's a price tag on everything. This is a capitalist economy, after all. Someone tells you how much he wants for his product, and you, the consumer, decide if you want to spend the money to get that product. Dana, on the other hand, means that you, the consumer, make your own decision about how much this product is worth. You choose how much you want to pay, and hopefully, you will be fair.

In this culture, dana makes a very powerful statement. When they first hear about it, people often respond with awe. They can hardly believe that this entire monastery and retreat center has been created through people's faith and generosity. In 1977, for example, we constructed a beautiful meditation hall, thanks mostly to about $150,000 collected from our Thai supporters, both in the United States and Thailand. The hall is truly awe-inspiring, with a seven-hundred-pound Buddha statue sitting on a high altar under a stained-glass window featuring an image of a Bodhi leaf. Our reliance on dana, our trust that the help will be there when we need it, is so rare in America that it seems to open people's hearts and minds. I think they trust us more because we clearly are not trying to take something from them. Instead, we're offering them something.

From the beginning, I also was very firm that there would be few cultural trappings at Bhavana Society. I didn't want the center to look like a Sinhalese temple, or an American meditation center, or a Japanese zendo. I wanted it to be a place where people of all traditions, of all ethnicities and national origins, would feel comfortable and at home.

That sometimes demands flexibility on the part of our guests. Asian people, traditionally, do not call ahead or register for functions at the temple. They simply drop in whenever they have a few things to donate, need some advice from a monk or nun, or want the monastics to bless a new child. On full-moon days, they always come to the temple. For them it's a wonderful place to relax with family and friends.

Americans, on the other hand, expect a more structured atmosphere. They make reservations before they arrive at the center. As soon as they get here, they check the schedule so they will know exactly what they're supposed to be doing every hour of the day. They expect to find silence and contemplation.

In the early days of Bhavana Society, when only a single door separated the meditation hall and the kitchen, we often had a culture clash. The Westerners would be seated quietly on their cushions in the meditation hall with their eyes closed. In the next room, a gaggle of Sinhalese and Thai adults and children chatted boisterously while preparing a big meal for the monks and nuns.

Nowadays we have all learned to live with each other's differences a little more easily, and I think it's a good thing. The Asians have come to admire the Westerners' dedication to the meditative practices, and the Westerners have developed appreciation for the sincere good intentions and generosity of the Asian visitors. Unfortunately, this type of mutual appreciation is all too uncommon in our world.

In 1983, civil war broke out in Sri Lanka. The conflict had been simmering ever since the country won independence from Britain in 1948. The two prominent ethnic groups—the Sinhalese (who are largely Buddhist) and the Tamils (who are mostly Hindu)—immediately started to bicker.

The Sinhalese felt the British had favored the Tamils by giving them better schools and better jobs. So they wanted compensation of some kind. In 1956 a Sinhalese man named Bandaranaike won a contested parliamentary election. As soon as he got into office, he carried out a campaign promise to make Sinhalese the official government language in Sri Lanka.

That enraged the Tamils and made them feel like outsiders. A secret antigovernment movement sprang up among the Tamils. A militant young man named Prabhakaran recruited young people as suicide bombers. He killed off several other Tamil leaders he considered his rivals. In 1983 Prabhakaran's Tamil "Tigers" made their first attack, killing thirteen soldiers. In response, riots broke out all over the country.

Ever since, it has been a bloody battle between Sinhalese and Tamils. During nearly twenty years of civil conflict, sixty-five thousand people have been killed.

The violence saddens me, and I try not to take sides. But in 1983 I read about five hundred thousand refugees, predominantly Tamils, who were stranded in refugee camps in northern Sri Lanka. At that time I was still in residence at the Washington Buddhist Vihara. I sent a letter to all the members of the vihara inviting them to donate to a relief fund for those refugees. A lot of people criticized me for supporting the Tamils.

I responded by saying that I didn't care if they were Tamils or Sinhalese—they were living beings who were suffering. For that reason alone, I wanted to help.

Another time, I was giving a Dhamma talk to a group of Sinhalese in Ottawa. Someone asked a question about the five precepts. As I talked about the first precept, to abstain from killing, I said it is an unconditional precept. This means that there are no circumstances in which killing is condoned.

The third (sexual misconduct) and fifth (alcohol and intoxicants) are conditional precepts, I said. They can be "bent" to accommodate certain situations. For example, the householder may enjoy sexual activity with his or her spouse. And a person can ingest certain medicines that contain alcohol, or even drink alcohol in moderation, if it doesn't interfere with mindfulness.

But that first precept, to abstain from killing, has no conditions. It is not even all right to kill to protect oneself, one's family, or one's country. I saw quite a few frowns in the audience when I said that.

Afterward, a man said to me, "Bhante, if you had given this talk in Sri Lanka, you wouldn't be alive tomorrow. Preaching nonviolence is not exactly popular there, right now."

In the United States, however, it wasn't my putative political views that got me in trouble; sometimes, it was my robe.

Once I visited a wealthy Sri Lankan physician who lived in Saint Louis. Four other monks were there as well, because he had invited us to chant for a special ceremony.

Before the ceremony, we decided to take a walk in a park across the street. Soon a police car pulled up along the curb next to us. The officer got out and asked us what we were doing.

"We're taking a walk," I said. "Have we done something wrong?"

The officer said there had been some burglaries recently in the neighborhood. And one of the residents had called police, saying there were strange-looking people in the park. Then the officer proceeded to give me the most thorough interrogation I had ever undergone.

Where was I from? What was I doing in Saint Louis? Where was I staying? Had I ever been convicted of a crime? What was my mother's maiden name? What was my father's name? What did they do for a living? Had I ever been married? Did I have any children? Who had invited me there? Why?

He also wanted to know how tall I was, how much I weighed, and if I had any distinguishing physical marks on my body. He then wanted to see my visa and my Social Security card.

I answered all of his questions, but what I really wanted to do was ask him one simple question: How many burglars do you know who wrap themselves in bright-orange robes and stroll through a park in broad daylight?

I also sometimes attract the attention of airport security guards. After all, I'm dark-skinned and I dress in bizarre clothing. My robe has lots of folds in which I might be hiding drugs or a weapon.

One time in Denver, I was waylaid by a security officer who didn't believe the vial of salt in my carry-on bag was truly salt. "I use it to gargle," I told her. "It's for my throat."

She insisted on calling airport police and a drug expert. As a result, I ended up missing my plane to Vancouver and had to wait eight hours for the next one.

Another time, coming home to Dulles airport after a teaching trip to Europe, I was met by an American friend. When he tried to walk through US customs with me, the customs officers pounced on us. He told them I was a Buddhist monk, coming home from a meditation retreat, but they were sure I was smuggling cocaine. It took a lot of talking to get past them.

I used to keep quiet in such situations, but now I am more assertive. I tell the customs officer that he has no right to harass me as long as I cooperate and open my bag.

"I have nothing to hide," I always say. Then I give the officer a nice smile and beam some metta in his direction.

CHAPTER TWENTY-SEVEN

Chief Sangha Nayaka

WHEN I WENT to Sri Lanka in 1985, a nominating committee of several monks asked me to receive one of the highest honors my monastic sect can bestow: the title of Chief Sangha Nayaka Thera for North America.

Literally, the title means something like "head of the community of monks and nuns." It's equivalent, maybe, to an archbishop in the Catholic Church. It means that you are the highest-ranking monk of your sect in that particular region (in this case, the United States and Canada). And it is a position you hold until your death.

I gave the offer some thought, but decided that it was not appropriate for me. I didn't think I had done any great service to deserve this honor. And there was a monk of our sect older than me, living in California, whom I thought merited this title more than I did. So I declined.

In March of 1996, I was teaching in Norway when the offer came again. The same group of monks telephoned me and asked if I would change my mind and consent. I declined once more. The same thing happened when I got to the next stop in my tour: While I was in Sweden they called, extended the offer, and I declined.

When I got to France, there was a fax waiting for me: "Please reconsider," it said. I didn't even answer the fax.

When my retreats were over, I returned to Bhavana Society. A visiting monk was there from Sri Lanka. He had been asked to hand-deliver a letter to me from the committee that so ardently wanted me to be Chief Sangha Nayaka.

Maybe it was time, I thought. I knew my relatives and friends would be happy. So I relented.

I was already planning to go to Australia that summer to teach. I said I would stop in Sri Lanka, on the way, and accept the certificate. I didn't think it would be a big deal and so planned to spend only one day there.

I arrived in Sri Lanka at 1:30 A.M. on July 4, 1996. I spent the night in the presidential suite at Vidyalankara Pirivena, the monks' college from which I had graduated in 1952.

The next morning I was driven to Kandy, the headquarters of the Siyam Nikaya sect of Theravada Buddhism in Sri Lanka. When we arrived, I was astonished to see a group of maybe two hundred people, waiting to greet me—all of them relatives or old friends. I had written to a few family members to tell them I was coming, but Venerable Dr. Vajira, the organizer of the event, had written to many more.

I stepped out of the van and saw faces I hadn't seen in forty years. Many I couldn't even recognize until they told me their names. My younger sister, Sita, had arranged a gala lunch for me and the fifty other monks who had come from all over Sri Lanka for this ceremony.

After lunch, I was trying to talk to as many of the guests as I could, when a monk approached to tell me I was expected at Pahamune temple—my teacher's teacher's temple. There, I was given a cup of tea and a brand-new set of orange robes to wear for the ceremony.

Soon a messenger arrived to tell me the procession was ready. "What procession?" I thought. I had no idea anything this elaborate had been planned; curious, I walked outside.

There was a long line of several hundred people. I had no idea who they were, or where they had come from. I was told to walk at the head of this parade, just behind a huge banner that read, "Welcome, Chief Sangha Nayaka Thera." Behind me would be dancers, musicians, drummers, conch-shell-blowers, and colorfully dressed children.

Everyone was in an extremely festive mood. I also saw some government officials in the parade, including the defense minister.

The parade route was about a quarter-mile long, and it took us to the sima at Malwatta temple. There, I was to offer gift trays to twenty of the high-ranking monks of the Siyam Nikaya sect, which is similar to what I had done on my higher ordination day forty-nine years earlier. Just like then, the room was packed with people, with a rope down the middle to divide laypeople from monastics. It was so hot that I perspired profusely. I was jet-lagged and had gotten very little sleep the night before. The heavy perfume of flowers on the altar, combined with the musky smoke of incense, made the air stuffy. I was hoping I wouldn't faint.

Venerable Dr. Vajira handed me the first tray and asked me to offer it to the supreme patriarch of the sect, who was sitting on a cushion to the right of the Buddha image.

I took the tray, approached the patriarch and knelt before him. He spoke a few words to me in a hushed voice about his gratitude for my Dhamma work.

Then, one by one, Vajira handed me trays to present to the nineteen other monks seated to the left, in order of seniority. Only one of my teachers was still alive to be there that day—Venerable Paravahera Pannananda Nayaka Mahathera. He was eighty-eight, and had come from Colombo to see me receive this honor.

When I held out the tray and bowed to him, I saw tears in his eyes. There were tears in my eyes, too.

After I sat down, a secretary monk opened a silver tube and unrolled the certificate naming me Chief Sangha Nayaka. He read it aloud, in both Sinhalese and English; then I was asked to come forward and receive the certificate from the supreme patriarch.

Several monks gave speeches in Sinhalese. The defense minister said a few words before being ushered out by his security guards. And then it was all over.

A crowd of people pressed in around me to offer congratulations. Within ten minutes, I was taken to a van and driven to the Temple of the Tooth, where we had a special devotional service. I was allowed to view the Buddha's relics before making a special offering of a silver tray heaped with fresh flowers.

My final duty that day was to pay my respects to the patriarch of the other chapter of our sect. He, too, expressed his pleasure at my being awarded this honor, and I presented him with a gift of a new robe.

Clearly, I was going to be in Sri Lanka for more than one day, so I settled in and enjoyed this time with my friends, family, and fellow monks. The next day the receptions started, each one at a different place. There were seven altogether, within four days. I just went from one event to the next, wherever I was driven.

One reception was at Vidyalankara Pirivena, my old alma mater, near Colombo. There, we were entertained by a famous band that normally only plays at state functions. The prime minister, Mrs. Sirimavo Bandaranaike, presented me with a certificate.

Another reception was at the temple where I had my first ordination. They, too, had a procession for me. The old schoolteacher from Malandeniya village was there, now a very elderly man, who had known me when I was a young novice. He walked the entire length of the procession beside the car I was riding in, holding on to the car and talking to me through the open window. I asked him to get in the car with me, but he wouldn't. Then I said I'd get out and walk with him, but he wouldn't hear of that either.

One night there was an all-night chanting in my honor, at a temple outside Kandy. I didn't participate; I just listened. Twelve monks chanted suttas to bless me. After chanting those suttas so many times in my life, to bless other people, it was a strange feeling to be the recipient.

Throughout the five days of celebration, I was touched that so many people wanted to honor my work even though most of it hadn't been in Sri Lanka. For forty-five years, I had devoted all of my energy to teaching Dhamma in other countries, not my own. But I heard many older monks encouraging their young students to follow my example and study languages so that they could teach abroad and bring honor to Buddhism and Sri Lanka.

Pride is a dangerous thing, though. It is a strong attachment and difficult to overcome. To combat it, I reminded myself that for all these years I'd simply been trying to live in accordance with the Dhamma, and to teach the Dhamma to others as much as I could. So really, there was nothing for me to be prideful about.

The last reception was in my childhood village, Henepola. It was held in the temple's preaching hall.

My brother Rambanda's widow was there, with four of their children. One of my uncles also came, and some of his grandchildren were there, too.

Three of my sisters, Bisomanike, Bandaramenike, and Sita Ekanayaka, and their children had made the trip to Kandy to witness the elaborate ceremony where I received the title of Chief Sangha Nayaka. But I think this simple gathering in our village meant more to all of us.

An old man from Henepola stood to welcome the crowd, and I barely recognized him. He said he was eighty-three years old, and his name was Puncibanda, which, incidentally, was my father's name.

"I remember when this preaching hall was built," he said, his voice cracking with emotion. "It was Bhante Gunaratana's father who built it. No one had any power tools in those days, and there was no place to buy good lumber. We had only crude, homemade bricks."

Tears slid down the old man's cheeks.

"But the temple needed a preaching hall. We had nowhere in the village where everyone could gather, so Mr. Puncibanda built us this hall. He built it so well that it's still standing today, seventy-five years later. And now we've come here to honor his son, who joined the Sangha, traveled afar to preach Dhamma, and has earned this great honor."

My sisters were crying by that time. I felt a lump rising in my throat, too, but I choked it back. Of course, monks can and do cry. Venerable Ananda, the Buddha's personal attendant, cried when his teacher passed away. I myself had cried several days earlier, when making the silver tray offering to my elderly teacher. I also cried at my parents' funerals, and even, as I've said, once during a speech about my mother.

This time, though, I was a Chief Sangha Nayaka Thera. The very utterance of that title inspired respect, and it was a title I would hold for the rest of my life.

I wanted to live up to the importance of that day and to honor those who had given me this honor. I wanted to embody the strength and beauty of a tradition 2,500 years old.

Even so, my eyes misted over. I couldn't help it.

I was, after all, just a son.

A son who had come home to Henepola.

CHAPTER TWENTY-EIGHT

Helping My Homeland

In 2004, a few minutes past midnight on the day after Christmas, a huge earthquake struck off the coast of Indonesia, spawning a tsunami that devastated more than a dozen countries on both sides of the Indian Ocean, including Sri Lanka.

It was one of the deadliest natural disasters in history. Hundreds of thousands of people were killed and thousands more went missing, washed away when the massive waves hit land. Many of my Sinhalese friends immediately started working on relief efforts for the scores of survivors who were left homeless.

In the week that followed, I was invited to appear on the *Larry King Live* show on CNN, along with a Roman Catholic priest, Jewish rabbi, Muslim scholar, several Christian pastors, and spiritual teacher Deepak Chopra. All through the show, rather than "Bhante G.," Larry King called me something that sounded like "BAHN-tuh-jee." We discussed the ideas of charity, compassion, and why a loving God would allow such suffering. When Larry King pressed me on the question of faith, I responded that Buddhists place their deepest faith in truth, in reality.

Soon after that, I went to Sri Lanka to participate in a conference, and when someone gave me a donation, I decided to pass it along to a tsunami relief fund. But deciding which organization should receive the money was tough. Millions of dollars were flowing into Southeast Asia at that time for tsunami victims, and inevitably there was a lot of controversy over which relief organizations were legitimate. I thought about the other pressing problems that predated this disaster—problems that had plagued my native country for a long time.

Although education is free in Sri Lanka, many children, especially those living in rural areas, do not go to school because they have no transportation or no money for clothes and school supplies, or their parents need them to work instead. I knew one family with two children, and the boys took turns going to school because they had only one nice pair of pants and one nice shirt between them. They also had only one notebook and one pencil. So they had a simple system: One day the older brother would go to school, wearing the pants and shirt, then the next day they would trade places. The other boy would erase what his brother had written in the notebook and put on the pants and shirt his brother had worn the day before. It was his turn to go to school.

I decided that a scholarship fund could help children like those brothers, and I decided I should use the money I had received to set up my own foundation. I recruited some Sinhalese friends living in Sri Lanka to serve as volunteer trustees. We hired a lawyer and deposited $10,000 in a bank in Colombo. We set up a system whereby our selection committee members would travel to villages in rural Sri Lanka and interview families who might need help funding education for their children.

Our efforts started in two places, the village where I was born and the village where I received ordination. They are two or three hours' drive from Colombo, and about six or seven miles apart. In each village, our committee would ask the local head monk to invite families to meet with them at the temple. Using a point system, they ranked each family's level of need, based on how many children they had, whether the parents worked, and how much money they earned.

For each family that was chosen to receive a scholarship, the mother was escorted to a local bank, where an account was opened in her name. We arranged for the bank in Colombo to transfer two thousand rupees once a month into the account at the local bank, so the mother would be able to go there and withdraw money for her child's school needs on a regular basis. Two thousand rupees is equivalent to about thirteen dollars—which is roughly two days' wages in Sri Lanka. As a child advances to higher levels of education, we increase the amount.

On our end, any donations that come into the scholarship fund are collected at Bhavana Society, and whenever we have $3,000 to $4,000 in hand, we wire it to the bank in Colombo. There is no middleman, and we have no overhead charges. Every penny of what people donate goes directly to the child. I'm happy about that, and I'm also happy about the fact that we have operated this scholarship fund for twelve years using only the interest on the $10,000 principal. We now have well over $100,000 in the fund, and it's continuing to grow. In fact, I have asked the trustees to find other villages where we can select students to receive scholarships.

I've also asked our trustees to help me expand the scholarship fund in another direction, one that may help us address the thirty-year war between Sinhalese and Tamils. Like so many conflicts in other parts of the world, this one springs partly out of mistrust born of a lack of communication. Sinhalese and Tamils speak different languages. So my idea is to start a language competition among children from the two ethnic groups. Sinhalese children will be taught to speak Tamil, and Tamil children will be taught to speak Sinhalese. Then our trustees will stage a speech competition, and the winning children will receive scholarships.

My hope is that these efforts will serve Sri Lanka by addressing two of its chief problems: poverty and ethnic clashes.

In the several years we've been awarding scholarships, I have received many letters from children who benefited from this fund. Often the letters bring tears to my eyes. These young people are so poor, but because of this scholarship, they've been able to attend school all the way through university. One young man finished his first university degree, then told our committee that he wants to go to graduate school. I advised him to learn English, so he will have a broader perspective of the world.

"That's the corridor that leads to your future," I told him.

CHAPTER TWENTY-NINE

Battles

THE FIRST DECADE of the twenty-first century threw many challenges at Bhavana Society, both from within and without.

In 2007 we received a disturbing letter from the Trans-Allegheny Interstate Line Company. The power conglomerate had plans to build a $1 billion, five-hundred-kilovolt transmission line that would carry electricity for 250 miles from the Midwest to Virginia, Maryland, and Washington, DC. In addition to traversing the Northern Shenandoah Valley, the line's proposed path involved clear-cutting a two-hundred-foot-wide swath at the western edge of our property, near where the monks' kutis were located.

We recognized immediately how the power line would scar the beauty of our land and discourage future visitors. Bhante Rahula went straight to work organizing a protest. In the monastery's summer newsletter, he described the situation and asked our supporters to write to their government officials.

"Apart from the potential health concerns due to close proximity to electromagnetic radiation," Rahula wrote, "this line would seriously infringe on the sanctity of our place of practice and the integrity of our contemplative way of life. The Bhavana Society vigorously protests the disfigurement of our beautiful forest monastery and unique spiritual refuge."

Our fight dragged on for months and attracted a lot of attention from various media, including an article that ran in the *New York*

Times on April 9, 2008. Rahula created a petition that was signed by more than one thousand of our followers and submitted it as part of his testimony before the West Virginia Public Service Commission.

It took a year and a half, a team of lawyers, and more than $11,000 in legal fees, most of which we raised via an emergency appeal to Bhavana supporters—but we finally won. Our lawyer was a smart man. When hundreds of people poured into the monastery for my birthday celebration in late 2007, he came to Bhavana and took pictures of the crowd, plus the endless line of cars parked up and down Back Creek Road. I believe that helped our case. Our lawyer argued that Bhavana Society truly is a sacred place, a place where people come from all over the world to find peace.

Eventually the power company decided on another route, one that was still quite near our property, but cut through our neighbors' land. We escaped—barely.

I credit the victory to Bhante Rahula, who worked tirelessly for months and was instrumental in getting the word out about our struggle. He never gave up on the goal of saving our beloved monastery, where he had lived and worked since 1987.

All of this made it so surprising when, not quite two years later, he decided to leave Bhavana Society. He told me he wanted to resign his position as vice abbot and once again become an itinerant monk, as he had been in his early monastic career. Rahula always had a wandering spirit and spent time every year mountain trekking all over the world. I think the administrative responsibilities of running a meditation center were not as attractive to him as the desire to develop his own practice and to be free to travel when he wanted to.

I understood his urge to move on and gave him my blessing, but it was worrisome for the monastery to be left without a second-in-command. So the next year I appointed as our new vice abbot Bhante Seelananda, a Sinhalese monk who had served Buddhist communities in New York and Canada. Unfortunately he, too, quickly decided he didn't wish to take on the duties inherent in running a monastery. Seelananda resigned the post in 2012.

Then came a period of limbo when we were without a vice abbot, and our board of directors kept asking me who would take over after my death. They worried that we didn't have a plan in place, and so did I. Many nights I lost sleep, thinking about the situation and mulling over possible candidates.

Finally, it hit me: What about Bhante Uparatana? I have known him since he was a boy; when he was only seven, he came to the temple in Sri Lanka where I lived. I knew his grandparents and his parents. I was his preceptor at his higher ordination. I sent him to monks' college, and then to university. Years later, after I came to the Washington Buddhist Vihara, I invited Uparatana to come to the United States. He lived and worked with me at the DC vihara until 1988 when I left.

Since then, Uparatana had created a thriving Theravada Buddhist temple of his own in Wheaton, Maryland. He had a large community of supporters and did a lot of social work and interfaith activities. He also taught meditation at American University, just as I had so many years ago. I was and am proud of him.

When I asked Uparatana, in the summer of 2016, if he would be willing to serve as Bhavana's vice abbot, we agreed that it would not be a residential position. He cannot leave his vihara in Maryland. But he cares about the continued existence of Bhavana Society, as I do, and he wants to help.

So we drew up a written contract, in both Sinhalese and English. It says that Uparatana will serve as vice abbot of Bhavana Society and advance to abbot upon my death. He will attend board meetings and work with the directors to assure that my guidelines for the operation of the monastery are continued—most notably that the center will always operate only on dana.

I now feel at peace, knowing that the future of Bhavana Society is in good hands, that my life's work will continue after I'm gone.

There's something else, though, about which I do *not* feel at peace. This sad tale involves my efforts to create a Western Buddhist monastery where monks and nuns can live together, studying Dhamma, practicing meditation, and teaching lay visitors.

I started in 1989, when I had been living in the United States long enough to recognize the growing demand for equal rights for men and women. I thought, "Why not? Why can't we ordain both genders here at Bhavana Society?" And so, at our very first ordination ceremony, a woman received novice ordination. After that, I ordained eight more women over the next twenty years.

As I mentioned earlier, I had significant opposition in the beginning from a few monks who held to the traditional Vinaya and disapproved of my plan. But I felt strongly that it was the right thing to do. And I believe that if the Buddha were alive today, he himself would have no objections to this. Both women and men have much to contribute to the modern Buddhist monastic order.

Even in the Buddha's own time, more than 2,500 years ago, he took the bold step of ordaining women, despite strong objections from some of his followers. But they dared not defy him, at least openly. It was only after he died that they raised their voices against the idea of a nuns' order. At the First Buddhist Council soon after the Buddha's death, Venerable Mahakassapa reprimanded Venerable Ananda, the Buddha's personal attendant, for supporting the Buddha's decision to ordain his mother, Pajapati Gotami.

At Bhavana Society, we set up the grounds so that nuns and visiting laywomen would be housed on the eastern edge of the property and monks on the opposite side. In the Buddha's time, that would never have been done. Bhikkhus and bhikkhunis lived at separate locations and rarely mingled, except when bhikkhus went to deliver Dhamma talks to the female monastics.

Looking back now, I suppose it was naive and idealistic of me to think that I could create a new tradition in the West, to have monks and nuns living in the same monastery. And it was perhaps even more foolhardy when I decided to establish a system of seniority that did not distinguish between male and female monastics. For example, I decreed that when we assembled to go for alms food at mealtime, we would line up according to who had been in robes longest, whether female or male.

"You can't do that," one monk told me. "According to Vinaya, even if a bhikkhuni has fifty Vassas"—which means she has been a nun for fifty years—"she must walk behind a monk who was ordained that very day."

This kind of attitude, this rigid clinging to an ancient custom that would likely offend and dishearten many of our visitors, was exactly what I had hoped to eradicate. But as I said, I was foolish. I should have known that trouble would eventually rear its head—and it did.

One monk was so angry about the new seniority rule that when a nun tried to walk ahead of him in the alms food line, he would physically block her way. If she tried to go around him, he would move to block her there, too.

Soon the bickering began.

Bhikkhus and bhikkhunis would start arguing as soon as meditation ended in the morning, a time when our speech should be peaceful and friendly. They would argue in the dining hall, after meals, during our work period.

If a nun was delegated to be the person who assigned daily chores—a role that rotated among the residents—inevitably one of the monks would declare that he didn't want to "take orders from a woman."

The arguments were incessant, and most all of them landed on my doorstep. Every day, I would find notes in the little mailbox on the wall next to my room. One person would be complaining about another person, and that person would be complaining about the other person. One monk came and knocked on my door, then started shouting at me. It all became so stressful, I would break down and cry as I tried to mediate their quarrels.

One day, when I sat down to eat lunch, a bhikkhuni knelt in front of me and asked me to help resolve the conflict she was experiencing with one of the bhikkhus. I felt like King Solomon being asked to divide a living baby in half to satisfy two women claiming to be its mother.

"If I support you," I told the nun, "this monk will be upset. And if I support him, you will be upset. I don't know what to say."

The nun nodded, tears rolling down her cheeks. She knew how unresolvable the situation was. Because this happened at the beginning of Vassa, the three-month period every year when monastics stay in one place, she could not leave. So for three months, she came to meals every day in tears. She didn't talk to anyone, especially any of the monks. And at the end of Vassa, she left.

That was 2010. Since then we have not had any bhikkhunis living at Bhavana Society. I have not ordained any more females. I know that many women in the Western Buddhist community—both ordained and lay—are upset and hurt that I didn't stand firm on this issue. Some have stopped visiting Bhavana Society. I feel very sad about it all.

My intentions, I think, were good: I wanted to ordain women as well as men. I wanted us all to live peacefully together, following the path of Dhamma in solidarity. But I underestimated how vehement my opposition would be. And I could not overcome the divisiveness, the constant quarreling. I am an elderly man now. My stamina is limited. I just want to live in peace and harmony.

Even though I no longer ordain nuns, I support their right to join the monastic order by attending any bhikkhuni ordinations to which I am invited. I also deliver Dhamma talks to a group of nuns by Skype, every full-moon day. Theravada Buddhist nuns are required to receive monthly instruction from a bhikkhu, and few monks are willing or able to do it.

This is my way of showing that, in my heart, I will always support the ordination of women.

I believe if the Buddha were here now, he would stand beside me.

CHAPTER THIRTY

Saved by a Man on a Bicycle

IN MAY 2012 I went to Canada for my annual visit. First I led a weekend retreat in Ottawa, then took a train to Toronto, where seventy people had assembled for ten days of meditation. On the second day of that retreat, I invited two monks, Chandrabodhi and Vijita, to accompany me on a walk around Lake Ontario. It was three miles just to get to the lake, and then we started to climb a hill next to it.

When we had almost reached the crest of the hill, I started to feel heartburn. I sat down on a bench and drank a little water, but the burning sensation grew stronger. I tried to get up and walk, but by then I was in intense pain and sweating profusely. I asked Chandrabodhi to use his cell phone and call the temple where we were having our retreat, to ask them to send a car. As he was doing that, I lay down on the grass and put my head in Vijita's lap. The pain continued to worsen, and I was having trouble breathing.

Chandrabodhi finished his call to the temple and said he thought we should call an ambulance, too.

"But it's three miles back to the parking lot," said Vijita. "And there are concrete barriers at the entrance of this trail. No ambulance is going to be able to drive up here. We'll have to carry you, Bhante. Let me run down there and get someone to help us."

Meanwhile, Chandrabodhi was calling 911 anyway. I could see the concern on his face. That's when I began to think about death. It was a fine spring day, and here I was, lying on the ground in a Toronto park, far from help. The pain was almost unbearable. Maybe this is the end, I thought.

At that moment, a man pedaling an old bicycle came into sight, riding toward us. He looked to me like he was homeless. His bicycle was pulling a crude wooden cart stacked high with newspapers, empty bottles, tin cans, pieces of wood, and a variety of tools: axe, knife, saw, and hammer.

When the cyclist saw me lying on the ground, he stopped. We asked him if he could help. Without a word, he hurriedly cleared the debris in his cart to make a space for me. They helped me get in, and we sped down the hill, me on my back in the rickety wooden cart and Chandrabodhi running alongside us.

When we reached the parking lot about fifteen minutes later, a fire truck and ambulance were waiting. Paramedics lifted me out of the cart and onto a stretcher. The next thing I knew, I was in a hospital with doctors and nurses bending over me.

They found that one of the arteries leading to my heart was 95 percent blocked. A stent was inserted, and two days later I was discharged.

When I got back to the temple where I had been staying, I asked my supporters if we could somehow find the man who had carried me on his bicycle cart. He had saved my life, and I hadn't had a chance to thank him. They went to the park to search for him, and lo and behold, there he was. They brought him to the temple to meet me.

His name was Ashad Ahamed, he said, and he was from Trinidad. He had immigrated to Canada with his parents when he was only five years old. Now he was twenty-seven and had long had trouble finding a job, so he collected recyclables and sold them to make a little money. He still lived with his parents.

Ashad said he often rode around Lake Ontario on his regular route, and that day his timing was a lifesaver for me. We invited him to come back to the temple the next day for lunch. When he did, he brought his parents and sister with him. The temple supporters had taken up a collection for him, and Ashad was genuinely touched when they gave him the money.

After I returned home from Toronto, my doctors advised me to eat less salt. Unfortunately, our monastery cook interpreted that literally: He put *less* at the end of the word *salt*—and now served food that was *saltless*. After eating a salt-free diet for two months, I began to feel more and more tired. My arms and legs were shaky, and I was dizzy almost all the time. I couldn't understand what was wrong.

In July, we held a retreat, and one of the participants was a doctor, a psychiatrist. When she saw how badly I was feeling, she said, "Bhante, I think we need to get you to a doctor. I'm worried about your sodium level. You need blood tests."

She was right; my sodium was critically low, so they admitted me to the hospital in Winchester, Virginia. I stayed there for five days. When I came back to Bhavana, I still didn't feel quite right, and my blood pressure was higher than normal.

On the seventh of August I went for my usual afternoon walk, but I could barely make it down our driveway to the main road. I came back and went to bed. When I woke up a few hours later, I knew something was radically wrong, so I telephoned my nephew Upali. He made several phone calls and finally reached a Sinhalese doctor he knew who lived in Pennsylvania. That man advised me to chew and swallow four baby aspirin tablets. He also recommended that we go to Johns Hopkins Hospital, in Baltimore, right away. But by then it was eight o'clock at night, and we didn't think it was a good idea to drive mountain roads in the dark with the risk that I might have another heart attack on the way.

So we waited until morning, and the next day I was admitted to Johns Hopkins through the emergency room. Over the next few days, doctors ran tests and discussed my history of heart trouble. Finally they decided I needed surgery, and it was scheduled for August 14. But on the thirteenth, I started having chest pain and severe dizziness, so they rushed me into surgery a day early. When the anesthetist came to have me sign consent forms, I told him, "Don't worry if I die

during surgery. I'm ready. I've been meditating on death since 1947."
He chuckled.

When I regained consciousness the next morning, I was in the
intensive care unit. A double bypass had been performed, using one
vein from my leg and another from my chest. Four nurses were watching me, sitting at each corner of my bed. As soon as I opened my eyes,
they started clapping. Someone explained to me later that if a bypass
patient is not going to survive the surgery, they usually die during the
post-op recovery period. So the nurses were celebrating my survival.

I stayed ten days in the hospital. When it was time to discharge me,
I was still very weak. A doctor told me, "From now on, you shouldn't
lift anything heavier than ten pounds."

I smiled at him.

"Okay," I said. "I guess I'll have to give up weightlifting."

Because I was still so weak, Upali took me to his home in Bethesda,
Maryland, to recover. I stayed there two months, and Upali took
wonderful care of me. He cleaned the urine bag of my catheter, saw
to my personal hygiene, managed the constant flow of visitors, and
arranged for home health nurses to come in and monitor my vital
signs. Upali is a wonderful person, very compassionate. I call him
my bodhisattva, because he is always helping other people. He and
his wife, Sumitthra, served food and drink to every single visitor who
came to see me. They were constantly on call. And on the day I finally
left, October 31, they both stood in the doorway and cried.

During the time I was convalescing at Upali's house, my younger
sister Sita died in Sri Lanka. And then my eldest sister, Dingiriamma,
Upali's mother, then living in the United States, started to go down-
hill. She lived in a nursing home, where I had visited her several times
in the past. Dingiriamma, as I've mentioned, was more like a mother
than a sister to me. She was nineteen years older, and when I was a
toddler, she used to nurse me. I spent a lot of time at her house with
her and her husband.

After she passed the age of one hundred, I tried to visit her more
often. She worried about me like a mother hen.

"Are you still traveling?" she would say. "I have told you to slow down. But you never listen. Where are you going next?"

"Oh, not too far," I'd say. "Maybe Singapore."

"All right, then. That's fine."

She had no idea where Singapore was.

Dingiriamma always asked me to give her a Dhamma talk when I visited. But her hearing was terrible. So I got an electronic amplifier that I could speak into; it made my voice quite loud, and then she could hear what I was saying. The only problem was, everyone else in the nursing home could hear me, too. Good thing they didn't understand Sinhalese!

On a cold winter day in early 2013, Dingiriamma was taken to the hospital in Bethesda. She died there on January 13. She was 104 years old. Now I am the sole surviving member of my family. My parents and all six of my siblings are gone.

People ask me if I'm sad about that. Actually, I'm not. I understand it as the truth of impermanence. When my mother died, I was forty-nine years old, and it hit me very hard. But Dingiriamma's death was easier to bear. By then, I was eighty-five and had decades of meditation practice behind me. I felt less sadness and more peace.

You know, we can learn a beautiful lesson from animals. Think about birds. When the baby chick comes out of the egg, the mother bird is very attentive, giving it a tiny amount of food many times a day, and each time watching to make sure it can swallow. For days she watches carefully over her chick and drops food into its open mouth whenever it cheeps.

Eventually, she sees that the baby is able to pick up a morsel with its own beak and swallow it. Then the mother bird knows that her offspring is almost ready to be independent. So when the baby cheeps for food, she doesn't respond every time. She wants the baby to learn to fend for itself, as it must. If the baby persists, she might even peck at it to drive it away.

In due time, the young bird flies away, and the mother's duty is done. Her chick is now on its own. They may never meet again. If the baby dies, the mother bird may not even know.

Or when the mother dies, the baby may be far away and not know. They shared an intimate relationship, but at the appropriate time they let go.

In the same way, we have to learn to let go of our loved ones— our mothers, fathers, brothers, sisters, husbands, wives, children. Of course, we will miss the love and support we derived from them, the feeling of closeness and companionship. But we also must reflect on the good things they did in their lives and be inspired by that.

In fact, that is the best way for us to prepare for our own end: We shouldn't worry about death and how it will come to us, but rather focus on what good we can do for others while we are still alive.

CHAPTER THIRTY-ONE

Coincidence—or Kamma?

NOW THAT I AM TURNING NINETY, I'm like many older people: I like to reminisce about the events of my life. Nine decades is a long span of time, and a lot of things, both fortunate and unfortunate, have happened to me. As a Buddhist, of course, I believe that the flow of experiences in my life is due to my kamma.

The law of cause and effect tells us that our volitional actions generate the events of our lives. Simply put, good comes to us only if we have done good deeds, either earlier in this life or in our past lives. Good thoughts and good intentions arise in us out of those past good deeds, and in the same way, bad deeds we've done in the past will produce bad thoughts, and bad intentions, in us.

For example, when I was only seven years old, I wanted to become a monk, even though I didn't fully know what that life would be like. And I wanted to learn English, even though I had no idea how to accomplish that goal. But those good intentions did not come to me automatically. They arose because I evidently had performed good deeds in previous lives. The good intentions that resulted out of those good deeds followed me into this life.

In the Dasadhamma Sutta, a discourse given to his monastic followers, the Buddha reminded bhikkhus of the "ten essentials" they should contemplate frequently. Number seven of those ten essentials is kamma:

"I am the owner of my kamma, heir to my kamma, born of my kamma, related to my kamma, abide supported by my kamma. Whatever kamma I shall do, whether good or evil, of that I shall be the heir." This should be reflected upon always by one who has gone forth.

Those same instructions are given to laypeople as the fifth of five "subjects of everyday recollection," or *abhinham paccavekkhitabbani,* in the *Abhinham paccavekkhitabbathana sutta* (*Anguttara Nikaya 5.6: Nivarana vagga*).

The role of kamma in shaping the events of our lives seems clear when I reflect on the many things I've experienced that we might otherwise call coincidences. Some of these coincidences are small, such as the time I misplaced a handkerchief while I was on sabbatical at the Forest Refuge in Massachusetts. It wasn't a big deal, because I knew I could easily replace the handkerchief. So I didn't worry. Several days later, I was walking on a path at the center and started sneezing. I really needed that handkerchief then! And as I opened my eyes after the sneeze, there it was, on the sidewalk a few paces in front of me.

It also happened quite a few times that I would think of a certain country I had not yet visited, and the next week I would receive an out-of-the-blue invitation to lead a retreat in that very country.

There also were a couple of humorous coincidences involving helicopters. Once, I was in my sister's hospital room with my nephew and niece. Outside her window we noticed a large concrete area in the middle of several hospital buildings. I told my nephew it was maybe a landing pad for emergency helicopters to bring in critical patients.

"No," he said. "Can't be. We've been here several times, and we've never seen a helicopter come in."

At that very moment, a helicopter came down and landed.

Another time, while leading a retreat in Germany, I walked daily through farmland surrounding the retreat center. Each day, I would be accompanied by another monk or layman attending the retreat.

Near a small lake on one of the farms, we would see a large, bare concrete square. I suspected it might be a helicopter landing pad, but none of the people I walked with each day knew what it was. One day, I was walking with a German man who lived in that area. We came near the concrete square next to the lake, and I told him I thought it was a helicopter landing pad.

"There's no reason for a helicopter landing pad to be here," he said.

No sooner had he uttered that sentence than a helicopter appeared in the sky, hovered above our heads, then dropped down and landed on the concrete pad.

I also can remember several occasions when I would think of someone I had known long before and wish I could get back in touch with that person for one reason or another. Then he or she would drop back into my life, as though my "call" had been heard. For instance, John Peddicord was a longtime student of mine who edited my very first book, *Mindfulness in Plain English.* I am eternally grateful to him for that and appreciate his talents. Unfortunately, we lost contact after the book was published. When I thought of asking him to help me with another book, I had no way to reach him. And then, one day I returned from my afternoon walk to find John standing outside the office building at Bhavana Society. It had been twenty-five years since we'd seen each other.

He told me he'd been living in Baltimore and California. I told him I was writing another book and could use his help, if he had the time.

"Of course," was his response. "I'll be happy to help."

Another time, I was thinking of a man named Harry Hill, whom we wanted to be the next administrative coordinator for Bhavana Society. He had visited the monastery several times years earlier, staying for weeks at a time. He had the necessary skills for the job and seemed like the perfect candidate. The only problem was, I had lost touch with him and couldn't find his contact information anywhere. I searched through my email, cell phone, and computer files. I also had our office manager, Kathy Nally, scour her files in search of a phone number or email address for him. No luck. Harry and I had no contacts in common, so I knew there was no other way to reach him. I gave up hope. The next day, Kathy came running to my room.

"Bhante, Harry Hill just called! He wants to come visit Bhavana next week."

And in 2004 I was teaching in Europe when my digital recorder broke. The recorder had been donated to me by a man named Laurence Bennett, who lived in Arizona. I loved that little device and used it to record talks I gave all over the world, then uploaded them to the Bhavana website for students to hear. After it broke on that trip, I was unable to record my talks in Germany, France, and England. By the time I got to Switzerland, I was thoroughly frustrated.

I arrived at the retreat center, got settled in my room, and was thinking intently about how I might find someone who could help me figure out what was wrong with the recorder. Then I walked outside and came upon a person walking up the steps at the entrance of the retreat center who looked familiar.

"Laurence! What are you doing here?"

"I just arrived. I'm here to attend your retreat."

"You came all the way from Arizona?"

"Yes!"

I asked him if he remembered donating the recorder to me several years earlier and told him it had suddenly stopped working.

"Let me look at it," he said.

Within five minutes, he had fixed the recorder.

Some of the other coincidences in my life were not so fortuitous.

At least three times, I have experienced frightening brushes with death. The first happened in 2003, when I was walking on Back Creek Road with another monk. We were almost back at the monastery when a large limb suddenly broke off a tree at the side of the road and crashed to the ground just in front of me. The limb was maybe six or seven feet long and very heavy. As it fell, it grazed the brim of my hat. If I had taken one more step forward, just another inch or two farther, it would have smashed directly onto my head.

A couple of years after that, I had another close call on Back

Creek Road. Again, I was taking my daily walk, this time accompanied by a lay visitor to the monastery. The winding two-lane road was icy because of freezing rain the night before. We were walking on the left side of the road, as usual, and when we came to a bend in the road, suddenly we saw a truck coming toward us, skidding on the ice. I moved farther off the road, as far as I could go, but the truck was careening directly toward me. I could see the passenger in the truck screaming and pressing her hands to the side of her head. My brain only had a second or two to process what was happening, but I remember thinking that this was the end of my life. I reached out my hand, and I guess in that instant the driver finally got the truck under control. It came to a stop about one foot in front of me. I touched the hood with my hand. The driver jumped out and immediately started apologizing. I told him it was not his fault.

Another time, in 2013, I was riding in a car with a lay supporter and his wife. I had given a talk in Fredericksburg, Virginia, and they were driving me back to Bhavana Society afterward. It was about 6 P.M., but not yet dark. I was sitting in the front passenger seat. When we came to a railroad crossing, my driver looked both ways and started to drive across. Then the unthinkable happened: Just as our car was on the railroad tracks, the gate in front of us clattered down, blocking our path.

We heard a loud noise and looked to our right. An Amtrak express train was speeding directly toward us, about three hundred yards away. It seemed to have come out of nowhere.

My driver reacted immediately, jamming the car into reverse—but it was too late. The gate behind us had also come down. We were trapped. The train would be upon us in another second or two.

With the car still in reverse, the driver pressed his foot on the gas pedal, and the car lurched backward about three inches, right up against the rear gate. We could go no farther.

The next instant, the train roared past, only inches from the front bumper of our car. It was so loud, it sounded and felt like an earthquake. The whole car was shaking like a leaf. I think we all were convinced we were about to die. In the back seat, my driver's wife let out a single scream and fainted. I don't remember feeling any emotion, just a sense of being completely stunned.

Then it was over.

The train disappeared down the tracks, and the gates lifted. Somehow, we were alive. The driver's wife regained consciousness and immediately started calling her children on her cell phone. For the rest of our trip, the three of us talked about how close we had come to dying.

But we hadn't died.

Our kamma that day did not create the conditions for death—only a visceral reminder of it.

CHAPTER THIRTY-TWO

Facing the End

I THINK I'M ALLERGIC TO BIRTHDAYS—at least the land-mark ones. Every five years for the last few decades, my students and friends have planned a big birthday celebration for me—and something always keeps me from attending.

When I turned seventy-five, in 2002, my Thai supporters planned a party and made hundreds of beautiful laminated Bodhi leaves with my picture on them, to give to everyone who came. Then an early December snowstorm in West Virginia forced the cancellation of the event.

In 2007, when I was turning eighty, I asked everyone not to do anything big. But they had already started preparing months ahead of time. Bhante Rahula commissioned many of my friends to write essays about me that he compiled into a handsome book titled *Preserving the Dhamma*. Invitations went out for a grand celebration scheduled for October, to avoid the possibility of winter weather and also to coincide with Kathina, the annual robe-offering ceremony when many laypeople visit temples.

The night before the celebration, I returned late from a teaching trip to Chicago, where I had given a number of Dhamma talks over the previous week. When I arrived at Bhavana Society, the people who had come for my party wanted to hear a Dhamma talk. I was very tired, but I didn't want to disappoint them, so I talked until 11 P.M. Then I was so keyed up, I could not sleep, even though I was exhausted. I took a sleeping pill.

The next morning, a junior monk mistakenly rang the wake-up bell at 3 A.M., instead of 4 A.M. as I had requested. I got up, with only two-and-a-half hours of sleep. I had a sore throat, so I took a little cough syrup, plus my regular allergy pills, which sometimes make me dizzy. During meditation, I was dozing off repeatedly.

The celebration was supposed to start at nine o'clock that morning. A few minutes before that, I was sitting on a bench on the porch, talking to people as they arrived. The next thing I remember, I was lying on the floor and monks were chanting over me. Someone else was taking my blood pressure. I had fainted and fallen off the bench.

As an ambulance drove me out of the monastery, I saw hundreds of cars lined up along Back Creek Road. People had come from all over the country to celebrate my birthday. I went to the hospital, and they had the party without me.

Five years later, for my eighty-fifth birthday, Bhante Seelananda planned a large birthday celebration, but I told him, only half joking: "Please don't do it. It may kill me this time!" As before, he wanted the celebration to be in October, to coincide with our Kathina observance. But when October rolled around, I was staying at my nephew's house, recovering from heart surgery. Again, the party proceeded without me.

And so it goes, as one grows older: My body has begun to fail, in various ways. I still walk every day, if my schedule allows, but the pace is slower and the distance shorter. Nowadays I'm happy if I can manage four miles. Recently I decided to alter my route, after a passing truck clipped me while I was walking on Back Creek Road. I was on the left side of the road, and as the truck came toward me, I lifted my right hand to wave to the driver. Then the truck's outside mirror smacked into the palm of my hand with a loud *thwack,* bending my fingers back at a severe angle. The pain was intense, as if my fingers were being snapped off. For the rest of the walk, my hand was numb, and I massaged it with my other hand. Fortunately, it felt better by the next day—but now I walk only on less-traveled side roads near the monastery.

In 2014 and 2015, I had cataract surgery, which was complicated when one of the cataracts shattered in pieces as the doctor was trying to remove it, necessitating a second surgery on that eye.

After increasing episodes of fainting, and my being diagnosed at one time as having nonepileptic seizures, we finally pinpointed the problem: I am lactose intolerant. The mucus produced when I eat dairy foods builds up and blocks my arteries, stopping blood flow to the brain. So I have switched to soy products and almond milk.

I also made other adjustments to my diet, mostly because of the medications I'm on since my heart surgery. I take two daily blood pressure pills, one cholesterol-lowering pill, one pill to prevent heart arrhythmia, one aspirin, and several vitamins and minerals. All of those substances have to be metabolized, of course, in the liver and kidneys, and some of them are strong enough to stress those organs. I don't want to add to that stress by eating unhealthy foods. So I'm very careful about what I eat and drink.

Of course, this sometimes causes difficulties when lay supporters bring meal dana offerings on special occasions. They want the food to be tasty, so they may fry it in oil or add cheese or milk to enhance the flavor. I see the look of disappointment and embarrassment on their faces when I ask them if the dish has oil or dairy in it. But Buddhist monks are supposed to accept whatever food is placed in their alms bowl, in the spirit of nonattachment. So I generally accept their dana and try to severely limit how much I ingest of something that I know may be harmful to my health.

In January 2016 I contracted pneumonia while visiting Sri Lanka to meet with the scholarship fund trustees. I spent two weeks in the hospital in Colombo, coughing incessantly and so weak that I couldn't move my arms or legs. A friend of mine hired a man to stay in my hospital room with me and take care of me. That man carried me to the bathroom, shaved me, bathed me, fed me. Back home, my supporters were so worried, they wrote my obituary and started discussing funeral plans. Finally, though, I was strong enough to be discharged, and after a week's convalescence in a supporter's home, I was able to fly back to the United States.

After that, I stopped traveling. For a while, I had been using wheelchairs to navigate crowded airports, but even that became too much. Travel in the post-9/11 era is rigorous, particularly on long international trips, and I simply can't keep up that pace anymore. Also, I find that when I travel, it disrupts my diet, my exercise routine, how much sleep I get, and how much time I have for meditation. And when I come home from a trip, I have colds, sore throats, headaches, dizziness. When I was younger, I could bounce back quickly from that. Not now.

Thanks to the internet, I can stay in touch with the outside world. I use Skype to communicate with students and deliver Dhamma talks to a group of bhikkhunis on uposatha days. I also continue to write, which is a satisfying way to spread the Dhamma.

In the last couple of years, I've been focusing more and more on Bhavana Society and the process of preparing it to function without me. We have a system set up that I think will keep things running smoothly after I am gone. There are six resident monks here now, and they have good hearts. Of course they will consult Bhante Uparatana, the nonresidential abbot, before making any big changes. There's also a board of directors and an advisory board of other monks to help them. I feel comfortable that these three groups will work together well, in conjunction with Bhante Uparatana, whenever critical decisions have to be made.

I've also been experimenting with letting the young monks lead retreats. I am there only on opening night to welcome the yogis and administer precepts. I also lead the closing session. The rest of the retreat is run by the resident monks. When we look at the evaluations filled out by yogis at the end of the retreat, they say they like this system. Some mention that they enjoy having a variety of monks teaching the retreat, as opposed to only one. My hope is that more monks will choose to take up residence here, continuing the Bhavana legacy of teaching Dhamma from the original Pali texts.

I feel confident that Bhavana Society will continue to flourish financially. There is a regular income flow from the royalties on my books, and that will continue after my death. We have a solid system for keeping track of and managing donations that come in. From the beginning, we have operated solely on a dana basis, which means that we don't charge set prices for any of our retreats or teachings. Visitors donate whatever they feel is appropriate. Their dana comes spontaneously, from the heart. And if they leave with a feeling of peace, if their experience here has helped them deal with difficulties in their lives, I feel good.

Operating on a dana basis means that we always spend only within our means. We don't want to borrow money from banks because we don't have a predictable, steady income with which to repay a loan. I have told our board, from the beginning: "We are not expansionists. We want to remain small and maintain our reputation with high-quality teaching and high-quality buildings." We can currently house sixty people at the monastery, and my plan is not to build any more housing, just maintain and improve our existing buildings. That's how we will stay viable.

I would like to be remembered as a simple monk with lofty ideas that he could not totally accomplish. I wanted to establish a well-running Theravada monastery where people could learn and practice the teachings of the Buddha. That is the most important thing I have accomplished in my life, thanks to the generous help of Matthew Flickstein in the beginning and so many other people in the years since.

I also wanted to ordain women and provide a place for them to live and teach alongside monks, but that goal was not achieved. My other aim was to write books that would help people learn meditation and Dhamma, and I'm happy I could accomplish that. Even our Buddha Vandana book serves as a valuable guide for daily devotional practice.

When I die, I don't want a lot of fanfare. I have written in my will that if I die at or within fifty miles of Bhavana Society, my supporters should have my body cremated and do whatever they want with the ashes. I don't care. If I die in another place, they can make any arrangements they want.

The truth is, I have no control over this body even now while I'm alive, much less after my death. So I don't have any particular wishes for how and when I'd like to die. I will leave as I came, without any plan or invitation.

I hope my supporters will not grieve my absence unduly. We humans are attached to each other, and this attachment makes us sad when someone we love passes away. But our clinging, our attachment, is not reality. It's a mere thought.

Can you cling to anything or anyone literally? No, because we— and they—are changing all the time. We have no control over that. And yet, in spite of this truth, we develop a thought, the thought of holding on. This happens because we don't see *anicca*, or impermanence. If we begin to see impermanence, we can train our mind to have a different thought, the thought of relinquishing and letting go.

When I look back over my life, I see it all as a dream. Thousands of people I've known are dead now, people in the village where I was born, in the place where I received ordination, where I went to monks' college. Thousands of people in Sri Lanka, India, Malaysia, the United States, Europe, South America, people all over the world are gone, and not a trace is left to recall any of them, except in my memory. It's just like the dreams I have when I'm asleep: I wake up, and sometimes I can remember my dreams, but I know they weren't real. So many of the people I have met in my life, places I have gone, talks I have given, things I have seen: All of it, gone. A dream.

I understand impermanence more clearly now, in my old age. When I wake in the middle of the night, I focus my mind on the changes I am experiencing at that moment. Maybe a tingling sensation in my body, an ache or a throbbing pain, the sensation of my mind waking up and the awareness of my breath going in and out of my lungs. In that moment, I'm happy because I see how quickly things change, and I know that this is helping me understand impermanence.

When the tiniest spark of feeling arises, in that feeling is a perception and a thought and a consciousness. It begins with contact, when two objects come together. At that moment, consciousness arises. Then arises perception and feeling. But all this happens so quickly, you cannot separate it. We use words to separate it, but the experience itself is inseparable. Even the mind cannot make the distinction. So there is no reason for us to be afraid of death or to mourn over it. The chain of change is going on all the time, and the end of that chain is called death.

Even a child can understand this. You tell a child, "Look at this flower. Watch the flower, from morning to evening." In the morning, the petals of the flower are fresh and beautiful. By evening, they have withered. What happened? That freshness, that color, that beauty was altered by the truth of impermanence. The flower changed—as does everything.

Oddly enough, in this highly technological period of human history, we still have an old-fashioned machine that shows us impermanence—the clock! That incessant ticking shows us not only the passage of time, it also shows us the truth of impermanence. From a clock, we learn this important lesson: Each moment is distinct from the previous one, and also distinct from the moment that comes after it, and the moment after that.

Whenever we close our eyes and meditate, we experience nothing but change. Whether it's a thought, a feeling, an idea, a memory, aches and pains in the body—all of it is coming and going, coming and going, all the time. The next moment, if it all stops, that is called death. It's nothing strange, nothing unfamiliar. Just the truth of impermanence. And we must familiarize ourselves with this truth.

Only then, finally then, will there be an end to our fear of death. Only then will our suffering cease.

Afterword

By Jeanne Malmgren

IN MY THIRTY-FIVE years as a Buddhist, I have been blessed with opportunities to meet a variety of teachers: Tibetan lamas, Zen masters, Theravada monks and nuns, American-born meditation instructors, and a Burmese *sayadaw* at a mountaintop monastery on the Irrawaddy River who didn't speak a word of English.

From each of them I learned something valuable, something that enriched the depth and texture of my life—and I bow in gratitude to them all. But like many people on a spiritual quest, I eventually found myself drawn to one particular teacher, someone whose personality and manner of imparting the Dhamma resonated with me. Someone I could trust and respect, without reservation. Someone who was the kind of person I aspired to be. For me, that someone is Bhante Gunaratana.

My first husband and I stumbled onto Bhante G. by accident. One spring day in the early 1980s, we were passing through our nation's capital on vacation and decided to drop in at the Washington Buddhist Vihara. Neither of us had ever visited a real live Buddhist center, but we were keenly interested in meditation. When we knocked on the door of the big house on 16th Street NW, Bhante himself answered. He gave us a tour of the premises, and I remember being awestruck by the shrine room, with its large Buddharupa draped in iridescent orange and gold tapestries. Bhante gave us a copy of the vihara's typewritten newsletter, and we slipped a five-dollar bill in the donation box.

A few years later, when we started our own meditation center in Florida, we invited Bhante G. to preside over our opening ceremonies. He was almost sixty years old, but looked much younger. I remember him standing in our yard outside the garage-turned-meditation-hall and hoisting a colorful Buddhist flag up the newly installed flagpole. I think we had only an inkling of how auspicious a beginning that was, blessed by Bhante's presence.

After Bhante Gunaratana and his supporters got Bhavana Society up and running in the late 1980s, I went to West Virginia several times. Sitting on my cushion and hearing Bhante's quiet voice break the silence at the end of each meditation period was always a touchstone for me:

> There is no concentration without wisdom,
> No wisdom without concentration.
> One who has both wisdom and concentration
> Is close to peace and emancipation.

I also loved staying in a rustic, one-room kuti in the woods, my only companions a kerosene lamp and the night sounds of the forest. Decades later, a photo of one of the kutis at Bhavana sits on my desk as a reminder of the peace I felt there.

In August 1988, I took part in the first Eight Lifetime Precepts retreat. It was a joyous occasion, all thirty or so of us dressed in white and nervously kneeling in the meditation hall. For the first time in the Theravada Buddhist world, Bhante G. had created something that allowed nonordained laypeople to embark on a deeper commitment to the path of Dhamma. By taking the Eight Lifetime Precepts, we were identifying ourselves in a formal way as Buddhist practitioners— but we didn't have to don robes or shave our heads to do it. During the ceremony each of us received a Pali name from Bhante. Mine was Medhavi, meaning "the wise." I was humbled and thrilled.

By the mid-1990s, my second husband and I were hosting residential meditation retreats in Florida, led by Bhante. One took place on

Captiva, a barrier island off the southwest coast of Florida. Captiva is accessible only by boat, so I thought it would be a nice, quiet place for us to meditate. To add to the ambiance, I decided we would paddle kayaks out to the island. This was a bad idea! On the opening day of the retreat, rough weather forced us to book a ferry instead. The ride across the channel was quite hair-raising: gusty winds lashing our faces and whitecaps spilling into the boat. It was only afterward that Bhante told me he is extremely uncomfortable on water, due to his near-drowning experience as a teenager (recounted in chapter 4 of this book).

Bhante G. is more at home in mountains, and he has climbed a few, including the 13,435-foot Mount Kinabalu in Malaysia when he was seventy-four years old. One of his favorite vistas, though, is quite near Bhavana Society. One gorgeous fall day when my husband and I were visiting, Bhante invited us to go there with him. We piled into my little pickup truck: Bhante in the passenger seat; my husband driving; me and Brown, the monastery dog, riding in the truck bed. As we rolled along winding country roads, I lay on my back, drinking in the brilliant reds and yellows of the trees overhead. It was one of the supreme moments of well-being in my life.

Another time I was on retreat at Bhavana, my meditation practice was being invaded repeatedly by regrets over a precept I had broken years earlier. After several days of struggle, I finally went to Bhante's office, head hung in shame, and confessed my transgression. My voice was shaking. Now he would know what a fraud I was, that I wasn't fit for the spiritual path. Surely he was going to tell me to pack up and leave. Instead, he looked at me, his face a calm pool of equanimity. No censure, no rebuke. Just a simple nod of understanding. Then he quoted a verse from the Dhammapada:

> Whoso was heedless formerly
> But later lives with heedfulness
> Illuminates the world
> As a moon freed from clouds.

Somehow, to be in Bhante's presence is both awe-inspiring and relaxing. He speaks directly from mind and heart, dispensing wisdom with a quiet grace, the ancient Pali rolling off his tongue as he recites Theravada scriptures. But he can also be warm and friendly, even downright funny. If you haven't visited him in a long while, he never forgets to ask about your family and, more likely than not, he'll launch into a story of his own. He changes his voice to play different characters, and at the end, when you get the punch line, he'll laugh along with you. He also might want to show you an app on his new smartphone. It turns out this "simple monk" is a techno-geek, even as he finishes his ninth decade.

I think what I appreciate most about Bhante G. is his ability to walk between and within two worlds. He is highly esteemed among the Buddhist monastic community, both in Asia and the West. They know him as a learned meditation master whose understanding of the Dhamma is deep and true, springing from a lifetime of study and practice. At the same time, he has an uncanny ability to connect with us "householders," although he has not lived even one day of his adult life as a layperson. He is a living bridge between the restless angst of our twenty-first-century minds and teachings that date back more than two millennia.

On my last visit to Bhavana, during the fall of 2016, Bhante and I spent two days working on the new chapters for this book. Our interview sessions were scheduled around his need for regular periods of rest and his after-lunch walk, which is shorter than it used to be, but which he still insists upon doing every day. I was mourning the recent death of my mother, so inevitably our conversation turned to that subject. Late one afternoon, after meeting with Bhante for several hours, I went to the meditation hall to clear my mind and do some walking meditation. Bhante's words "It's all a dream" were still rolling around in my head as I paced slowly back and forth.

Suddenly, out of the corner of my eye I saw something streaking toward the plate-glass window next to me. It was brown, about the size of a softball, and moving fast. *BOOM!* The sound of impact was shocking in that silent hall. For a moment I could feel my brain struggling to register what had happened. Then, out of the blankness rose a single word: "bird."

I left the hall, put on my sandals, and went outside. Next to some shrubbery beneath the arched window, I found a wood thrush on its side on the ground: intact, beautiful, legs already stiffening. I sank to my knees and murmured verses of protection over the still, small body. Death is real, and it ends the dream.

When Bhante Gunaratana dies, I will grieve, as will his thousands of students worldwide—those who have studied with him in person, those who know him from his books, those who took his correspondence courses or met him on his world travels, people in places as far-flung as Calgary and Rio and Kuala Lumpur. For decades we have depended on him for spiritual nourishment and inspiration. It began with his book *Mindfulness in Plain English,* inarguably a classic in the field, a resource that has brought millions to the path of meditation. His steadfast devotion to the Buddha's teachings, and his ability to bring the Dhamma alive for modern people, is his genius, his great gift to us.

With hands folded in front of my heart: Thank you, Bhante.

May you be well, may you be peaceful, may you be safe.
May all beings benefit from your lifetime of service.
Sadhu, sadhu, sadhu.

Index

About the Authors

BHANTE HENEPOLA GUNARATANA, a native of Sri Lanka, is the author of several Wisdom titles: *Mindfulness in Plain English, Eight Mindful Steps to Happiness, Beyond Mindfulness in Plain English, The Four Foundations of Mindfulness in Plain English, Meditation on Perception,* and *Loving-Kindness in Plain English.* A Buddhist monk for more than seventy-five years, he is North America's highest-ranking monk of the Siyam Nikaya sect of Theravada Buddhism. After coming to the United States in 1968, he earned a PhD in philosophy from the American University in Washington, DC. He has led meditation retreats all over Asia, Europe, Australia, and North and South America. In 1988 he founded Bhavana Society (www.bhavanasociety.org), the forest monastery/retreat center in West Virginia where he now lives.

JEANNE MALMGREN has been a student of Bhante Gunaratana since 1985. After a long career in journalism, she earned a master's degree in clinical mental health counseling and now has a private psychotherapy practice. She also writes about healing arts, teaches classes and workshops in mindfulness, and leads meditative hikes in the Blue Ridge Mountains of South Carolina, where she lives. She can be reached at www.upstatecounselor.com.

Also Available by Bhante Gunaratana

Mindfulness in Plain English

Beyond Mindfulness in Plain English
An Introductory Guide to Deeper States of Meditation

Eight Mindful Steps to Happiness
Walking the Buddha's Path

The Four Foundations of Mindfulness in Plain English

Loving-Kindness in Plain English
The Practice of Metta

Meditation on Perception
Ten Healing Practices to Cultivate Mindfulness

The Mindfulness in Plain English Journal

The Mindfulness in Plain English Collection

About Wisdom Publications

Wisdom Publications is the leading publisher of classic and contemporary Buddhist books and practical works on mindfulness. To learn more about us or to explore our other books, please visit our website at wisdompubs.org or contact us at the address below.

Wisdom Publications
199 Elm Street
Somerville, MA 02144 USA

We are a 501(c)(3) organization, and donations in support of our mission are tax deductible.

Wisdom Publications is affiliated with the Foundation for the Preservation of the Mahayana Tradition (FPMT).